THE OTHER
OLYMPIANS

THE OTHER OLYMPIANS

A True Story of Gender,
Fascism and the Making
of Modern Sport

MICHAEL WATERS

EBURY
PRESS

1

Ebury Press, an imprint of Ebury Publishing
20 Vauxhall Bridge Road
London SW1V 2SA

Ebury Press is part of the Penguin Random House group of companies
whose addresses can be found at global.penguinrandomhouse.com

First published by in the United States by Farrar, Straus and Giroux in 2024
First published in the United Kingdom by Ebury Press in 2024

www.penguin.co.uk

A CIP catalogue record for this book is available from the British Library

Hardback ISBN 9781529910193
Trade Paperback ISBN 9781529910216

Printed and bound in Great Britain by Clays Ltd, Elcograf S.p.A.

The authorised representative in the EEA is Penguin Random House Ireland,
Morrison Chambers, 32 Nassau Street, Dublin D02 YH68

Penguin Random House is committed to a sustainable future
for our business, our readers and our planet. This book is made
from Forest Stewardship Council® certified paper.

CONTENTS

A NOTE ON NAMES, IDENTITIES, AND PRONOUNS

The Other Olympians chronicles the lives of several European athletes—Zdeněk Koubek, Mark Weston, Willy de Bruyn, and Witold Smętek—who publicly transitioned gender in the 1930s. Though all were assigned female at birth, and were perceived by the public as women throughout their athletic careers, I refer to all using only male pronouns and only the names they chose after transitioning, in accordance with their publicly expressed identities and with the best practices outlined by the Trans Journalists Association. (At a few junctures, you might see me quote from 1930s sources that include the name "Koubková." That is Koubek's feminized last name, since in Czech even last names are gendered.)

It is tempting to place a contemporary label like "trans" or "intersex" onto these athletes, but I try to use these labels sparingly throughout the book. It is difficult to fit any of them into a contemporary identity category. Today, many people understand that sex and gender are two separate categories: gender is a psychological and socialized identity, while sex is assigned, often at birth, based on your physical body. But in the 1920s and 1930s, people did not differentiate between gender and sex as we do today. Though you can find allusions in the archives to a psychological or social understanding of gender, when writers talked about being a man, a woman, or an "invert," they were generally referring to biological sex rather than to a social understanding of gender.

A few times, I allude to Koubek and Weston as approximating trans identity, because both men, at various points, described their connection to maleness in psychological terms. In these moments, I am using "trans" broadly, as an umbrella term to capture a number of different possible identities.

Any portrait of each man's identity is muddled, however, by that lack of delineation between sex and gender. To receive gender-affirmative surgery, Koubek and Weston each needed to emphasize their normatively masculine *physical* traits, both in public and to their doctors. If they simply said they felt a psychological connection to male identity, they probably would not have received healthcare. For this reason, news reports about both men suggest that they each had biological traits typically associated with both male and female sex categories. Perhaps today, either Koubek or Weston would have gravitated more toward a label like "intersex," which refers to the possibility that they were born with a mix of traits traditionally demarcated as both male and female. It is difficult to know. When we discuss them today, we should leave some space for a multitude of possible identities.

GLOSSARY OF ACRONYMS

In the early twentieth century, a disparate series of organizations issued sports policies. Though I have tried to simplify the bureaucratic details of sports governance where possible throughout *The Other Olympians*, here are some key acronyms to keep in mind as you read.

AAU Amateur Athletic Union (US-based sports organization that oversees American track-and-field sports; a key constituency of the American Olympic Committee)

CAAU Czechoslovak Amateur Athletic Union (Czechoslovakia-based track-and-field organization; the Czech equivalent of the AAU)

FSFI Fédération Sportive Féminine Internationale (the sports organization, started by Alice Milliat, overseeing the Women's World Games)

IAAF International Amateur Athletic Federation (the governing body of track-and-field sports; in 2019, it rebranded as World Athletics)

IOC International Olympic Committee

Part I

TRIUMPH

CHAPTER 1

THE DAY BEFORE the world changed, Carl Diem walked into Berlin's new sports stadium in high spirits. It was the morning of June 27, 1914, and Diem, a gangly thirty-two-year-old, was there to visit Germany's pre-Olympic games, a dress rehearsal for the forthcoming event.[1] In two short years, athletes from across the United States and Europe would convene at the very same stadium for the real Olympic Games. Diem needed to make sure it was perfect.

No one had a bigger stake in the 1916 Olympics than Diem. The previous October, German officials had appointed him secretary of the Organizing Committee for the Olympic Games, a coalition of politicians and athletic officials tasked with setting the schedule, venue, lodging, layout, and financing for the competitions. It was a high honor for someone so young, especially given Diem's unconventional background. As a teenager, following a short-lived career running track, he had dropped out of high school to write for newspapers.[2] His critiques of Germany's weak athletic infrastructure drew the notice of the country's sporting elites. They elected him, at the age of twenty-one, to serve on one of Germany's top sports organizations.[3]

A decade later, Diem was the face of the next Olympics. Since his appointment to the Organizing Committee, he had traveled across Germany, giving speeches to dubious sports officials about the need to prepare their teams for international competition. Germany was a gymnastics-focused country, with three times more gymnasts than any other type of athlete,[4] but Diem wanted to make the country a real competitor in sports like track and field.[5] The fresh-faced dropout was still distressed that at the 1912 Olympics, Germany had finished an embarrassing fifth in the national medal count.[6]

Diem delivered lectures in Hamburg, Frankfurt, and Cologne, courting politicians for money over high-end Rhine wines and champagne.[7] At night, as trains whisked him from city to city, he stayed up late plotting out the finer details of the Olympics. And his efforts weren't limited to his home country. He took a steamboat to America, where he met with Woodrow Wilson and gifted the US president a German sports pin.[8] Later, he visited the headquarters of the International Olympic Committee in Paris and returned to Berlin with a grand plan to blanket Germany with sports fields and playgrounds.

That Saturday, Diem's vision of an athletically elite Germany seemed to be arriving. Thousands of top athletes warmed up for track-and-field competitions.[9] Germany's head of state, Kaiser Wilhelm II, studied the crowd from a canopied box seat. During the day's competition, the kaiser's nephew proved the indisputable star. The twenty-one-year-old prince cruised through the distance run and the weight-throwing competitions. The press loved the spectacle, which meant so did Diem. With the backing of the kaiser, he was invincible.

No one involved could have known it then, but that spot—that gleaming new Berlin sports stadium—would, twenty-two years later, become the setting for a turning point in world history. It would become synonymous with fascism and racial discrimination; with new heights in athletic achievement and a major leap forward in radio technology; with propaganda and spectacle and social control; and, more quietly, with the birth of a regime of gender surveillance in sports.

In twenty-two years, the fates of a loose group of sports professionals—a Czech athlete who publicly transitioned gender, the organizer of a breakaway sports competition for women, a closeted queer Missourian sprinter, an ambitious American executive, a Nazi sports doctor, an aging half-Jewish bureaucrat, and Diem himself—would all collide here during one of the most notorious Olympic Games in history. The result would be the creation of an Olympic sex testing policy and apparatus that, even as its origins have been forgotten, continues to define sports—and, to an extent, society—today.

o o o

Once upon a time, this place was a patchwork of trees. In the second half of the nineteenth century, the population of Berlin, one of the largest cities in the newly formed German Empire, was exploding. The city's elites demanded more—more space, more fresh air, and more distance from the bustle and grime of the inner city—and so they turned to the massive Grunewald Forest on the western edge of Berlin.[10] Packed with conifers and birch trees, the Grunewald had, for centuries, hosted Prussian aristocrats looking to hunt wild boar and deer.[11] Now rich Berliners wanted to make it their new home. On the outskirts of the forest they erected ungainly mansions, often over the protests of environmentalists, who in turn organized a Berlin Forest Protection Day to stop the development. They popularized a song that criticized the clearing of the Grunewald as a "wood auction."[12] But opposing the development was futile: around 1909, the new neighborhood drew the attention of a small group of

German officials who were looking to build a stadium big enough to host the Olympics.[13] These officials fixated on a grassy area just outside the forest, which had everything they needed: a mostly undeveloped area not far from downtown Berlin, populated by residents rich enough to subsidize the construction.

The German Stadium (Deutsches Stadion) opened in 1913 after a furious two hundred days of work. It was the second-largest sports venue in the world, home to a track, two gymnastics fields, a soccer field, a bicycling course, and a swimming pool.[14] The German Stadium was the stuff of dreams, a symbol of its country's new athletic prowess. Tourists flocked to it, and athletes battled to compete inside it. Carl Diem later bragged that in those days, "There was life from morning to night" at the stadium.[15] When the Olympics came to town, he assumed, the German Stadium would blow away the world.

Sunday, June 28, 1914, was the second and last day of the pre-Olympic competition at the German Stadium. In the morning, sharpshooters filed onto the field for the shooting championships.[16] Between rounds, marching music blared throughout the stadium. At around 11:30 in the morning, the German shooters were preparing for the end of the competition when, suddenly, the music stopped. The black, red, and white flag of the German Empire dropped to half-mast.[17] The breaking news was hard to believe: a young Serbian revolutionary had killed Archduke Franz Ferdinand, heir to the Austro-Hungarian Empire and a close ally of the German state. Sitting in the audience, one German official, a Prussian general, reacted immediately. Diem recalled a single sentence: "This means war."[18]

It did, in fact, mean war. But it would take an agonizing few weeks to get there. Exactly one month later, on July 28, the Austro-Hungarian Empire declared war on Serbia, activating a web of geopolitical alliances. Two days after that, Russia mobilized against the Austro-Hungarian Empire. Germany, a dutiful ally of Austria-

Hungary, declared war on Russia, then on France, then on Belgium. On August 4, Britain launched its forces against Germany.

Germany's Olympic dreams unraveled. Diem enlisted to fight in the German army that August, hoping for a swift end to the hostilities. He told reporters he would wait to send out invitations to the 1916 Olympics until there was peace. "We can be reasonably sure that modern war will not last so long," he said.[19] But it wasn't meant to be. On October 1, German officials dissolved the Organizing Committee and suspended all events at the German Stadium. Instead, sheep grazed on the neglected field.[20] The following April, when German soldiers deployed chlorine gas at Ypres, Belgium, the war entered a gruesome new phase. The 1916 Games were canceled. When the dust settled, in the final days of 1918, Germany had not just lost the war but also found itself expelled from nearly all global institutions, including the International Olympic Committee. Diem, a true believer in the Olympic project, was crushed. It was going to be a long road back.

ZDENĚK KOUBEK GREW UP HEARING WHISPERS of independence. Born on December 8, 1913, in the Czech city of Paskov, a snow-covered village along the southeastern border with Poland, he was, technically, a subject of the Austro-Hungarian Empire. But the empire was fast losing its grip on the region. Koubek was barely six months old when Austria-Hungary attacked Serbia, sending Europe careening toward war. Koubek's father, who worked as an overseer in the mansion of an Austro-Hungarian aristocrat, had little choice but to join the army. The empire dispatched him to the town of Plava, on the Italian border.[1]

With their source of income gone, Koubek's mother and five older siblings moved some one hundred miles away to a suburb south of Brno, a small city packed with cobblestone roads, museums, movie theaters, and German restaurants. Nearly two-thirds of Brno was ethnically German,[2] and many locals spoke a language that blended Czech and German.[3] Under the Austro-Hungarian regime, German residents exerted near total control of the city. When a group of Czechs proposed creating the first Czech-language university in Brno, German residents responded that the Slavic "barbarians" would ruin the city's "German" character.[4] Once the war broke out, resistance became dangerous. In February 1915, the Austro-Hungarian Empire executed seven Czechs whom it accused of spreading enemy propaganda.[5] It further suspended forty-seven Czech-language newspapers from publishing and required the remaining papers to run prewritten propaganda articles. "Paper after paper was strangled," one Czech observer recalled.[6] Czech critiques of the empire slipped underground, heard only in whispers on trams and in cafés.[7]

Huddled in their new apartment, Koubek's family subsisted on dinners of polenta, stale bread, and—to Koubek's particular chagrin—turnips, as the country sacrificed meat and flour to feed soldiers in the war effort. Only in 1920, two years after the close of the war, did Koubek discover such luxuries as sausage. By that time, the Austro-Hungarian Empire was no more, and the British, American, and French armies supervised the creation of a new government in Koubek's home region, a state called Czechoslovakia. It was to be a representative democracy of over thirteen million people—a configuration of Czechs and Slovaks who had broken away from the Austro-Hungarian Empire, plus the region's existing German, Hungarian, and Jewish populations. Change came fast.[8]

In 1918, the country's new National Assembly elected its first president. Women gained the right to vote. The double-headed eagle, once a symbol of Austro-Hungarian power, disappeared from public buildings.[9] Films depicting Czech soldiers who had broken away from the Austro-Hungarian forces to fight for Russia or France or Italy were screened widely across the young nation and became the basis for a new Czech national self-mythology.[10] Czech-language universities opened,[11] and buildings were given Czech names to erase their Germanic origins. Prague's New German Theater rebranded as the Smetana Theater.[12] In cases where politicians opted to leave relics of the old empire intact, some activists took matters into their own hands. Czech vigilantes forcibly removed a number of imperial statues, at times descending into violent clashes with ethnic Germans who tried to defend the monuments.[13] In downtown Brno, a linguistic guerrilla war took hold: Germans defaced posters written in Czech, while Czechs graffitied those written in German.[14]

The new Czech state had no history, no self-identity. Even its most ardent supporters frequently worried about its fragility;[15] those fears drove some to embrace violence. One particularly dangerous group was the legionnaires, a network of Czech soldiers who had broken away from the Austro-Hungarian army to fight for the Allies during the war. Though hailed as war heroes, some legionnaires couldn't give up the fight, even after Czechoslovakia became independent. They instigated attacks on German, Hungarian, and Jewish residents, fearing that racial and ethnic minorities posed a threat to national cohesion.[16] They once attacked the pregnant wife of a British ambassador after they heard her speak English in the street and mistook it for German.[17]

The legionnaires also went after leftists. On June 26, 1920, in Olomouc, a city just outside Brno, one thousand members of the left-leaning Social Democratic Party gathered for a conference.[18] The legionnaires, fearful of a socialist takeover, decided to frighten them. One hundred and fifty of them left their barracks and broke up the meeting, locking the doors and fanning out across the room, guns and knives raised. One soldier stabbed the speaker in the back. The ambush inflamed the left, whose leaders began exhorting Czech people to express their "just anger."[19] It became an existential crisis for Tomáš Masaryk, the president of Czechoslovakia. But instead of punishing the legionnaires, he instructed the Social Democrats to more clearly demonstrate their loyalty to the new Czech state.

Though they were ethnically Czech, Koubek's family didn't have

time to consider the growing pains of an independent Czechoslovakia. The family was barely staying afloat. When Koubek's father
returned home from the front lines, he struggled to find a job. Eventually, he decided to try his hand as a carriage driver in downtown
Brno, hoping that the growing number of wealthy visitors to the city
could help him eke out a living. Koubek, clad in boots and patched-up
trousers, often rode with him on horseback.

○○○

Koubek could not quite place how, but he grew up knowing he was
different. Most people perceived him as a girl, including his mother
and father, who wrote that he was female on his birth certificate
and who assigned him a feminine name that he would later reject.
To the world, he was a girl, though eventually he'd understand
himself not to be. Koubek's mother forced him to start wearing a
blue bow in his hair, which Koubek hated. He stared at himself in
the mirror and scowled. He thought the bow made him look like an
obedient poodle, and soon the nickname stuck: the boys at school,
especially the mean ones, nicknamed him "the poodle." In a small
act of rebellion, Koubek wore trousers that he borrowed from his
brothers, but he kept the ponytail and bow intact to please his
parents.

Outside of class, most of the girls refused to talk to him. His only
female friends were named Anka and Božka, and they had a habit of
tormenting the boys. They laughed when the other kids confused
zebras and rhinos in biology class or when they mixed up the names
of Holy Roman emperors in history. When a classmate placed hedge-
hogs in a confessional stall at the local church, Anka and Božka
gleefully ratted him out to their teachers. Humiliated, the boys often
threatened to fight them—until Koubek stepped in. Koubek had
learned to throw a fierce punch, and he used it to protect his friends.

Years later, when Koubek was trying to explain his new life as a man to the general public, he claimed, perhaps with a touch of exaggeration, that he had developed a fearsome reputation throughout the school. Whenever an argument escalated into shouting, some student inevitably threatened to call him for help.

Social life in the suburbs of Brno revolved around campfires. The neighborhood kids gathered on the outskirts of the woods to bake potatoes, stage wrestling matches, and organize sprinting contests. They usually raced from a firepit to a rusted billboard advertising shoe cream somewhere in the distance—a stand-in for the finish line. The sprints were not taken lightly. The winner got to walk away with the coveted prize of four sizzling baked potatoes, and they fought hard: once, a boy Koubek's age tripped and fell into a ditch in the middle of his run. He hobbled back to the group with a broken knee and a layer of mud clinging to his face.

Koubek was eight years old when he joined his first sprint. He had never been much of a runner, but he decided to try. From the moment he heard *go*, Koubek shot out ahead of the four girls he was competing against. He pictured himself as a deer, galloping away from a hunter. He was just a few meters from the finish line when someone shouted his name from behind. Koubek slowed to see what had happened. In that instant, the girl who had shouted his name leapt ahead of him. She won by just a fraction of a second. Koubek was devastated that he'd fallen for such an obvious trick. The boys whooped and hollered, savoring the rare chance to tease their most fearless classmate. Koubek choked back tears and ran straight toward the woods, not stopping until he found his way home. He resolved never to run again.

○○○

The older Koubek became, the more peculiar he found the rituals of femininity. When he was fourteen, he enrolled in a Czech convent school in Brno, where he fit in even less than before. He experimented with an embroidery class, but his designs were so disfigured that one of his teachers told him he made the angel Gabriel look like a chimney sweep. Another nun, disgusted, threw his work into the trash. The only time he felt in step with femininity was in choir class. Koubek was a soprano, and the other students always remarked that he had a beautiful voice. But one April, during his early teen years, his pitch started to drop, fast. Soon he stood out as the sole baritone in the otherwise all-girls' choir. His teacher, who had once embraced his talents, became concerned that the sea of soft voices would be "profaned" by his "base rumbling" and decided to intervene. She wrote on Koubek's report card that he "does not have an ear for music." Koubek was summarily ejected from choir.

It didn't help that Koubek's new friends started cultivating crushes on their mediocre-looking male peers. One friend was falling for a boy whom Koubek thought gnashed his teeth too much in class. When the question turned to which boys had caught Koubek's attention, Koubek had no answer. He didn't know how to say he felt nothing. Why wasn't he more like the girls, dreaming of princes in storybooks? He tried not to let it bother him, but it did. *Will I ever in my life have somebody?* he asked himself.

On Sundays, when suitors came over to his family's house to court his two older sisters, his parents told him to wait outside so he wouldn't spoil the mood. Koubek often perched at the crown of the cherry tree in his backyard, where he could stare out at the Brno countryside. There he developed an obsession with detective novels. He read every book about Leon Clifton, the popular fictional Czech detective.

From his spot on the cherry tree, Koubek also plotted out business ideas. He was nothing if not an entrepreneur. During school breaks, he bought baskets of fruit from a local farmer, and with his younger brother and dog in tow, he paraded around the neighborhood shouting "Fruuuuit for saaaale!" He sold apples and berries to his neighbors at a steep markup. Koubek was thrilled when he earned enough to make his business's first big investment: a wagon to carry the produce.

Koubek had never run track formally, and he hadn't run at all since that first failed sprint at the campfire in Brno. As he grew older, his contempt for sports only grew. He refused to participate even in informal athletic competitions with his friends. Role-playing games, he thought, were far more dignified than sports. On the streets of Brno, he scowled at people who jogged past him, training for some unknowable sprint. Runners were far too thin, he thought, and probably a little bit mentally unwell. Anyway, Koubek didn't come from money. His father was barely making ends meet as it was. Having the time and money to invest in athletics was an unimaginable privilege for someone like him. "People should have more important things to worry about than competing with each other," he huffed in a later essay.

CHAPTER 3

AS A CHILD, Alice Joséphine Marie Million didn't expect to see the world. She was born in Nantes, France, on May 5, 1884, to working-class parents who owned a small grocery store.[1] The oldest of five children, Alice always had an independent streak: in 1904, when she was just twenty years old, she moved to London and married another Nantes transplant named Joseph Milliat.[2] Alice took his last name, Milliat, and clung to it when he died unexpectedly four years later, leaving her widowed at the age of twenty-four.

Though she was born a few decades before Zdeněk Koubek, Alice Milliat, like her Czech counterpart, had hated sports as a kid.[3] In Milliat's case, gymnastics classes at school were a particular source of frustration. But after losing her husband, she reinvented herself. She learned to row and play soccer. When Milliat moved back to France several years after her husband's death, she joined Fémina Sport,[4] a newly formed women's sports club. In a country where ritzy athletic clubs monopolized women's competitions, Fémina Sport made a point of recruiting athletes from the working class.[5]

Milliat soon discovered that she had stumbled into a larger movement. The arrival of World War I catapulted women's sports into the mainstream in Europe and the United States. Just as women poured into factories to take over male-dominated jobs, so, too, did they ascend the ranks of traditionally masculine leisure activities. An American news report declared in 1919 that, in the wake of the war, women track-and-field athletes "are no longer looked upon askance."[6]

Sporting short brown hair and a wardrobe of somber clothes, Milliat rarely registered as a threat, and she used that to her advantage. In 1915, she became the president of Fémina Sport.[7] Two years later, she assimilated a pair of rival women's sports clubs into France's first women's sports league, which she called the Fédération des sociétés féminines sportives de France (Federation of French Women's Sports Clubs). She kept pushing. It was "profoundly abnormal," she thought, that she was one of only two women in leadership in the league.[8] In 1919, when she was elected president of the new federation, Milliat decided to clean house. She rewrote the group's bylaws to require that women make up the majority of its eight-person executive board.[9] She also recruited female referees and coaches to oversee soccer and track-and-field competitions and pushed for more female club managers.

Soon after she took control, Milliat had to contend with a common complaint about women's sports: the claim that it amounted to a public health catastrophe. Medical professionals had insisted there was a link between women's sports and declining birth rates as far back as 1888, when one physician wrote that women needed to "abandon cycling to the stronger sex" because bike seats could damage their reproductive organs.[10] Milliat knew that public tolerance of her project often depended on the degree to which her players seemed properly feminine. When reporters questioned the morality of operating a women's soccer team, Milliat countered that soccer was not "unwomanly," because women played the game differently from men. "They play fast, but not vigorous," she insisted.[11] One of her sprinters was married with four kids, Milliat made sure to point out, as if that bolstered her team's feminine credentials.[12] "You'd better believe that we are women and that we intend to remain women!" an underling of Milliat's once told the press.[13]

It wasn't long before Milliat hit a ceiling in her home country. French women athletes were so few and far between that Milliat's adult female players had to resort to competing against young boys.[14] Few soccer fields would let women practice.[15] Being a sports executive, she lamented, meant constantly having to fight "the primitive spirit of male domination."[16]

Sometime in 1919, just months after the close of World War I, Milliat decided to expand her movement outside France. From her small apartment in Paris, the most that her day job as a stenographer could afford her,[17] Milliat wrote a letter to the most powerful sports executive she could think of, urging him to introduce more international sports competitions for women. She addressed the letter to Pierre de Coubertin, the founder of the modern-day Olympics, and dropped it off in the mail.[18]

o o o

Unfortunately for Milliat, Pierre de Coubertin had other things on his mind. On April 28, 1919, as the leaders of France, England, and the United States were negotiating the Treaty of Versailles, Coubertin joined seven other sports leaders in Lausanne, Switzerland, for the first postwar meeting of the International Olympic Committee, the governing body of the Olympics. Coubertin was planning for the grand return of the Olympic Games in 1920, in Antwerp, Belgium. He wanted these Olympics to be a symbol of postwar international cooperation, but he couldn't decide which teams should be allowed to take part.[19]

The fifty-six-year-old was a French baron, raised on private schools, dinner banquets, and fencing lessons. Standing before the gathered members, he looked the part: thick bristling mustache, bushy eyebrows, brown top hat, receding white hair. He was never ashamed of the aristocracy that built him. It was part of his appeal: *The New York Times* once praised him as "a man who comes from the best conservative stock of France." Throughout his life, he ended his official Olympic correspondence with the sign-off "Baron."[20]

Coubertin's most pressing concern in Antwerp was Germany. He already had close ties to sports officials in the country, having befriended Carl Diem, that chief planner of the canceled 1916 Olympics, in the years leading up to the war, and he had a soft spot for the young German.[21] Before the war, they had exchanged handwritten postcards, hiked together up Swiss mountains, and visited operas, theaters, and museums across Paris. Diem had expressed his "veneration" for the French leader. Still, Coubertin worried that allowing Germany to return to the Olympics was bad politics. It seemed inappropriate to welcome athletes from a country that had unleashed poison gas on the open battlefield.

As had become his habit, Coubertin punted the decision. He and the other IOC members ruled that the country hosting the Olympics should have the right to decide whom to include; they most likely knew that Belgium, the next host, would not invite Germany. Predictably, when the Olympics resumed the next year, Germany, Austria, Turkey, Bulgaria, and Hungary—the Central Powers and their allies—found themselves shunned from competition.[22] The postwar healing would have to wait.

In some ways, the indirect decision to exclude Germany marked an ideological departure for Coubertin. When the baron kicked off the modern Olympic Games in 1896 in Athens, Greece, he claimed he wanted to use sports to bridge geopolitical divides. The real story was more complicated. Coubertin first explored the idea of organizing an international sports competition while studying at a university in Paris in the early 1880s, when he had militarism on the mind. He became convinced that France's defeat in the Franco-Prussian War a decade earlier was a failure not of military tactics but of physical strength.[23] The solution, he decided, was better athletics. Only as he started touring other countries to see how to improve the French teams did his ambitions widen. If he could bring European countries into a shared sports league, maybe, he thought, he could reduce the need for war itself.

In practice, however, the early Olympic Games were a thinly veiled playground for white aristocratic men. Coubertin hoped the Olympics would help bring "to perfection the strong and hopeful youth of our white race"[24]—an early tell of which kinds of people he envisioned competing in the games and which he did not. Coubertin described sports in African countries as "behind the times"[25] and African people as "still without elementary culture," and he imagined that the "civilizing mission" the French government had embarked upon—his chosen euphemism for colonialism—would bring about change. Sports, he once suggested, could help people from African countries "clarify thought."[26]

In 1916, twenty years after its founding, the International Olympic Committee had representatives from only one African and one Asian country, compared with the forty-seven representatives it boasted from Europe, the United States, and Australia.[27] The insularity of the IOC wasn't aided by the fact that a little less than half of its first forty-two members were, like Coubertin, part of the European aristocracy.[28] All were men; the IOC didn't appoint its first female member until 1981, nearly a century into its existence.[29]

Alice Milliat would have struggled to find a person less receptive to her plea than Coubertin. By the time her letter arrived, Coubertin had grown weary of the question of women's sports, which seemed to reemerge, cicada-like, every IOC meeting. His stance was crystal-clear: women's athletics would not "constitute a sight to be recommended before the crowds that gather for an Olympiad."[30] Because sports were about "virilizing bodies and souls,"[31] women could achieve the "ruggedness" and masculinity of a successful athlete, Coubertin told IOC officials, only "when nerves are stretched beyond their normal capacity, and morally only when the most precious feminine characteristics are nullified."[32]

Women did manage to secure places in a select few sports, largely because of a bureaucratic quirk of the Olympics. Each host country—not the IOC itself—was empowered to select the events that would be staged. At the Paris Olympics in 1900, nineteen women attended, a paltry number compared to the 1,318 male athletes.[33] In 1904, when St. Louis hosted the Olympics, just eight women participated. Women could enroll only in sports like tennis, which were associated with the upper class. Track and field, more accessible to the working class, was entirely off the table. Even so, Coubertin "greatly regret[ted]" even these minuscule exceptions.[34] He wasn't alone: the American Olympic Committee affirmed that it would not allow women to compete in any event "in which they could not wear long skirts,"[35] effectively removing swimming, track and field, and soccer from the Olympic program.

When Coubertin failed to respond to Milliat's letter, the ambitious Frenchwoman decided to take matters into her own hands. She approached sports leaders from England, Switzerland, France, Italy, and Norway about organizing an international women's competition. In March 1921, she held a practice event on a pigeon-shooting field outside a local casino in Monte Carlo.[36] A columnist for *The Daily Telegraph* was there and left impressed, observing, "There is no real cause to fear any corruption of English womanhood by athleticism."[37] Women had just won the right to vote in the United States, the UK, the Netherlands, and Canada—why shouldn't they also have the right to sports?

Buoyed by the success, Milliat invited seven top sports officials to a Paris restaurant that October.[38] As waiters rushed through the maze of tables, balancing glasses of champagne and plates teeming with cream of spinach and ham,[39] Milliat announced the formation of an international league for women's sports. She called it the Fédération Sportive Féminine Internationale—more commonly referred to today as the FSFI. It was to be structured like the IOC and would organize an international competition for women every four years.

The next year, Milliat, as head of the FSFI, held the first Women's World Games in Paris. Women athletes jumped at the chance to take part. Seventy-seven athletes from Czechoslovakia, France, England, Switzerland, and the United States ultimately made the trip to France.[40] Over twenty thousand people attended,[41] and the event garnered positive coverage in publications like the *Los Angeles Times*[42] and *The Boston Globe*.[43] Arriving visitors received a pamphlet outlining the week's events, which included a speech from Milliat explaining that the Women's World Games could contribute to "the betterment of woman, whatever class of society she comes from."[44]

Milliat was hardly the prototypical executive. Few women held leadership positions in sports at the time, and even fewer advocated so explicitly for gender diversity in leadership. French newspapers, threatened by the power she had accumulated, attempted to malign her as an autocrat, comparing her to Mussolini and Napoleon.[45] But Milliat had the personality to lead an international sports league in other ways. Fluent in French, English, and Spanish, she had an ear for language and a knack for using it to get what she wanted. When her federation selected a new country to host the Women's World Games, Milliat started teaching herself the local language so she could better communicate with her hosts.[46] She worked to expand the reach of her federation beyond Europe, traveling to Japan in the hopes of convincing the country to host a competition there.[47] Sports committees in India, Palestine, and China wrote to Milliat, asking how they could join.[48]

Yet despite her caricature in the press, Milliat was no radical. Even amid her crusade for women's sports, she felt the relationship between sports and women's health was unsettled, with a full analysis not due for "several generations,"[49] and she pushed for medical interventions to protect her players in the interim. When participants in the Women's World Games finished a sprint or a soccer match, doctors, at Milliat's request, examined their heart rates and breathing frequencies and made sure there was no damage to their reproductive organs. She could often be heard touting the femininity of her athletes to reporters.[50] She wasn't trying to blow up the sporting apparatus—she just wanted to carve out space within it.

○○○

Far from the beacon of athleticism and international cooperation that its founder envisioned, the early Olympics, which began in 1896, were marked by chaos. In an era before sports medicine became a field of study, athletes drank champagne and brandy and took cocaine and strychnine—a common rat poison—to sharpen their focus ahead of competitions.[51] Sugar cubes soaked in nitroglycerine were a common prerace snack. Runners, dehydrated and often intoxicated, had a habit of collapsing in the middle of races.[52] Temporary structures erected for visitors sometimes caved in; a faulty bridge sent one Olympic athlete careening to his death.[53] Some athletes arrived to their competitions late. Others were known to quit their race halfway through to sit at a café. At least one sprinter was chased a mile off course by a pack of stray dogs.[54] Félix Carvajal, Cuba's first Olympian, started his race so famished that he reportedly stopped at a roadside food stand in the middle of his run and took a thirty-minute lunch break. Somehow, he still managed to finish in fourth place.[55]

Track-and-field routes often wove through population centers, and the lack of instant replay meant accusations of cheating were rampant. Tales abounded of marathon runners who disappeared in the middle of competition, only to mysteriously resurface, as if through a shortcut, at the front of the pack.[56] Fred Lorz, a marathon runner at the 1904 Olympics, quit his race after nine miles and hitched a ride back to the stadium. When he arrived, spectators, to his surprise, hailed him as the first-place finisher.[57] He eventually admitted the truth, but not before posing for celebratory photos in the crowd.[58]

Also unresolved were the rules of the competitions themselves. At the 1908 Olympics in London, the four-hundred-meter dash sparked significant controversy. The judges, all British, threw out a presumed American victory because of accusations that the top-place finisher had gotten in the way of his British runner-up during the sprint.[59] In the sticky July heat, tensions ran high, and British spectators began chanting "foul" at the American.[60] The problem, it turned out, was a discrepancy in the British and American track-and-field rules. While the Americans allowed "track tactics" in the final one hundred meters of a race,[61] a definition that could include physically blocking a competitor, Britain banned "wilfully jostling or running across or obstructing another competitor." Because all the referees were British, they enforced the latter rules. The American side was furious. "This race was deliberately taken away from us," one official said.[62] American Olympic officials decided to credit their own sprinter with a gold medal, even though the official Olympic records listed the Brit as the winner.[63]

So when the Olympics came to Stockholm, Sweden, in 1912, a middle-aged Swedish businessman named Johannes Sigfrid Edström wanted to avoid a repeat of these disasters. It was clear to anyone who paid attention that Pierre de Coubertin, the creator of the modern Olympics, didn't exactly delight in the fine details of planning the games. The baron's interest was in spectacle, not governance.[64] But if the Olympics were to be taken seriously, Edström knew, they needed clearer rules of competition.

Edström, who sat on the Organizing Committee for the 1912 Games, was a titan of industry, and a wealthy one at that: he controlled a massive electricity company in Sweden, the General Swedish Electrical Limited Company,[65] best known for manufacturing generators and trolley cars. Square-faced, with short, parted hair and a wardrobe abundant with gray suits, Edström easily could have passed for an ex–Olympic athlete. In truth, though, he was always more of an engineer. After graduating from a technical school in Zurich,[66] he moved first to Pittsburgh, then to New York, to work for Westinghouse and General Electric, two of the biggest electrical companies in the country. Soon, he met his wife, a schoolteacher and suffragette from Illinois named Ruth Randall.[67] Randall became closely involved in Edström's work; the two often debated policy over breakfast.

After returning to Europe, Edström gained a reputation as a fixer, capable of solving large transit-oriented problems. Cities like Zurich regularly called him in to help electrify their transportation systems.[68] The work also shaped him into a savvy political operator, a skill he began to apply to sports administration at the turn of the century. Soon after he secured a spot on the Organizing Committee for the 1912 Games, Edström positioned himself as Coubertin's ally.[69] When a debate around the pentathlon—a series of five exercises that included fencing, swimming, horse-riding, shooting, and running—created a rift between Coubertin and the Swedish organizers, Edström astutely pushed the Coubertin point of view.[70] Coubertin thought he'd found a kindred spirit.[71]

It didn't take long for Edström to cash in on that goodwill. He began reaching out to track-and-field representatives from across Europe, inquiring about whether they would attend a rule-making meeting ahead of the 1912 Olympics. Together, Edström said, they could standardize international regulations for track-and-field sports to avoid the controversies that had reared up in London.[72] When Coubertin found out, he fumed at the Swedes for challenging the authority of the IOC. A letter from the president of Sweden's Organizing Committee failed to calm him down, so Edström stepped in. He assured the IOC president that "the work of the IOC will not in any way be disturbed" by the track-and-field congress: it was, instead, a way to make the IOC's job easier.[73]

The sweet talking worked. Coubertin backed off. In July 1912, just before the Olympic Games in Sweden, seventeen countries met to outline how they would govern track-and-field sports. The group agreed to make their meetings an annual event, focused on creating rules for Olympic competition and registering world records.[74] A year later, in August 1913, Edström named the group the International Amateur Athletic Federation—the IAAF for short. Edström was elected its president. The German athletic leader Carl Diem, whom Edström had befriended in recent years, was also chosen to serve on the IAAF,[75] inaugurating what would become decades of collaboration between the two men.

The IAAF, Edström assured Coubertin, would operate in a subordinate position to the IOC, creating rules related to track-and-field sports but deferring to the ultimate authority of the IOC if disagreements arose. It was not unlike a federalist governing system: the IOC would be like a federal government, with the power to set universal laws when it pleased, while the IAAF was more like a state government, legislating where the IOC did not over its specific field of focus. Throughout the next two years, Edström kept Coubertin regularly in the loop about all the developments from the IAAF.[76] But tensions lingered. When Coubertin learned that the IAAF planned to meet in Paris in 1914, just a few days before the IOC had scheduled its own official meeting there, Coubertin called it a "direct and personal insult to the I.O.C."[77] Edström, sensing that a fight wasn't worth it, convinced his members to relocate the meeting to Lyon instead.

The IAAF was among the first of what would become a sprawling array of "international federations," or regulatory bodies where leaders from each set of Olympic sports—soccer, swimming, rowing, cycling, track and field, and so on—crafted rules for themselves. The IOC could not possibly make every decision, about every sport, for itself; that was where the federations came in. These international bodies soon set rules around which athletes were eligible to compete in their sports, including, in many cases, instituting policies around sex testing.

When it was founded, the International Amateur Athletic Federation was meant to be a behind-the-scenes organization that settled technical debates over how to, say, draw track lines. At first the IAAF mostly issued small decisions. It hired the American manufacturer Spalding to create prototypes for all Olympic-level track-and-field equipment,[78] so that every country had a standard. It appointed an international group of judges, to minimize host-country bias, and created a panel of five experts to review any protests that athletes lodged.[79] It reviewed world records[80] and argued over how wind should factor in. If the wind velocity was much higher during one Olympics than the other, should the IAAF adjust the times of the world record holders accordingly?[81]

In its first years of existence, the press paid almost no attention. But under Edström's leadership, the IAAF began steadily accumulating power. Nowhere was that more apparent than in the growing debate around women's sports. As Alice Milliat's crowning achievement, the Women's World Games, gained steam, it put the IOC in a bind. The all-male board, especially Coubertin, didn't want to allow women to compete in the Olympics. But they also worried that ignoring the phenomenon would cleave their influence in half. The more the Women's World Games grew in popularity, the more it risked taking away the spotlight from the all-male Olympic movement. The IOC faced a galling choice: it could continue to ignore women's sports and allow their power to split along gendered lines, or it could bring women into the fold and hope to do away with the Women's World Games in the process.[82]

When Edström first learned about the Women's World Games, he took the latter position. He started warning colleagues that the IAAF needed to "handle the female athletes" by bringing Milliat under its control.[83] If he could convince Milliat to abandon the Women's World Games and instead become a subordinate member of the IAAF, then both Edström and Coubertin could maintain their power. Whether the IAAF or the IOC had anything concrete to offer Milliat's organization was not part of the discussion. Edström saw women's athletics as his for the taking, and he asked his colleagues to "point out to the leading women that we will ourselves govern the female sport."[84]

In 1922, Edström appointed a committee of six executives to investigate whether to allow women to participate in track-and-field sports at the Olympics.[85] Though he did give Milliat and another prominent woman athlete spots on the committee, he made sure to curtail their power. He wrote to one male committee member, in reference to Milliat, "I should be very thankful if you are not too much influenced by the French women." He was open to negotiating with Milliat, but he wanted to do it on his terms. If Milliat didn't agree to give up the Women's World Games and join the IAAF, he said, "we will have to fight her Federation."[86]

ONE MORNING IN THE FALL OF 1927, Zdeněk Koubek wove through the bustling sidewalks of downtown Brno, balancing four cups of coffee on a tin tray.[1] There was an art to navigating the city during rush hour. Dodging the lattice of cars, ambulances, horse-drawn carriages, museum trams, and pedestrians all jockeying for space along the city's tight cobblestone streets made Koubek feel like a magician.

Koubek slowed in front of a crowd gathering outside a clothing store. Everyone seemed to be fixated on the store's front windows, which featured an assortment of half-dressed mannequins. The shop was changing the outfits ahead of the winter season. For a moment, the models looked nude. It was enough to cause a scandal among the city's commuters. A few men stood in the road, on their tiptoes, vying for a glance. Koubek paused, it turned out, for a few seconds too long. When a shout came from down the street—his name—Koubek jerked upright, nearly spilling the coffee on himself. He raced over to the haberdashery down the street and slipped inside. "We are all hungry, and you just gape in front of a shop window," Ms. Boženka, Koubek's coworker, snapped as soon as he pushed open the door.

Boženka was only eighteen, four years older than Koubek, but she liked to act much older. This was part of their dynamic. She knew everything; he didn't. She got to yell; he was quiet. He was an apprentice; she was a full employee. Boženka had a reason for her impatience. Koubek was not exactly a hard worker. He was prone to distractions, the changing of mannequin outfits not least among them. He couldn't help but go scarlet whenever women came into the store to try on lingerie. Boženka usually had to take over for him.

Koubek decided to win Boženka back with some light flattery. "When I was outside observing how the changing of that window display aroused such interest, I was thinking that our boss could do a similar sort of advertisement." He summoned his flirtiest voice: "You, Ms. Boženka, sitting there and stringing up our silky stockings, my goodness! There would be more people in the street than at a demonstration!"

Boženka started to blush, then caught herself. "Girl, why don't you take more care of yourself? You look like a runaway from an orphanage," she told him. "The first impression at the counter means everything for attracting a customer or a suitor! You are not going to have any luck in this regard."

She wasn't wrong. For an apprentice at a clothing store, Koubek didn't dress with a particularly refined sense of fashion. While Boženka showed up to work in deep red lipstick, Koubek mostly donned ratty gray clothes. There wasn't much he could do about it. On his meager salary, he couldn't afford nice clothes—and anyway, he didn't feel the need to dress up for men. He didn't understand why. He simply wasn't that into boys. "Well, I am not looking for such luck, in any case. I want to learn how to sell from behind the counter and not throw myself before men's eyes. I know that I do not turn heads like you, Boženka," he said. Then he lowered his voice, remembering that that day, he had a plan to get on Boženka's good side. "For that matter, I have a secret for you," he told her. "But I don't dare hand it over to you, lest you get angry with me."

Boženka's face lit up. "C'mon, quick, tell me what you've got. What happened?"

Koubek reached into his blouse and fished out a small white envelope that a customer had handed him the day before.

Boženka snatched the note. "I want you to tell me who the letter is from."

Koubek couldn't believe she wasn't understanding. "You know, the young guy who has come here every day since the beginning of the holidays and is now up to his neck in socks and buttons," he said. "He's got enough socks to satisfy a centipede and enough buttons to start a museum." The customer, a doctor, dressed crisply and spoke proper Czech, making a point of correctly pronouncing every soft "i." It was frustratingly obvious to everyone but Boženka herself that he was in love with her. Whenever Koubek, not Boženka, assisted him at the register, his disappointment was evident. The doctor, Koubek told Boženka, was too shy to ask out Boženka in person, so he'd appealed to Koubek for help. Koubek told Boženka to open the note. "There is a folded piece of paper inside."

Delighted, Boženka read aloud from the doctor's calligraphic handwriting. He was requesting a date with Boženka that upcoming Sunday. Tucked inside the envelope were tickets to a track-and-field meet of Moravian Slavia, a sports club based in Brno. And to thank Koubek for arranging it, he'd included an extra ticket for the young apprentice.

Boženka handed Koubek the ticket, grinning. Koubek scowled. Sports tickets? That was the gift? Ever since his failed track-and-field match years earlier, he'd hated sports. "If it were at least a ticket to the theater, or the cinema . . . ," he said.

"What are you doing, you goose?" Boženka said when Koubek threw the ticket on the ground. "You'll see, you'll like it a lot in the end!"

Koubek glared at her but gave in. It wasn't like he had other plans. "OK, fine, we'll go on Sunday to your stupid track-and-field match."

○○○

That weekend, Koubek met Boženka and the doctor outside the haberdashery. Koubek was taken with how pretty Boženka looked, dressed in a blue hat and an English coat. He had much less to say about the young doctor, who, it turned out, didn't seem too keen to talk to Koubek, either.

The doctor was in a rush, and he hailed a taxi. The match, he explained, started in an hour, and he was planning to compete in two of the events—the high jump and the hurdles—which meant he needed to get there early. Boženka tried to sound chipper. "The whole week we were standing behind the counter, so it would be nice to spare our legs on a Sunday!" she said. But Koubek couldn't get past the expense of it all. Taking a taxi was a luxury he'd never been able to afford. On the ride over, as he watched the price on the taxi meter tick up, Koubek made the sign of the cross.

The trio got off at the Brno Riviera, a sports field just a few kilometers outside of downtown where the local club Moravian Slavia practiced. The doctor jogged off to the locker room, and Boženka and Koubek headed to the stands. About thirty minutes later, when a group of athletes dressed in blue tracksuits began jogging onto the field, Koubek refocused his chagrin on them. He thought their pre-event warmups looked silly. Grown men shaking their legs, bouncing up and down—who, he wrote in an essay published years later, would waste their time training for something this silly?

An announcer clutching a bullhorn told the audience that the hundred-meter dash was about to begin. The doctor joined five other men at the start. They all kneeled. A man sporting a Charlie Chaplin mustache fired a pistol, and the athletes were off. Koubek was surprised to find himself transfixed. There was something electrifying about the way the men ran—the rush of air past their bodies, the freedom of movement. Koubek thought back to the feeling of sprinting at the bonfire, and he realized he wanted to try again.

The doctor came in dead last, and Boženka looked disappointed. Koubek tried to comfort her, but unfortunately, he wasn't very skilled. He started telling her it didn't matter that her date fared so poorly, before segueing into his own monologue. "It must be really beautiful to be a track athlete and run freely in the fresh air," Koubek said. He didn't know how he would make it work. Athletics were for rich people, he knew—people who could afford the cab fare to the Brno Riviera, who could take time off work to train. He didn't have those luxuries. "I just wish that once, maybe only once in my whole life, I could wear that shirt with a star on it and see how it would go for me out there."

○○○

In the following months, Koubek couldn't get enough of track and field. He ditched the detective novels he'd grown up reading and instead devoured the sports section of every newspaper he could acquire. He cut out photos of some of the most prominent sprinters of the day—the American Charles Paddock, who had won gold at the 1920 Antwerp Olympics, and the Norwegian pole-vaulter Charles Hoff. Most of all, he fell in love with Hitomi Kinue, a track star from Japan who was on her way to becoming the most famous woman athlete in the world. He started training, too—mostly on his own time, running laps and practicing high jumps after hopping the gates of the Brno Riviera, the stadium he had visited with Boženka.

Koubek stashed all the photos and clippings in an old suitcase that his brother had given him. While working at the haberdashery, he imagined himself like Hitomi—gathered in a stadium in front of tens of thousands of spectators, sprinting to victory as cameras flashed and audiences chanted his name. "It must be beautiful," he wrote later, "to run victoriously through the tape at the finish line, to reap unrelenting ovations." He got so lost in thought that, at work, Boženka frequently snapped at him: "Why are you gawking?"

His job performance, already not exactly worthy of praise, suffered from his newfound obsession with sports. Once, a customer asked to buy three meters of cotton, and Koubek absently replied that he could offer her one hundred meters at 10.5 seconds. When the customer looked confused, Koubek added, to assuage her, that the offer was better than the track-and-field world record.

Koubek was sixteen going on seventeen when he got his opportunity to become part of a real sports club. After months of training, he joined a small-time women's group in Brno. He was so fast that he drew the attention of an official from the University Sport Club of Brno (VS Brno), a league associated with the University of Brno. A friend told the official that Koubek was "a girl with the devil in their body." Intrigued, the official invited Koubek to sign up.

Koubek was more than thrilled to don the VS Brno jersey. Within weeks of joining, he was outrunning the girls and spent most of his time training with the boys' team. Koubek's quick rise didn't always earn him fans. "Girl, if you think that you will catch a groom that way, you are thoroughly mistaken," one woman told him. Koubek just smiled at her. He knew better than to fight back.

To balance work and sports, Koubek developed a strict schedule, which involved blowing out his gas lamp and going to bed at nine o'clock on the dot every night. Not that there were many temptations to stay up—he couldn't afford to have a nightlife. At VS Brno, Koubek stood out not just for his drive but also for his fearlessness. When a top sprinter whom Koubek later identified by the name Karla Sychrová arrived to compete against the team, most of the Brno players complained that it wasn't a fair match, that Sychrová had too much experience.[2] Koubek volunteered to go up against her anyway. He told Sychrová that he wasn't afraid.

To everyone's shock, Koubek beat her handily in the high jump, buoyed by a misstep in Sychrová's second jump. Koubek was declared the winner, and the crowd erupted into cheers. Sychrová's face turned red. In the locker room, she slammed the door so hard that a chalkboard came crashing to the ground. "What a little snake!" Sychrová said of Koubek. The young athlete, she complained, "looks like some disheveled, freckle-faced boy from an American film." Koubek was mortified. The next day, he went to the creamery on Czech Street, in downtown Brno, that Sychrová owned. "Miss, I'll take a quarter liter of milk and one bun, and please forgive me for beating you yesterday. Please don't be angry with me!" he said. Koubek braced for a scolding. Instead, the two became friends.

Almost as soon as Koubek joined VS Brno, friends and rivals alike began commenting on his appearance. This experience wasn't new to Koubek—nearly every successful woman track-and-field athlete, including his idol Hitomi, had at some point been accused of having masculine traits—but the comments cut deep, because a part of him knew them to be true. He did have enough traditionally masculine features—short hair, thick arms, sharp jaw—that once in a while strangers on the street perceived him as a boy. At work, he was often addressed as "Sir." More important, though, he had never felt comfortable in feminine spaces. Though Koubek preferred not to think about it, sometimes he had no choice but to confront the reality of his gender. Several months into his time at VS Brno, for instance, a female teammate scoffed at the suggestion that Koubek might one day make it to such athletic heights as the Women's World Games, Alice Milliat's global competition. "She was so clumsy when she first joined us," the teammate said. "And that's not all. Maybe she isn't even a woman at all. Her arms, legs, and voice are like a boy's."

No one on VS Brno took the comment seriously—no one except Koubek.

○○○

In September 1918, a sixteen-year-old painter left their family home to attend a prestigious design school in Prague.[3] By the time they graduated a year later, they had developed a particular fascination for the budding Surrealist movement. They soon shed their birth name, instead opting for the gender-neutral moniker Toyen.[4]

Though assigned female at birth, Toyen at times described themself using male pronouns. Toyen kept their hair bobbed, and they liked to wear pants and smoke.[5] One of their friends recalled that Toyen "wore coarse cotton trousers, a guy's corduroy smock, and on her head a turned-down hat."[6] At times, they could be found wearing a suit and a beret. A 1930 caricature in a weekly paper called Toyen "that male, that female, that neuter."[7] They did not always cross-dress, often appearing in heels or skirts, but their unconventional relationship to gender left an impression on their friends, one of whom remembered that Toyen "refused, when she spoke of herself, to use the feminine endings."[8] To earn a living, Toyen took to designing books and bookplates, but it was their sketches of faceless or blindfolded girls, androgynous people, and sex between women that captured the attention of their contemporaries.[9]

When Koubek was growing up in Czechoslovakia, Toyen was not famous enough to be a household name, but they became a stand-in for the small—yet growing—queer consciousness at the margins of the young nation. In 1924, just a year after Toyen began asking friends not to refer to them by their birth name, a Czech writer published *Homosexuality in the Light of Science* (*Homosexualita ve světle vědy*), a mammoth book that posited that many of

Czechoslovakia's famous historical figures were queer.[10] It was a radical work of history, and seven years later, in 1931, it inspired a group of queer Czech activists to establish the country's first queer newspaper, a journal that eventually came to be known as *New Voice* (*Nový hlas*).[11]

Compared to the rest of Europe, Czechoslovakia was relatively forward-looking on the topics of sex and sexuality. Tomáš Garrigue Masaryk, the president of Czechoslovakia, was a strong supporter of feminism. He tossed out restrictive laws, including a requirement that women who worked for the government could not marry,[12] and appointed a number of women to the country's parliament. Still, the dominant strain of Czech feminism centered on monogamous marriage to men.[13] And Masaryk himself had little sympathy for sexual liberation. Ideally, he argued, most people would have only one sexual partner in their lives.[14] In early 1926, his Ministry of Justice flirted with removing the country's ban on homosexual acts, but the reform was ultimately dropped.[15]

The real queer consciousness in Czechoslovakia was happening in underground newspapers like *New Voice*, using ideas borrowed from nearby Germany. Weimar Germany was the global hub of queer research and activism, and at its center was Magnus Hirschfeld, a sexologist whose early research into people who are today called trans, intersex, and queer shaped the world's understanding of sex. Beginning in at least 1908, Hirschfeld convinced German police to accept a "transvestite" certificate, which would exempt his patients from anti-cross-dressing laws.[16] In 1919, he opened the Institute for Sexual Science on the corner of Beethoven Street and In den Zelten in downtown Berlin, where he began treating a steady trickle of patients who lived at the margins of gender and sexuality.[17] He provided early forms of vaginoplasties and other surgeries that aided gender transitions.[18] Often, once his patients transitioned, he offered them jobs. One of his first patients, Dora Richter, worked for him as a cookmaid. "Only a few companies hire transvestite staff," a surgeon at Hirschfeld's institute wrote, according to the historian Leah Tigers, "so we employed them as best we could in our own institute."[19]

The Institute for Sexual Science became the nucleus of the German queer scene. Not far from the institute, a client of Hirschfeld's ran a bar called the Petite Lion that she described as a "Meeting Place for Transvestites."[20] It was one of nearly a hundred gay and lesbian bars across Berlin, according to Hirschfeld's own estimate. For a time, that number seemed only destined to grow. "One bar closes, another opens," the sexologist wrote.[21] Hirschfeld wasn't only interested in queerness. He also tried to map the sexual proclivities of all Germans, inviting members of the public to his so-called Questionnaire Evenings, where he compiled statistics about their sex and masturbation habits. Though he remained closeted, Hirschfeld quietly had affairs with multiple men, including his final life partner, the young PhD student and sexologist Li Shiu Tong.[22]

Throughout the 1920s, Hirschfeld toured the world, giving 178 lectures,[23] mostly on homosexuality, across Europe, China, Indonesia, the Philippines, and Egypt. His central thesis on sexual identity—that homosexuality was not an illness but rather a character trait—seeped into international discourse. His timing was also impeccable. Hirschfeld was speaking to a global audience that had already been exposed to the idea that biological sex might be inherently unstable. The rising field of sexology was producing groundbreaking new research about the nature of hormones, glands, and other sex traits every day. Each discovery seemed to throw the established sex categories deeper in flux.[24] In the years immediately after World War I, some close readers of the news began to understand "female" and "male" not as stable, distinct categories but as permeable states of being: everyone had both male and female traits, according to sex science,[25] and sometimes, in rare cases, a person's ratio of male and female traits might actually shift. A man could suddenly become more feminine; a woman could suddenly become more masculine.

Journalists regularly produced tales, often embellished for sensational effect, of switching sex categories. Mutability started with animals, then laddered up. Beginning in 1912, newspapers reported that the average oyster could change sex "without apparent cause" multiple times throughout its life.[26] The Scottish geneticist F. A. E. Crew added to the frenzy in 1923 with his own report of a so-called sex reversal. In a paper published that year, he said he had successfully turned a hen into a male chicken. Crew wrote that he believed "a determined male or a determined female"[27] could transform their sex organs.

These scientists often suggested that biological sex in humans was just as permeable. From a lab in the sleepy town of Cold Spring Harbor, New York, the American biologist Oscar Riddle watched as a female blond ring dove underwent, supposedly, a sex transformation. The bird developed tuberculosis,[28] at which point Riddle noticed that it began squawking like a male and its measurements began to mirror a male dove's. When the bird died, in 1916, Riddle claimed it had developed male genitalia and by that time looked, for all intents and purposes, like a male pigeon.[29] Riddle felt he had stumbled across a scientific miracle. He wrote up his findings into a paper, "A Case of Complete Sex-Reversal in the Adult Pigeon," which the Chicago-based journal The American Naturalist published in 1924.

When Riddle's paper went to press, it caused a minor news sensation. "Science may find a way for a girl who wants to be a boy," the United Press wire service declared, citing a speech Riddle gave to a zoological group about the paper's findings.[30] In the speech, Riddle called sex reversal in humans "wholly probable" based on his research.[31] Other newspapers trumpeted sex change in humans as the next scientific frontier. "Want Your Girl to Be a Boy? Call on Dr. Riddle," one newspaper headline exclaimed.[32] Explanations for how this happened varied wildly from scientist to scientist, but Riddle, at least, was adamant that an animal's biological sex was tied to its metabolism—the speed at which its body processed and broke down food.[33] Experimenting with metabolism could result in animals swapping sexes. For his dove, he told reporters, tuberculosis had been the key ingredient. Tuberculosis had sped up the bird's metabolic rate, and those changes radiated out until eventually the dove took on the physical characteristics of a male.[34]

Sex, in Riddle's understanding, wasn't a biological definite. It was shaped by outside forces, like disease or physical exertion. If a person wasn't careful, their body might change without their knowledge. Riddle became convinced that sex reversal could happen to anyone. As his scientific stature ballooned, he began giving interviews warning of the dangers of spontaneous sex change.[35] After all, stories of people who transgressed the boundaries of male and female seemed to pop up every few years in local newspapers. In one instance, in 1911, the New York–based *Buffalo Enquirer* reported on a pair of fifteen-year-olds who, although raised as girls, had petitioned to change their legal sex. The paper noted that "as they grew up, these two girls felt that girls' dresses and girls' education were becoming unsuitable to them" and "their voice became so deep that they were jeered at in school." The court dutifully approved the petition.[36]

In these first decades of the twentieth century, scientific upheaval and glimmers of queer visibility combined to create a historical moment in which sex and sexuality could, at times, feel limitless. That didn't mean it was safe to be queer. For someone like Koubek, whose gender didn't match up with how others perceived him, publicly presenting as a man would have been illegal. Authorities were regularly enforcing Czechoslovakia's criminal ban on

cross-dressing. In 1933, *New Voice* wrote that the number of ar-
rests for cross-dressing was on the rise throughout Prague. Viola-
tors, the paper reported, usually spent a week in jail.[37]

Koubek never mentioned Hirschfeld, Toyen, or *New Voice* in
the personal essays he later published, but he seemed to understand
the visceral dangers associated with donning men's clothing. As his
fame ballooned, so did his fears about his gender. He was mortified
when, in his late adolescence, he found himself needing to shave
every day to keep the stubble off his face. At athletic competitions,
he refused to change in the girls' locker room, instead opting to
travel straight from his apartment to the track field. He didn't have
the time to sort through what those experiences might mean. He
was too busy feeling afraid.

What Koubek couldn't have known, of course, was that he
wasn't alone.

○○○

For as long as Mark Weston could remember, he called himself a
tomboy.[38] When Weston was born on March 30, 1905,[39] in a small
cottage in Plymouth, England, his parents assigned him a traditionally feminine name that he would ultimately discard. Like Koubek,
he was raised as a girl, but it always felt like a poor fit. When he was
a child, he recalled in later interviews, his mother tried to teach him
needlework, only to find that it took Weston four years to knit a
single sock.[40]

Mark Weston was the family's second child. His brother, William, was seven years older.[41] His father, Stephen C. Weston, worked
as a stoker on a navy steamship called HMS *Vivid*.[42] Growing up,
Weston took after his father's love of ships. He started boating com-
petitively, which led him to explore other sports. Weston tried his
hand at cricket and soccer. In high school, he got good enough at
both sports that he started teaching the boys' teams how to play.[43]

Weston soon gravitated to the women's sports scene in Plymouth. In August 1922, when Weston was seventeen, his home city fielded its first track-and-field team.[44] Weston became a member about a year later.[45] Though he started off running track, he made much more of a splash in the javelin-throwing and shot put competitions. In the summer of 1924, the Plymouth team dispatched him to London for a nationwide tournament. He walked away with gold in the shot put.[46] A month later, his put broke the British women's record by over three feet.[47]

The next year, he left his hometown team to join the more prestigious Middlesex Ladies' Athletic Club,[48] a budding sports group that practiced in a South London stadium. Weston was a rising star, but he couldn't afford for sports to become anything more than a part-time hobby. Across Europe, most clubs required that athletes compete as "amateurs," meaning they could not earn any money from their sports. If they did, they could be banned from both the Women's World Games and the Olympics itself. Those restrictions meant that top athletes usually had sources of wealth beyond their day jobs. Weston's family was poor, so he cycled through jobs to support his parents even as he rose through the ranks of British sports. He began doing needlework in a clothing factory in Plymouth[49] but eventually switched to working as a nurse at a local hospital. There, he developed a passion for massage, and he trained to become a professional masseur with a focus on alleviating arthritis.[50] He was so busy with work that he rarely took the four-hour train trip to London to practice with the rest of his team.

Weston's coach decided to train him by mail. Weston practiced alone on the shore in Plymouth, throwing limestone rocks in place of a shot put as seagulls circled overhead.[51] Other times, he rowed through the harbor by his parents' cottage.[52] Newspapers noted that Weston was "rarely seen" in London—and when he did make an appearance, he shied away from the press.[53] He seemed uncomfortable with his own growing fame. One July night, Weston took a midnight train from Plymouth to London for an inter-club competition. He crammed all his events into a single day, saying he could only spare the one day off work.[54] He managed a clean sweep of the shot put, javelin, and discus events. That night, before he had time to celebrate, a train whisked him back to Plymouth.

A reporter for the *Western Morning News*, the main newspaper that covered the Plymouth area, marveled at the fact that an athlete with seven gold, two silver, and three bronze medals was living "quietly and unheralded" in his mother's cottage, seemingly anonymous even in his hometown. The reporter had to "insist" that Weston even agree to an interview.[55]

Initially, Weston tuned out the growing fervor over butch women athletes. In 1922, the British paper the *Daily Herald* published a story declaring that women who participated in "masculine" sports like soccer or track and field risked creating a third category of sex. Out of women athletes, "a new type of human being, neither male nor female, is likely to develop." The *Daily Herald* quoted a biologist who said that all people had both masculine and feminine elements inside them. For women, repeat competition "tends to develop only the male in her"—leading to what the *Daily Herald* quipped would be a soccer team comprised of the "neuter eleven."[56]

The possibility that sports could destabilize the male-female sex paradigm itself was far from a niche concern. A British newsreel of the Women's World Games in 1922 broadcast clips of women competing in the high jump with the caption: "The new theory that 'sport may kill sex' does not worry them!"[57] These gendered anxieties were most intense for women of color. The sports that were regarded as the most masculine—and the most corrosive to the health of women—were often track and field, where the largest share of working-class women, especially Black women, participated.[58]

Weston later explained that he didn't think much about his gender during this period.[59] Mostly he was excited by the chance to leave home. As he toured England, he towed along an autograph book and shyly asked any British Olympian he met to contribute a signature. Once, during a newspaper interview, Weston took the time to show off the signatures he'd collected to a reporter.[60] He was a fanboy at heart.

If crisscrossing England by train felt like an adventure, Weston was on the precipice of a much bigger thrill. At the end of July 1926, Weston tried out for the second Women's World Games,[61] which were to be held the following month in Gothenburg, Sweden. On August 9, *The Daily Mirror* announced the British had chosen fourteen athletes to dispatch to Sweden. At the bottom of the lineup was Mark Weston's name.[62]

Maybe it was a coincidence that Alice Milliat chose Gothenburg, the Swedish city near where IAAF president Sigfrid Edström had grown up,[63] as the site of the Women's World Games. But it was a happy turn of events for Milliat, in no small part because of the effusive reaction she received on Edström's home turf. Sweden's royal prince Gustaf Adolf agreed to serve as patron of the games,[64] a symbolic endorsement of her project, and the Swedish organizers paid the full cost of hotel accommodations for every visiting athlete.[65] Meals at a local school were also offered for free, as was a welcome banquet for the athletes at Gothenburg's ornate Plaza Hotel.[66] On August 27, Sweden's King Gustaf V sat for the opening ceremony. Though other Swedish IOC members attended, Edström notably did not.[67]

Edström, as head of the IAAF, was still working to convince Milliat and her allies to give up the Women's World Games. It wasn't exactly succeeding. Milliat was becoming suspicious of Edström's motives, and he of hers. Yet there Milliat was, in Edström's home city, accepting a welcome from the highest levels of Swedish government.

For Mark Weston, the Women's World Games did not bring a breakout moment. In his signature event, the shot put, Weston failed to medal,[68] and he hardly appeared in any write-ups of the event. Outside of his hometown newspaper, few seemed to notice the young shot-putter.

○○○

Koubek and Weston were not alone. By the early 1930s, a handful of athletes across Europe were privately asking similar questions about their gender—forming the outlines of an as-yet-invisible community of people who would soon upend the sporting world.

One of them, Willy de Bruyn, started his cycling career by accident. He was always fast—in races around his village, he easily outpaced the neighborhood kids—but he was ashamed to be seen as an athlete.[69] Sporting success, he thought, was unfeminine. In his tiny village of Erembodegem, Belgium, he was preoccupied with fitting in. By the time he was fourteen, in 1929, de Bruyn had found a job in a cigarette factory, where he worked for eight hours a day feeding rolls of cigarettes into heavy machinery. He hated it, but his family, who owned a local bar, needed the money.

Then, in 1930, he walked into his family's bar and saw an ad for a women's cycling race. The competition was informal, organized to celebrate a local holiday, but there was a cash prize attached: three hundred Belgian francs, equal to about a week's salary at the cigarette factory. De Bruyn won easily. The second-place cyclist didn't cross the finish line until several minutes after de Bruyn, an eternity in a thirty-kilometer race. As word of de Bruyn's cycling prowess spread across his village, friends encouraged him to enter competitions up and down Belgium. A local bike manufacturer gifted him a new bike, believing de Bruyn could help promote the brand.

At fifteen, de Bruyn began sweeping cycling competitions. When he wasn't working at the factory, he was training for his next race. He saw the prize money as a way to support his family. But cycling also provided a merciful break from thinking about his gender, which had begun to occupy an increasing share of his headspace. "I grew more and more convinced that I was not a young woman at all," he wrote later. He didn't understand where his feelings were coming from, so he started reading: he devoured as many books as he could find about the nature of biological sex. He discovered, he recounted later, that intersex soldiers had fought under Napoleon and that the ancient Greeks had their own intersex god, Hermaphroditus.

The work of Magnus Hirschfeld, that influential German sexologist, had a particular impact. De Bruyn trembled when he read about one of Hirschfeld's patients, a worker at a printing house who began living as a man for the first time at age twenty-five and was still able to marry and form a family. De Bruyn wanted that, and he wanted it badly.

De Bruyn, Weston, and Koubek did not yet know about one another. But in their simultaneous questioning, they were beginning to unwittingly articulate a challenge to the sex essentialism of the sports world and, consequentially, of society at large. They couldn't have fathomed how intertwined their lives were about to become.

CHAPTER 5

CARL DIEM NEVER GAVE UP on the stadium his country had built for the 1916 Olympics. One way or another, he thought, that little patch of land near the Grunewald Forest was going to usher in the future of German sports.

In 1919, soon after the cessation of the war, Diem settled on a new way to make Germany unbeatable: he would harness the fledgling power of science. Scientific breakthroughs seemed to crop up every day, from Technicolor films and commercial aviation to Albert Einstein's theory of relativity. There was no reason why it couldn't be applied to sports.[1] He suggested in a memo that Germany create a school devoted to the study of sports science.[2] When the German College of Physical Exercise (Deutsche Hochschule für Leibesübungen) was founded a year later, in 1920, it became one of the first universities in the world focused on sports, and it chose a familiar location for its headquarters: the German Stadium, the home of the scrapped 1916 Olympics.[3]

In the halls of the German Stadium, researchers filmed hurdlers and played back the tapes to point out flaws in their form.[4] Just as the Industrial Revolution had brought a new kind of mechanization into the workforce, especially in the manufacturing sector, the German sports apparatus reoriented itself around machinelike precision. One sports journalist praised the "systematic and strict" training of the typical German athlete, who was taught to "rid himself of all sorts of bad little habits" and who "adopted the detailed new improvements."[5] German coaches set strict diets and training routines for their athletes. All sorts of new inducements were tested: researchers studied how ingesting an array of products, including kola nuts, chocolate, coffee, testosterone, and cocaine, impacted athletic performance.[6] To discuss the latest discoveries in the science of sports, coaches and athletes flocked to a lecture hall in the basement of the stadium.[7]

For the first time in the country's history, German cities bankrolled a flurry of new sports construction projects. In 1920, the country had 10 sports stadiums. By the end of the decade, it boasted 125.[8] A second sports university, the Institute for Exercise in Hamburg, soon opened, following the example of the Berlin prototype.[9] In women's sports in particular, Germany became a "powerhouse," as the historian Erik N. Jensen explained later.[10] Germany didn't place the same limits on women's training as the United States and England, which allowed German women to practice freely. Some German writers, in fact, hailed women athletes as vanguards. German female track stars, they wrote, were the "carriers of our race" and "future mothers of the next generation."[11]

It was in early 1924 when Diem received the news he'd been waiting a decade to hear. Pierre de Coubertin, the aristocratic founder of the IOC, wrote him a letter, wanting to know whether the Germans would be willing to return to the IOC.[12] Coubertin didn't make any grand statements about a need to end postwar animosities or about the current cataclysmic state of the German economy, which was just recovering from a bruising period of hyperinflation. It probably frustrated Diem that this man he admired was so unwilling to apologize, but he wasn't going to waste his time arguing. In his reply, Diem suggested that his colleague Theodor Lewald be appointed to represent Germany on the committee.[13]

Twenty-two years Diem's elder, Theodor Lewald was an avid sports fan,[14] though never much of an athlete himself. Before the war Lewald had been Diem's most important ally in bringing the Olympics to Berlin. In 1914, Lewald, who was then the minister of the interior for the German Empire, had convinced Germany's parliament to allocate 200,000 marks to subsidize the Olympic Games.[15] Lewald and Diem had the same interests, though Lewald had the savvier political instinct. He spoke five languages and was a loyal and dedicated public servant.[16] No matter how much paperwork might be sent to his house one evening, he would inevitably have read, annotated, and left it out to be retrieved the next morning.[17]

When Diem told Lewald the news that he'd nominated him for the IOC, the former interior minister was thrilled. Lewald was eager to embark on a new project. Since the war, Lewald's time in government had been a bit too eventful for his tastes. In November 1918, the kaiser, whom Lewald had served for over a decade, abdicated the throne and fled to the Netherlands. Lewald drafted the kaiser's final statement to the German people.[18] With the stroke of Lewald's pen, the monarchy was over. A year later, legislators had agreed on a new constitution, a document Lewald helped write.[19] The Weimar Republic then began in earnest. But by 1923, Lewald had grown tired of the republic, and he left government service to focus on building up the German sports ecosystem. To an aging establishment figure like Lewald, German politics likely seemed increasingly unhinged. That November, the far-right politician Adolf Hitler had attempted to stage a coup in Munich, locking down a large beer hall and calling for the arrest of prominent members of the city council. The coup failed, and Hitler received a sentence of five years in prison. But it seemed to mark a dangerous new era of German politics. Lewald wanted no part.

Lewald was already president of Germany's largest sports organization,[20] and from there, it wasn't a big leap to the IOC. The following May, in 1925, Lewald traveled to Prague for a blockbuster session of the IOC.[21] It was the first committee meeting that Germany had attended in over a decade—a major geopolitical moment, though few acknowledged it at the time. Lewald's arrival at the IOC marked the start of a new phase in Germany's relationship with the Olympics. Eventually, of course, it would blow up in all their faces.

◦◦◦

Amsterdam was the first test of Diem's and Lewald's years of investment in improving the German sports infrastructure. After the first two postwar Olympic cities—Antwerp in 1920 and Paris in 1924—had refused to extend invites to Germany, signs of international healing finally materialized after the IOC session in 1925. Diem and Lewald were relieved when the organizers of the 1928 Olympic Games in Amsterdam asked Germany to send a team.[22]

The two men wanted to use the event as Germany's springboard back onto the world sporting stage. And who knew—maybe a strong showing from Germany would revitalize their dream of a Berlin-hosted Olympics. Lewald had already asked the IOC to choose Berlin as the host of the 1932 Olympics, to no avail. The IOC awarded the 1932 Olympics to Los Angeles instead.[23] But a good German showing in Amsterdam could turn the tide for 1936.

When the Amsterdam Olympics finally arrived, Diem and Lewald boarded a train to the Netherlands alongside the nearly three hundred German athletes who were eligible for the games.[24] Diem and the athletes elected not to stay in Amsterdam, instead settling in the seaside town of Zandvoort, less than twenty miles outside the city. Diem preferred to sleep far from the "battlefield," he wrote later.[25] City life could conjure up distractions, especially in a place as vice-ridden as Amsterdam, and Diem didn't want to leave anything to chance for his athletes. The stakes for Germany were too high. In the days leading up to the Olympics, to calm his nerves, he went for swims in the North Sea, jogged up and down the beach, and sat in the sand and let the waves lap at his feet.

When the modern Olympics first began, in 1896, they wielded little international clout. Even sports figureheads struggled to understand what they were. Harvard College was skeptical of whether to grant a leave of absence to track athlete J. B. Connolly to attend the first Olympics, which were held in Greece. When Connolly tried to explain the meaning of the games, a dean replied, "You know you only want to go to Athens on a junket."[26] But by the start of the Amsterdam Games, the idea of the Olympics as a prestige event was worming its way into the global consciousness. The phrases "Olympic record" and "Olympic champion" had entered the lexicon,[27] and private companies were beginning to take an interest in the event. In 1928, Coca-Cola, eager to expand its international footprint, dispatched around one thousand cases of product to Amsterdam with the US team.[28] Branding their signature soda a "health drink," Coca-Cola employees manned kiosks across Amsterdam and hawked it to passersby.

The Amsterdam Olympics were a watershed moment in sports history. Half a million spectators attended,[29] and the Dutch introduced new traditions, like the first-ever lighting of the Olympic torch, into the Olympic canon. The organizational apparatus of the Olympics, however, had not caught up to the event's budding prestige. Many competitions started late,[30] and the Dutch queen Wilhelmina, who was supposed to preside over the opening ceremony, backed out at the last minute because she was on vacation in Norway.[31] Local shopkeepers were annoyed that the Dutch state hadn't lifted a law requiring that they shutter their doors at 8:00 p.m., insisting that they were losing out on precious tourist dollars.[32] Initially, the national government had planned to subsidize the cost of the Olympics, but the Dutch parliament ultimately refused to pass a spending bill. Sports, they insisted, were un-Christian, and they could not support the sight of women athletes dressed in "indecent" clothing.[33] As a result, "nothing seemed to have worked as it should," a prominent sports journalist complained.[34]

The Dutch queen's absence offended Lewald, who complained to Diem that it amounted to a personal affront. Diem, for his part, was preoccupied with other organizational failures. He remembered the living quarters as particularly underwhelming. Once the games began, he moved his team to an empty barracks on the Schiphol Airfield, which had clearly not been cleaned in anticipation of their arrival. The athletes had to gather buckets and mops to make the place livable.[35]

Once the Olympics kicked off, those concerns melted away. From the sidelines, Diem and Lewald watched as something incredible happened. German athletes were squaring off against the world for the first time since the war—and they were winning. Germany ended the games in second place in the medal count, behind only the United States. It was an even better finish than Diem had imagined.[36] "The performance," Diem later wrote in his memoir, "was the most perfect thing I've ever seen in my life."[37]

They decided to ride the momentum. Buoyed by Germany's success in Amsterdam, Lewald pushed for Berlin to host the Olympics in 1936.[38] Though Diem urged Lewald to wait, insisting that a bid for the Olympics was "premature," Lewald went ahead anyway. "We have him alone to thank for broadcasting the games to Berlin," Diem wrote later.[39]

Lewald's first move was to cobble together an airtight pitch. For the IOC, the most important feature of a hosting bid was the financing. The IOC had very little money of its own, which meant it picked host cities that promised to pay for the Olympics themselves.

Germany had one key advantage in this respect: it had already built a stadium for the 1916 Olympics, the German Stadium. Sure, that old building needed improvements, but at least Berlin wouldn't be starting from scratch.

Lewald wrote letters to the mayor of Berlin, urging the city to set aside funds to revamp the German Stadium.[40] The money never materialized. By the start of 1929, Lewald was growing more desperate. Two other neighboring German cities, Cologne and Frankfurt, were considering submitting bids to host the Olympics, and unlike Berlin, they had recently built new stadiums.[41] Lewald again begged the mayor of Berlin to commit to financing the stadium's upgrades, but the city simply didn't have the funds. On October 29, 1929, as Lewald was still lobbying for money to pay for the Olympic Games, the US stock market crashed. It would take mere weeks for the German economy, already hobbled by World War I, to fall into a tailspin.

Even before the Great Depression, Lewald's efforts were not always embraced by his home country. Anger lingering from World War I often permeated the conversation around sports. One newspaper noted that participating in a global sports competition represented a betrayal of German nationalism. Ideologues associated with the Nazi Party, still a fringe group at the time, called it a "race-less" enterprise that intended to create a "union of nations."[42] Others, of course, simply worried about the money. In a country as bankrupt as Germany, few saw the point in devoting so many public funds to a sports competition.

The Depression made the public sour further on the prospect of financing a bid for the Olympics. As the new financial realities set in, Lewald tried a new approach. In 1930, he convinced the IOC to hold its annual meeting in Berlin, a setting that he hoped might sway members toward supporting the city's bid for the Olympics.[43] From May 25 to May 30, Germany pulled out all the stops to impress the visiting delegates. Greeting the committee members was

Weimar Germany's interior minister, who gave a speech highlight-
ing Germany's many athletic bona fides, including its fifty sports
organizations and its eight million registered athletes.[44] After the
daily IOC sessions, Lewald planned a week of festivities, which included visits to the State Opera House to watch German gymnastics, a trip to a Prussian castle, an airplane show at the Tempelhof
Aerodrome, and an elaborate dinner hosted by the country's secretary of state.[45] Lewald closed out the session with a trip to the German Stadium. Committee members left the 1930 IOC session
impressed. One American sports official told the press, undoubtedly to Lewald's delight, that Berlin was "likely to be the scene of
the 1936 Games."[46]

Sunny diplomacy was not Lewald's only tactic to secure the
1936 Olympics. After the IOC trip to Berlin, he also set about sab-
otaging his opponents. Twelve cities had, in some form, bid to host
the 1936 Olympics,[47] but really it came down to only two others:
Barcelona and Rome. Lewald paid for a meteorological study showing that both cities would have bad weather conditions during the
Olympic Games. He then leaked the study to the press.[48] He wrote
letters to other IOC members, urging them to support his bid and
promising them that Berlin had the funds to pay for the entirety of
the Olympics itself. This wasn't true, but Lewald considered it, at
worst, a white lie. He knew the political system well. Surely, he
thought, he'd scrounge together the money by 1936.

The following April, Lewald traveled to Barcelona for the IOC's
1931 session, where committee members were finally planning to
select the next host of the Olympics. Many delegates opted not to
attend. Seismic protests had wracked Spain following the abdica-
tion of its king less than two weeks earlier. Lewald was not dis-
suaded, and over the sound of rifle shots,[49] he offered the IOC his
closing pitch for a Berlin-hosted Olympics. Germany was an athletic powerhouse, and unlike Barcelona, its major rival to host the
Olympics, it wasn't facing any major political turmoil. Plus, giving

Berlin the Olympics would be a powerful symbol of international unity following World War I.

It was hard to tell which was more persuasive: Lewald's uplifting case for Berlin or the chaos on the streets of Barcelona. Either way, Lewald's plan worked. Following the session, the IOC chose the venue of the 1936 Olympics through a mail vote. On May 13, 1931, as the Great Depression was hollowing out the United States and Europe, the IOC declared Berlin the winner, 43–16.[50]

Within months, Diem and Lewald were touting Germany's grand return to sports. When a *Los Angeles Times* reporter flew to Germany to report on the country's plans for the 1936 Olympics, Diem took him on a tour of the German Stadium. The Organizing Committee, Diem told the newspaper, was going to remodel the German Stadium and add twenty-five thousand more seats. The reporter was infatuated. Germany, he declared, was back.[51]

MARK WESTON LEFT the 1926 Women's World Games in Gothenburg, Sweden, without making much of an impression. Instead, the event minted a different celebrity: the nineteen-year-old Hitomi Kinue, the sole contestant from Japan.[1] Hitomi had taught herself track and field early in her adolescence, practicing for hours a day on fields across Okayama Prefecture.[2] She first garnered the affection of her home country in 1923, when, at only sixteen years old, she shattered Japan's previous high-jump mark.[3] A year later, at an event in Okayama Prefecture, she set an unofficial women's triple-jump world record.

By day, Hitomi worked as a journalist, penning feature stories about sports or interviewing Manchurian warlords for the *Ōsaka Mainichi shimbun*. The paper became the singular benefactor of her sports career.[4] In 1926, her boss funded her trip from southern Japan to Gothenburg,[5] a journey that sent her through Russia on the Trans-Siberian Railroad.[6] At Gothenburg, Hitomi won gold twice—in the long jump and the broad jump—and silver in the discus.[7] Hitomi was thrilled when the Japanese national anthem blared over the speakers for the forty thousand spectators to hear.[8]

The Women's World Games turned Hitomi into a star. *The Washington Post* and *The New York Times* soon devoted articles to her, though in their obsession, shades of racism were apparent. The British press dubbed her "the brilliant little Japanese athlete";[9] a German newspaper was shocked to see that Hitomi had a "splendid body no different from those of female athletes from Europe and America."[10] Speculation about her biological sex was not out of bounds, either. Starting in 1926, gossip magazines repeated an anecdote from Hitomi's high school years, in which a swim coach had refused to let her join a women's swimming competition out of concern that she was a man. The same year, a Japanese commentator wrote admiringly of Hitomi's physically masculine characteristics. Noting that Hitomi had arms and legs "stronger than those of most men," the writer declared that "it would be difficult to find such proportions, even among a hundred thousand male athletes."[11] Though Hitomi was assigned female at birth, and only ever publicly identified as a woman, even she could not evade the gender anxieties of the era.

Coming on the heels of her Gothenburg win, the 1928 Amsterdam Olympics seemed certain to elevate Hitomi to new heights. The young sprinter arrived in Amsterdam by way of London, where she had once again swept England's top athletes. A writer for the *Washington Evening Star*, who interviewed Hitomi in Amsterdam a week ahead of the Olympics, marveled at her "magnetic personality." She was the only woman on the Japanese Olympic team, but she got along well with her male teammates. The reporter was scandalized to discover that she played billiards with the rest of the men.[12]

For a female track star like Hitomi, the Amsterdam Olympics felt different, and not just because the Germans had been invited. The IOC and its track-and-field-focused subsidiary, the IAAF, were allowing women to participate in track-and-field sports for the first time, crafting a slate that spanned the high jump, discus, relay, eight-hundred-meter dash, and one-hundred-meter dash.[13]

The inclusion of more women's sports was almost certainly a response to the success of the Women's World Games. Sigfrid Edström used it as an olive branch to Alice Milliat. He invited Milliat to that year's meeting of the IAAF, where he praised her for her "good cooperation" and once again pitched her on abandoning the Women's World Games and joining the IAAF instead. "We are looking forward to the time to come, when Madame Milliat and her friends will unite with us completely," Edström told the group.[14] Milliat thanked him, though she said that if she were to give up the Women's World Games, she would need a bigger concession. She wanted a ten-event program for women track-and-field athletes, which she called a "full" program even though it was still far shy of the twenty-three track-and-field events available to men.[15]

Notably absent from the 1928 Olympics was a women's track-and-field contingent from England. The leaders of British women's sports, who, like Milliat, wanted the Olympics to add more track-and-field events for women, decided to make a statement. They were going to boycott the 1928 Olympics.[16] It was a significant decision, given that the British women's team was heavily favored to sweep. For Mark Weston, it may have been career hindering. Though he would have been a long shot to secure a spot at the Olympics given his mediocre showing at the Women's World Games two years earlier, his career was peaking right around the Amsterdam Olympics. Now, because of the boycott, he had lost his best chance at qualifying. He'd never get another shot at the Olympics.

ooo

Hitomi was supposed to cruise to victory in the one-hundred-meter dash, usually one of her strongest competitions. But when she didn't make it to the finals, she was crushed. Her face felt hot. She couldn't stand the possibility of going home empty-handed. On a whim, she decided to enter the eight-hundred-meter race, one of the track-and-field competitions that the Olympics was making available to women for the first time. Hitomi had never run it before, but she wanted to try.[17]

On August 2, Hitomi lined up alongside sprinters from Poland, Germany, the United States, Canada, and Sweden. The race lasted for two laps. After the first time around the track, Hitomi trailed far behind the other women, in sixth place. Her chances of medaling looked grim. Hitomi pushed herself to go faster. One by one, she passed every woman ahead of her, until she crossed the finish line just eight-tenths of a second behind the gold medalist.[18] Lina Radke, a German sprinter, set a new world record—2 minutes and 16.9 seconds—and Hitomi won silver, earning Japan's first women's Olympic medal.[19]

Those accomplishments barely made it to print. After the race, both Radke and Hitomi staggered, and may have collapsed, from exhaustion.[20] That wasn't uncommon in track-and-field sports in an era when plenty of sprinters still believed drinking brandy before a run would improve their endurance. But the next day, international commentators seized on it as proof that the eight-hundred-meter sprint amounted to nothing short of catastrophe for women. The *Chicago Tribune* wrote, erroneously, that five of the sprinters had fainted at the end of the race; *The New York Times* said that half the women "fell headlong on the ground" and insisted that an eight-hundred-meter sprint was "too great a call on feminine strength." To the *Times* of London, the finishers resembled "prostrate and obviously distressed forms lying on the grass at the side of the track after the race." *Ladies' Home Journal* had more aesthetic concerns: the top finishers, it complained, looked like "glorified tomboys."[21]

These dispatches were heavily embellished, but they fueled their own narrative. Commentators seized on the reports to claim, once again, that track-and-field sports were fundamentally wrong for women. After witnessing the eight-hundred-meter sprint, rather than marvel at Hitomi's incredible comeback, the writer for the London *Times* left feeling "that such things should not be."[22] Edström's organization, the IAAF, was well aware of the mutiny in the press. Days later, when the committee next met, its members pulled the women's eight-hundred-meter dash from the Olympic lineup in a 12–9 vote, claiming that it was endangering women's health.[23]

The sudden backlash to women's track-and-field horrified Milliat, but she had few allies to lean on. By the time the teams left the Netherlands, the power center of the IOC had shifted. Pierre de Coubertin, the founder of the modern Olympics, had retired from the organization,[24] and in his place as president was Henri de Baillet-Latour, a Belgian count who styled himself a reformer. Baillet-Latour wanted to do away with Coubertin's autocratic governing style, which tended to involve Coubertin making unilateral decisions and only soliciting the opinion of the IOC later.[25] Instead, he declared that "work must now be done collectively."[26]

Baillet-Latour's reformist mindset didn't extend to women's sports. Baillet-Latour had always opposed expanding the slate of women's track-and-field sports for the Amsterdam Games. Though outvoted, he went out of his way to tell Milliat that he didn't want to get her hopes up. Adding women's track and field to the Olympic slate was an "experiment," he had written to her ahead of the Amsterdam Olympics, with no guarantees for the future.[27]

Like Edström, Baillet-Latour wanted Milliat gone. The contempt that Baillet-Latour and Edström held for her was unmistakable. When the IAAF invited Milliat to its meeting in Paris in April 1926, Milliat—who was the only woman in the room—was tasked with serving as the "secretary," taking notes on the discussion.[28]

Her ideas were not taken seriously. When Milliat complained that
the IAAF taking over women's sports would reduce opportunities
for women athletes, Edström chastised her for being "on her high
ways again."[29] Milliat had begun telling colleagues that Edström's
plan "consists simply of the dissolution of the FSFI,"[30] her organization that oversaw the Women's World Games. It was all too apparent that women's sports were just politics to these executives. Neither
Baillet-Latour nor Edström actually wanted to nurture competitions for women. And it was this stance that made them particularly susceptible to the creeping doubts surrounding the femininity
of many top athletes.

After the controversy at the Amsterdam Olympics, Baillet-
Latour felt vindicated in his skepticism. He moved to gut women's
sports. At the 1930 meeting of the IOC, the same meeting that Theodor Lewald was using to pitch Berlin as an Olympic host, Baillet-
Latour proposed limiting the Olympic competitions for women
only to gymnastics, tennis, skating, and swimming[31]—essentially
rewinding women's sports back to where it had been at the start of
the century. This was bad news for Edström, who was trying to
coax Milliat into giving up the Women's World Games by showing
that the Olympics would be a suitable steward.[32] The best way to get
her to relinquish the Women's World Games, he insisted, was to
ensure that at least some women's sports remained on the Olympic
slate.

Edström had reason to be nervous. Milliat's organization, while
not quite profitable,[33] was ballooning in popularity. Milliat, he
warned in his letters to sports officials, wanted "with all her power
to carry on her Games with a similar ritual as the Olympic Games."[34]
If the IOC let her continue, the Women's World Games could become "just as famous" as the Olympics itself—the nightmare sce-
nario for Edström, who still saw his control over global track-and-field
sports as deeply fragile.[35]

Edström worked behind the scenes, urging various delegates to reinstate women's track-and-field sports for the 1932 Olympics. In a letter to Baillet-Latour, Edström implored the new IOC president to "be fair" and reiterated that the IAAF "has always been faithful to the Olympic cause."[36] He was successful, sort of. By a vote of 16–3, the IOC agreed to allow a pared-down slate of women's track-and-field sports at the next Olympics. The eight-hundred-meter dash, however, would remain banned.[37]

Milliat was unimpressed. She was already planning the next installment of the Women's World Games, and her organization was talking about *more* sports for women, not fewer. She wasn't content to give in to the IOC's whittled-down athletic program, and she wasn't planning to give up the Women's World Games.[38] Edström grew frustrated with Milliat's resistance. To contain her, he turned to his newest friend for help: a bespectacled American named Avery Brundage, who always seemed to have a scheme up his sleeve.

o o o

By the end of the 1920s, Mark Weston was struggling to hide his renown in his hometown of Plymouth, England. It was a testament to the smallness of the city: the fact that a Plymouth resident had made it to the Women's World Games at all was news. Weston's poor showing didn't matter. A newspaper, certainly exaggerating, referred to him as the "latest and greatest discovery in the women's athletic world."[39] Local officials began requesting his presence at events and fundraisers. He gave a shot-putting exhibition at a carnival in 1928,[40] then again a year later at a fundraiser for a local hospital.[41] When Weston left for a competition in Germany in 1929, a crowd of fans waited for him at the train station, clamoring for his autograph.[42]

The next year, in 1930, Weston nearly dropped out of the Women's World Games in Prague.[43] He didn't want to travel so far for a competition he was sure he would lose. When his coach found out he was planning to forfeit his spot, she sent him an urgent letter: "You really must come. The committee are relying on you as our hope in the field event." Weston relented. He boarded a train for Czechoslovakia with his mother, father, and a close friend by his side.[44]

Hitomi Kinue also had to be talked into attending the games in Prague. She was so busy with her journalism work that she considered quitting sports entirely. The prospect alarmed Alice Milliat, who wrote a personal letter to Hitomi, urging the young star not to give up on her career.[45] Privately, Milliat probably knew she couldn't afford any missteps. After the catastrophe at the Amsterdam Olympics, she needed the next Women's World Games to make a splash. Hitomi, by far the biggest star of the Women's World Games, whom *The Guardian* had taken to calling "the greatest girl athlete the world has ever seen,"[46] could make or break the event. Hitomi gave in and took the Trans-Siberian Railroad to Czechoslovakia. This time, she was not alone: five other Japanese women, disciples of hers, had also qualified for the games.[47]

In Prague, Weston placed poorly in the discus event,[48] and his teammates didn't fare much better. Hitomi earned another gold, but she was disappointed to place second in the overall medal count.[49] The German women, now a force of international renown, swept most of the competitions. Weston blamed it on funding: Germany, he said, had spent years funneling money and resources into women's athletics, while the British athletes were forced to skate by with almost nothing.[50]

On September 13, a few weeks after the Women's World Games, Weston traveled to Berlin for a separate competition. There, he was surprised to find that the city was bending toward violence. The first day of competition, a clash between Nazis and Communists left one dead and eight wounded.[51] As soon as Weston's shot-put event ended, at 7:30 p.m., German officials abruptly told the teams to leave the country. When Weston asked why, a press representative warned of "election disturbances and goodness knows what."[52]

The next morning, in the largest popular vote in Germany's history, the Nazi Party stunned the country with its election success, bringing its total number of seats in the Reichstag, Germany's parliament, from 12 to 107, just a couple dozen behind the ruling Social Democratic Party.[53]

That year, 1930, would turn out to be Weston's last trip to the Women's World Games. And though Weston didn't admit this until later, it was also the year when he began to feel most uncomfortable with his assigned identity of woman.[54] Playing in a woman's sports league, he realized, no longer fit him.

ooo

Even though it was held in his home country, Zdeněk Koubek didn't attend the 1930 Women's World Games in Prague as a spectator, but his teammates brought him back a program. Koubek cherished it. Among the pages was a black-and-white photo of Alice Milliat, plus a list of the participating athletes.[55] Koubek could have traced his fingers across Hitomi's name. He carefully preserved the pamphlet in the suitcase where he kept his other sports memorabilia.

Hitomi seemed to be like him—an outsider in women's sports whose gender presentation was a frequent source of speculation. But Hitomi's life was about to take a tragic turn. Koubek, like the rest of the world, could only watch when, the following March, doctors checked Hitomi into a hospital in Osaka after she started coughing up blood.[56] She stayed there into the summer. On August 2, 1931, she died from respiratory failure. The news shook the sports world. *The New York Times* ran a long obituary.[57] In Prague, where Hitomi had built up an unlikely fan base, track-and-field aficionados built a monument in her honor, which was finished a year later.[58] Upon reading the news, on his way home from a track meet,

Koubek was devastated. He had "longed" to meet the woman he called "that most popular athlete in the world," he wrote later. Now he would never get the chance.

Hitomi's body was not even cold when critics once again began questioning her womanhood. A male writer penned an essay in a Japanese women's magazine titled "A Discussion of Hitomi Kinue," in which he highlighted her supposedly masculine traits and speculated that Hitomi was "40 or 50 percent male and 50 or 60 percent female."[59] The cruelty with which male commentators wrote about Hitomi doubled as a warning for other athletes: win too much, and you, too, will come under scrutiny.

The commentary around Hitomi likely hit close to home for Koubek. As much as he tried to avoid thinking about his gender, occasionally his discomfort with being viewed as a woman surged back. On New Year's Eve in 1931, just a few months after Hitomi's sudden death, Koubek's older brother Miloš invited him to a variety show at a restaurant in Brno. To cap off the night, Miloš planned to perform a rendition of the popular duet "The Playboys" with his friend. But as midnight approached, Miloš found his friend lolling over a table, twelve empty beer glasses stacked in front of him. Koubek volunteered to do the duet instead. "I know that couplet by heart," he told his brother. "I even practiced it at home with the guitar. Lend me some men's clothing and in a flash you'll have a duet."[60]

"The Playboys" was written for two men, so the group supplied Koubek with full male attire. In the dressing room backstage, he slipped on a black suit. Koubek watched through the mirror as a stylist appended a wig and a black beard to his chin. He couldn't help but marvel at how natural it looked on him. "[I] recognized in [my] soul that a beard suited [me] very well," he wrote later. In his descriptions, Koubek didn't yet conceive of himself as a man— in his life, it was not like he had many models for transitioning gender—but he recognized, undeniably, that he felt an affinity for masculinity.

A bell sounded, and Koubek and his brother hurried onto the stage. When the piano started, the two of them burst into song:

> *We like to go out on the town, sometimes the whole night*
>   *long*
> *Until we start to groan that we're feeling somewhat wrong.*
> *In our beds the next day*
> *Is where we'll have to stay.*
> *We feel so strange, and sort of bad,*
> *An experience we've never had.*
> *We are happy bar hoppers who know how to live like*
>   *kings,*
> *The girls love us, especially those who like the finer things.*

The audience roared, not least because Koubek seemed so plausible as a man. By the end of the night, Koubek—still in his beard, suit, and pants—hit the dance floor. The audience was thrilled to see him in masquerade, and no one seemed to bat an eye when he gravitated only toward the women in the room. When he let their bodies press against him, he played it off; anything went on New Year's Eve. At the end of the night, one woman fell into his arms and whispered, "If I didn't know that you were a girl, I would fall in love with you and ask to take you on a date tomorrow."

It scared Koubek how happy the comment made him.

ooo

Sometime in early 1932, an application to enroll in the national track-and-field championships in Prague arrived at the office of VS Brno. When Koubek asked his coach to fill out the form, he was refused. Bankrolling a player's trip to Prague was expensive, the coach said, and it wasn't like Koubek would win. Outraged, Koubek threatened to join a rival club. Eventually, VS Brno relented. In an 8–7 vote of its executive members, the club agreed to give Koubek a stipend of 25 crowns per day for his trip to Prague.

Months later, on a sweltering July day, Koubek clambered onto a train to Prague. The third-class cabin was all out of seats, so Koubek sat on his suitcase, which he'd stuffed with sweet buns, salami, and coffee. The train windows were rolled down, and at every stop on the way to Prague, salesmen shouted out offerings of snacks that Koubek couldn't afford to buy: "Beer, chocolate, liquor, hot dogs!"

In Prague, Koubek slept in the spare room that the president of a rival team, Dr. František Bléha, had offered to him. Bléha was a delegate of the FSFI,[61] and an effortlessly friendly host at that. When Koubek arrived well past midnight, Bléha greeted the young athlete with hot tea and desserts. Koubek, now eighteen years old, had never been to Prague, and everything he saw there felt positively cinematic—the cacophony of honking cars, the castles, the Gothic cathedrals, the looming office buildings. The following morning, Koubek walked all across the city and visited as many tourist sites as he could. He stopped on the steps of the National Museum to eat an ice cream. "Good god, how would it be possible to take in the totality of all this beauty in not even two full days?" Koubek wrote later.

At three o'clock in the afternoon, Koubek arrived for his event dressed in a jersey emblazoned with his black "VS" insignia. He'd slipped it on at Bléha's house, because he didn't want to change in front of the other athletes. Koubek watched the early races from the sidelines. First was the eighty-meter sprint, then the one-hundred-meter, then the two-hundred-meter. When a megaphone rang out announcing the beginning of the high jump, Koubek felt a rush of excitement. He hurried onto the field and lined up, his chin held high, alongside his competitors. He placed a close second, just five centimeters shy of the top finisher. A day later, Koubek returned for the eight-hundred-meter dash. The sun was shining when he stepped onto the track. It wasn't exactly a highly trafficked event—there were more athletes on the field than there were fans in the stands, he remembered—but the race was hard fought. Koubek finished second. The next day, a national newspaper, *The Czech Word* (*České Slovo*), mentioned Koubek in its pages. On the train ride back to Brno, he opened the newspaper and studied his name in print. It was the first time he had received any type of publicity.

Questions about his gender persisted. Later that year, VS Brno dispatched him to a track-and-field competition between Czechoslovakia and Poland. At passport control on his way to Poland, a border agent, confused by Koubek's masculine appearance, stopped him and started asking questions. At one point, the agent threatened to give Koubek a medical examination. Somehow Koubek talked his way out of it, but the interaction haunted him. "That was the first administrative doubt expressed about whether [I] was positively a female," Koubek wrote later.

When he arrived in Poland for the competition, Koubek won gold twice: in the eight-hundred-meter dash and in the high jump. When he passed back through the border, he brought his trophy to the border agent who had questioned his sex. "See, I didn't lie to you," he told the agent. "Here you have real documents that I am indeed Koubková," he said, referring to the feminized version of his last name, "and not some man who wants to flee across the border."

○○○

As the Depression swept the world, it sank Germany's Olympic project deeper into financial peril. Theodor Lewald, having secured the Olympics for his home city, now had to fund it. He was furiously writing letters to anyone he could think of: sports organizations, the Berlin city government, rich benefactors.[62] But the financial crash had donors spooked. No one was willing to give him money. By June 1932, as Lewald was preparing to leave for the Los Angeles Olympics, he admitted to a friend that he had lost hope. "When we will begin the construction work for the 1936 Olympic Games, I dare not say," Lewald wrote in a letter on June 4. "Who can even predict when the necessary resources will be made available."[63]

The following month, Diem and Lewald boarded a six-day steamship to New York with a pared-down German team. Because of the financial crisis, the German Olympic Committee had the money to send only about eighty-nine athletes to America, a third of the number it had chosen for Amsterdam four years earlier.[64]

When they arrived in Los Angeles, Diem and Lewald were surprised to find the topic of the Great Depression delicately elided. Despite the catastrophic state of the American economy, the government of California had scrounged together some $2.5 million to fund the games,[65] equal to about $54 million today. Signs of resistance were evident only to those who looked closely: ahead of the games, for instance, worker activists took to the state capitol in Sacramento bearing signs that read, "Groceries Not Games! Olympics Are Outrageous!"[66] When pressed on their support for public subsidies of the event amid an economic catastrophe, Los Angeles politicians said only that they saw the Olympics as a "depression buster."[67]

The dominant mode of the Los Angeles Olympics was one of bombast. A group of three local newspapers, plus the film studio Metro-Goldwyn-Mayer, had committed to sponsoring the games[68] in addition to the money provided by the state government, and they didn't seem to spare any expense. Olympic athletes, guests, and politicians attended parties inside the MGM studio or in Los Angeles nightclubs. Hollywood stars like Bing Crosby, Cary Grant, and the

Marx brothers could be spotted in the stands at Olympic competitions or at the roving slate of after-parties that popped up across the city.[69] There were so many parties that some visiting officials purported to be attending at least three per night.[70]

Private industry was all in, too. Kellogg's, Safeway, and Piggly Wiggly blanketed the stadiums with advertisements. Everywhere on the street, street vendors, capturing the fervor of the moment, sold "Olympic" hot dogs and soft drinks.[71] Tickets were cheap, and they were easy to buy: visitors needed only to call a number to place their order, and a network of phone banks would process it for them.[72] Los Angeles had even remade itself aesthetically in anticipation of the event. The city spent a whopping $100,000 on planting a network of thirty thousand palm trees alongside its roadways, giving itself the aura of a desert paradise.[73]

Lewald and Diem were taken by the spectacle. This, they thought, was the future of the Olympics—a melding of culture and political power, marked as much by celebrity, media, and corporate self-interest as by sport itself. As they shuttled between track-and-field events, Lewald and Diem took copious notes, hoping to find inspiration for the 1936 Olympics.[74] They snapped photographs of everything they saw. New innovations, like the creation of the first Olympic Village and the introduction of triple-tiered medal platforms for winners, especially caught their eye.[75] Diem liked that each delegation in Los Angeles was given their own living quarters, complete with a dining hall and a chef well-versed in that nation's cuisine.[76]

For the two men, perhaps the most notable part of the Los Angeles Olympics was what happened on July 31, the day after the opening ceremony. Back home in Germany, millions of people turned out to vote in the federal elections. The atmosphere was tense. Nearly every home in Germany put up a flag for their preferred political party: a swastika for the Nazis, or a hammer and sickle for the Communists. It was a physical manifestation of a divided country. In one building in Berlin, a resident hung a Nazi banner with the words "A people without arms—a people without honor—a people without bread." A neighbor responded with a Communist slogan: "We are settling accounts—we want bread!"[77]

Diem and Lewald were still in Los Angeles when they heard the final results. By a slim margin, the Nazis were now the largest party in the Reichstag.

Part II

ENTER THE NAZIS

CHAPTER 7

AVERY BRUNDAGE NEVER REALLY KNEW HIS FATHER. In 1892, when the future sports leader was five years old, his family moved from Detroit to Chicago.[1] Afterward, Avery's father, a building contractor named Charles Brundage, abandoned them. Avery hated to talk about it. "I never met the man," he said later.[2] Instead, Avery grew up with his mother, a clerk, and his younger brother, Chester. To earn money on the side, he started delivering newspapers.[3] Every morning after he finished his route, he took a cable car seven miles to his high school. He was a promising student. At thirteen, an essay he submitted to a newspaper contest won him a trip to Washington, DC, where he attended the second inauguration of President William McKinley.[4]

Brundage picked up sports in high school. In a vacant lot in the back of school, he dug sand pits to practice his jump. Heavy rocks and stones were stand-ins for shot puts. By the time he was a senior, a local paper called him "the find of the season."[5] A stocky, six-foot-tall sprinter, he was often pictured in glasses, giving him the air of a professor rather than an athletic star.[6]

Brundage enrolled at the University of Illinois Urbana-Champaign as a civil engineering major. He would often complete his problem sets ahead of everyone else, then lean back in his chair and leaf through the sports pages of the *Chicago Tribune*.[7] When he graduated in 1909, a prominent athletic club in Chicago invited him to join. Brundage then placed third in the national championships for the "all-around,"[8] a multipart competition that included a broad jump, a hammer throw, a pole vault, and a one-mile run. Ever ambitious, he "soon had visions of a new world record," he wrote later.[9] He was working at a prominent architecture firm, where he oversaw increasingly lavish new building projects.[10] At night, Brundage set aside the construction contracts and went for two-hour runs under the stars.[11]

The training paid off. In 1911, Brundage won the US national track-and-field championship.[12] Newspapers declared him "without a peer" in the United States.[13] The following summer, a telegram arrived for Brundage from the headquarters of the American Olympic Committee in New York: "You have been selected a member of the American Team."[14]

It was a dream come true. Brundage quit his architecture job and took the train to New York, where he boarded a steamship to Sweden. Stockholm thrilled him.[15] The Swedish stadium was wondrous, one of the most impressive up to that point in Olympic history—a gleaming, U-shaped structure made of granite and brick, with seats for twenty-seven thousand spectators.[16] In between competitions, he met prominent track-and-field sprinters from across Europe, including his future friend, the German athlete Karl Ritter von Halt. Brundage came in sixth in the pentathlon, a failure for which he would never forgive himself.[17] But the Olympics left a lasting impression. The eclectic mix of nationalities, the exquisite talents of the athletes, the spectacle of the opening and closing ceremonies—Brundage was insatiable.

Though Brundage would later portray himself as an underdog,

his family was well-connected in Chicago. His uncle Edward J. Brundage was a prominent Chicago politician who would soon become the attorney general of Illinois. Brundage's uncle offered unintentional glimpses of the ugly side of Chicago politics. When Brundage was young, his uncle convinced the mayor to abandon a plan to shut down a baseball field in Brundage's uncle's district in exchange for a supply of stadium tickets.[18]

By the 1920s, Chicago was a bastion of corruption, especially in the construction business. Brundage, returning to the industry after his loss at the Olympics, gained a reputation as a straight-edged player. Colleagues called him "Honest Ave."[19] When a construction manager asked for a $100,000 bribe, Brundage reported him to the police.[20] He hated cheats. What he valued in sports—as in business— was integrity. Sports seemed like a space apart from politics. "The track athlete stands or falls on his own merits," Brundage explained once.[21] He seemed to sour on salary-based professional sports soon after the 1919 World Series,[22] when the Chicago White Sox, Brundage's hometown baseball team, bet against themselves and then intentionally lost the game, setting off an enormous scandal.

Amateur athletics, Brundage decided, were the purest form of sport. He praised the Olympics for its tenets of amateurism, which meant that athletes couldn't earn money from their sport. Olympic athletes chose their career, he thought, purely for the love of the game. To Brundage, the amateur rules at the Olympics meant that athletes were "judged solely on their merit, regardless of social position, wealth, family connections, race, religion, color or political affiliation."[23] He believed "sport is the only true democracy," because "whether you are rich as Croesus or as poor as Job's turkey," any athlete, he thought, could take part.[24]

It wasn't the most logical perspective. Not being able to earn a salary from sports ensured that only people with wealth and family connections could participate. But Brundage seemed to truly believe his way of thinking. He also truly believed he was living proof of the up-from-your-bootstraps narrative. He had a habit of portraying his own rise in the sporting world as an example of the opportunity that amateur sports could bring, often eliding the benefits that his race, gender, and family prominence brought him. Decades later, a reference in a German magazine to Brundage's "life of ease" as a young adult infuriated him. "You may inform them that every penny that I have ever had has been earned through my own efforts," Brundage instructed a colleague.[25]

In 1915, Brundage launched his own construction business—the blandly titled Avery Brundage Company—using $2,000 he had saved.[26] It didn't take long for him to build up an impressive client list. A decade later, the Avery Brundage Company had become one of the most important construction firms in the city, responsible for erecting dozens of high-end apartment buildings, a Ford Motor manufacturing plant, a Chevrolet warehouse, the Illinois Life Insurance Company Building, and multiple ritzy hotels.[27] In 1929, just before the Great Depression ground construction projects to a halt, Brundage was worth over $250,000, equal to $4.3 million today.[28]

Still, Brundage couldn't shake his love for sports. On the side, he became involved in the Amateur Athletic Union (AAU),[29] the organization that governed track-and-field sports in the United States. In 1925, he became its second elected vice president.[30] It was a relatively minor executive post from which he had no trouble parlaying real political power. Three years later, he assumed the presidency.[31] He had a forceful but effective personality: he wasn't afraid to disqualify top American athletes whom he believed had broken his rules.[32]

Brundage's rise in the American sports world drew the attention of Sigfrid Edström, the head of the IAAF. By the end of the decade, Brundage was president not only of the Amateur Athletic Union but also of the American Olympic Committee, the umbrella organization to which the AAU belonged.[33] In September 1929, when Edström visited Chicago, where his wife had grown up, he decided to court the new American power player. Brundage and Edström met for lunch. The two seemed to hit it off.[34] Brundage—as a sports official, a political conservative, and a staunch believer in the amateur doctrine, which stated that Olympic athletes should not be paid for their sports—became a natural ally of Edström's.

Edström asked Brundage to join the 1930 meeting of the IAAF Congress.[35] There, Brundage was elected to join the IAAF's Committee on Women's Sport, the subcommittee on which Alice Milliat also sat.[36] A few months later, in January 1931, Edström offered him a high-ranking position on the IAAF: chair of the Rules and Records Committee,[37] a title that would give him significant influence over the rules of international track-and-field sports.

For Edström, who was devoting much of his time to his takeover of Alice Milliat's organization, Brundage became the ideal second fiddle. It helped that Brundage was no fan of Milliat's, either. Brundage said later that Milliat "made quite a nuisance of herself" with her demands that the IAAF and the IOC elect more women leaders.[38] Edström seemed to feel safe complaining about her to the younger American. In the letters they fired back and forth between Stockholm and Chicago, Edström lamented that the Women's World Games had caused "so much trouble" for sports leaders. Of Milliat's organization, he wrote, "We should like the whole thing to disappear from the surface of the earth."[39]

Brundage had a generally skeptical opinion of women's sports. Though at some points he issued ostensibly positive statements about how, "under proper supervision," women athletes could do "some wonderful things,"[40] more often he viewed women with suspicion. In December 1932, Brundage, in a moment of frustration with a high-profile American competitor, expressed support for banning women athletes from the Olympics entirely: "You know, the ancient Greeks kept women out of their athletic games. They wouldn't even let them on the sidelines." Maybe, he said, "they were right."[41] But like Edström, Brundage could see the bigger picture. Bringing women's sports under the control of the IAAF wasn't about endorsing those sports per se. It was a political calculation to keep the power of the Olympics intact.[42] It was better to have someone like Alice Milliat working *for* the IAAF, and therefore the Olympics, rather than against it.

Soon after Brundage joined the IAAF Council, he developed a close friendship with another man who would shape his career for decades to come: Karl Ritter von Halt, a German banker who had, since 1925, served as the director of Germany's athletic federation.[43] When von Halt was elected to the IAAF in 1932, the two of them—plus Edström—formed a close-knit trio. Like Brundage, these men had attended the 1912 Olympics in Sweden: Edström as one of the organizers and von Halt as a twenty-one-year-old decathlon athlete who carried the German flag at the opening ceremony. Together, they called themselves the "Beer Drinking Society,"[44] and they held private meetings throughout Europe and the United States, at which von Halt often brought Bavarian beers.

All three men developed an obsession with enforcing the amateur rule. In April 1932, when they discovered that Paavo Nurmi, a famous Finnish gold medalist,[45] had pocketed a large travel stipend that they claimed amounted to a professional payment, Brundage and Edström pushed to ban him. Providing the ammunition was Karl Ritter von Halt, who led the investigation. Von Halt concluded that Nurmi had, in fact, deposited some $300 worth of traveling expenses[46] (over $6,000 today).

The public did not receive the trio's push to designate Nurmi a "professional," and therefore eject him from the Olympics, warmly. Edström, as the head of the IAAF, took the blame. In Finland, residents boycotted the city's trams, which were manufactured by Edström's company.[47] When Finnish sports officials penned angry letters demanding that Edström reverse his decision, Brundage stood by Edström. Edström leaned on him for emotional support. "I have been strongly attacked in the Finnish newspapers," he lamented to Brundage in one letter, in the fall of 1932. He comforted himself in the belief that "only amongst the plebeian population" is anyone "displeased with the disqualification."[48]

The scandal cemented Brundage as a forceful supporter of the Olympic movement. For decades, Edström had been seeking a strong member in the Americas to help him expand the Olympics beyond Europe.[49] Brundage seemed like the perfect person. And when another, much larger controversy threatened to destabilize the legitimacy of the Olympics itself, Edström, along with the new IOC president, Henri de Baillet-Latour, leaned on Brundage to make it go away.

○○○

On January 24, 1933, members of Germany's old guard filed into Berlin's city hall[50] with an impending sense of doom. The republic they had nurtured since World War I seemed to be on the verge of collapse. Industrial production in Germany had fallen by half, and by the end of 1932, as much as one-third of the country's population was out of work.[51] Thousands of homeless young people crowded the streets of Berlin, begging for money or food.[52] Lines for the unemployment office wrapped around multiple city blocks. People bartered potato peels and firewood.[53] One guide led visitors on a tour of Berlin called "Crisis, if You Please," where they saw abandoned factories, homeless encampments, unemployment lines, and other signs of "the metropolis in crisis."[54]

Two months earlier, in the second federal election that year, Adolf Hitler's Nazi Party had again secured a plurality of seats in the Reichstag, placing the fascist leader just shy of leadership power. The Nazis were buoyed by the votes not of the poor but of the elite; the wealthiest neighborhoods voted for the fascists in the highest numbers.[55] Hitler's main roadblock to power was Germany's president, the aging conversative leader Paul von Hindenburg, who had held the position since 1925. Ranking slightly below von Hindenburg was the chancellor: in December, a conservative, Kurt von Schleicher, had become chancellor with Nazi support, but his tenure looked fragile. The conservative parties were fractured along ideological lines, and rumors were swirling of yet another coming cabinet shakeup.[56]

The possibility that Hitler might ascend to leadership had kicked Theodor Lewald, the former bureaucrat who, alongside Carl Diem, was now the principal organizer of the Berlin Olympics, into action. Hitler was vociferously opposed to the Olympics, and prominent Nazis had long dismissed Lewald and Diem as representatives of "bourgeois-internationalist" ideology.[57] The seventy-two-year-old Lewald was nothing if not a pragmatist, and he wasn't going to let political turmoil in the German government spoil his dreams of a Berlin-hosted Olympics. That month, to insulate the Olympics from political headwinds, Lewald decided to register the Organizing Committee for the 1936 Games as its own nonprofit, with himself as its head. That way, it could function independently of the German state.

Next up, Lewald needed to stage the Organizing Committee's first official meeting. On that late January evening in 1933, at his invitation, a group of old allies slipped into the redbrick city hall building and climbed up to the council room. Among the arriving men was Heinrich Sahm, the politically moderate mayor of Berlin who had supported Paul von Hindenburg's presidential reelection campaign against Adolf Hitler the year prior.[58] Other attendees included Carl Diem and Lewald's two colleagues on the IOC: Adolf Friedrich of Mecklenburg, a former governor of German-colonized Togo in West Africa, and Karl Ritter von Halt, the friend of Avery Brundage.[59]

Lewald greeted the Organizing Committee and ran through his agenda. First up was the question of money. There was no delicate way to put it: the Organizing Committee was strapped for cash. Lewald's years of lobbying had turned up little. The German central government, whom Lewald had met with about sponsoring the Olympics, rejected out of hand his proposal that it contribute 7.5 million Reichsmarks to the Olympics.[60]

Lewald tried to focus on the positives—the Organizing Committee would not have to pay for everything alone. He pegged the expected revenue from ticket sales at 3 million Reichsmarks, a significant windfall when combined with other sources of help.[61] The Reich Post Ministry, too, had agreed to sell an Olympic-themed stamp, from which they would donate some profits into the coffers of the Organizing Committee.[62] It was a good start, Lewald thought—it just wasn't going to be enough to fund the Olympics on its own.

The Organizing Committee zagged between other logistical items. For the Olympic hymn, Lewald announced he had convinced the playwright Gerhart Hauptmann, who, in a few months, would apply to join the Nazi Party, to write a poem.[63] The Organizing Committee also agreed to send an invite to President von Hindenburg to serve as the official patron of the Olympics.[64] The men adjourned with assurances that they would meet again in the coming months.

If Lewald exited the meeting feeling optimistic about the future of the Olympics, six days later it all fell apart. The German president, Paul von Hindenburg, appointed Hitler chancellor of Germany, giving the fascist leader outright power for the first time.

○○○

At first, more moderate Germans stressed, it wasn't supposed to be a big deal. Von Hindenburg was appointing Hitler purely as a *political* decision, to harness Hitler's influence and funnel it toward support for the more moderate conservative factions in Germany. Von Hindenburg essentially thought he could control the Nazi leader. A January 31 *New York Times* article on Hitler's appointment stressed that Hitler had sworn to follow the country's republican constitution. "The composition of the Cabinet leaves Herr Hitler no scope for gratification of any dictatorial ambition," the *Times* announced.[65]

That fiction didn't even last a full month. On February 27, an arson attack set the Reichstag ablaze. When the fascist leader first saw the fire, "his face glowed red with excitement," according to an observer. Eager to institute a dictatorship, Hitler declared, "We will show no mercy anymore; whoever gets in our way will be slaughtered."[66] With dubious evidence, Hitler blamed the Communist Party for the fire, and he arrested many of his political opponents. Imprisoning adversaries had the added benefit of making the elections uncompetitive, and a week later, on March 5, the Nazis won an outright majority in the Reichstag.

With Hitler firmly entrenched in power, Lewald's nightmare seemed to be coming alive. The Berlin Olympics were again thrust into doubt. A coalition of Nazi student groups began insisting that the Olympics "must not be held in Germany,"[67] while a Nazi paper called Diem and Lewald traitors for taking money from Jewish businesspeople, including from the publishing magnates the Ullstein family.[68] The virulent antisemitism that the Nazis propagated threatened Lewald personally. Lewald's father was born Jewish, though he had converted to Christianity at a young age.[69] Lewald never had much of a relationship to Judaism, but he knew that didn't matter to the Nazis.

On March 6, the day after the Nazis won their outright majority in the Reichstag, Lewald wrote to Hitler to express his "warmest congratulations" and to request a conversation about the upcoming Olympics.[70] Ten days later, he shuffled into a meeting with three men—Nazi propaganda minister Joseph Goebbels, interior minister Wilhelm Frick, and Hitler himself. Lewald wanted the Nazis to guarantee a loan of 6 million Reichsmarks to fund the Olympic project.[71] He made his case on grounds he felt would be familiar to the Nazis: public relations. The "enormous propaganda effect" of the Olympics, he told Hitler, would more than pay for itself.[72] The Berlin Olympics could be a way for the Nazis to spotlight their new nation.

Hitler seemed intrigued. Yes, he told Lewald, the German state would guarantee the loan. Echoing Lewald, he later explained to his advisors that he saw the Olympics as a tool to "win over world opinion" by displaying Germany's "great cultural achievements."[73]

It was Lewald's first big break in years, but it proved to be short-lived. A week after the meeting with Hitler, the Nazis passed the Enabling Act, which gave Hitler broad dictatorial control over the country. On April 1, Hitler instituted a boycott of Jewish businesses, and on April 7, he expelled Jewish people from government service. The sports world soon followed. On April 28, Hitler appointed an ardent Nazi named Hans von Tschammer und Osten to become Germany's sports czar, the top sports official in the country.[74] Among von Tschammer's first moves was to crack down on Jewish athletes. By the end of the year, Jews were expelled from nearly all sports organizations, with the exception of two Jewish sports clubs.[75]

The violence against Jewish citizens put Lewald's own standing in jeopardy. Lewald was chairman of the Reich Committee for Physical Exercise, a prominent German sports body. In early April, the group voted to ban the "not fully Aryan representatives" from future meetings. Lewald was forced to resign.[76] Next, Nazi newspapers agitated for Lewald to be fired from the Organizing Committee for the 1936 Games.[77] Von Tschammer, the new Nazi sports leader, was happy to oblige. He initially demoted Lewald before attempting to remove him. But in a nimble feat of politicking, Lewald managed to talk his way out of a resignation. If the Nazis pushed him out of the Organizing Committee, Lewald warned, the IOC would revoke Berlin's host status. Lewald had deep ties to the IOC; von Tschammer did not.[78]

The rise of the Nazis had other political ramifications for international sports. Carl Diem, the original proponent of the 1916 Games, did not join the Nazi Party, but he also did not seem particularly repulsed by the new fascist state: he applied, without success, for the position of Nazi sports czar that von Tschammer received instead.

Meanwhile, Karl Ritter von Halt, the prominent IAAF member who was close friends with both Avery Brundage and Sigfrid Edström, joined the Nazi Party in 1933.[79] Edström wrote later that von Halt had to join the party because his job as a director at Deutsche Bank required it, adding that "in his heart he was not a Nazi at all."[80]

On the contrary, there is plenty of evidence that von Halt was a true believer. In his role at Deutsche Bank, he began funneling gifts and unsecured loans directly to Heinrich Himmler, the eventual architect of the Holocaust. According to the historian Peter Longerich, von Halt became a member of Himmler's inner circle of friends, where he attended private meetings to discuss politics and the future plans of the Nazi government.[81] In von Halt, the Nazis now had a high-profile representative on the IAAF—though if this turn of events bothered Brundage and Edström, they didn't seem to show it.

○○○

As Theodor Lewald struggled to keep his job atop the Organizing Committee, Jewish leaders across the world began to ask how the International Olympic Committee could, in good conscience, allow such a hostile country to host the forthcoming Olympic Games. On April 14, 1933, Avery Brundage received a letter from the editor of the *Baltimore Jewish Times*, urging the sportsman to take a stand against the Berlin Olympics.[82]

Brundage responded that he expected the Olympics "will not be held in any country where there will be interference with the fundamental Olympic theory of equality of all races." Brundage did not mean his letter to be a rebuke of Germany; he was trying to emphasize that, to his mind, Germany was in fact going to rise to the occasion. To his chagrin, when the *Baltimore Jewish Times* published his letter, it was misinterpreted. The Associated Press affixed the story with the headline "Brundage Predicts Games Will Not Be Held in Germany."[83]

Though Brundage was quick to clarify his comments, a political movement was already beginning to coalesce around the idea of stripping the Olympics from Berlin. An alliance of labor groups and Jewish groups began calling for the IOC to jettison Berlin as host. The Labor Sports Union, a worker-run sports organization, demanded a boycott of the Berlin Olympics.[84] At the same time, halfway across the world, leaders in Japan released a statement calling for the IOC to move the Olympics, preferably to Rome.[85]

When news of the burgeoning boycott movement reached Berlin, the Organizing Committee worked to avoid a PR disaster. The criticisms coming out of America—that the Nazis were violent fascists, that they were not giving an equal shot to Jewish athletes and athletes of color—were accurate, but Lewald, fearful that a boycott by the United States could derail the entire Olympic Games, worked hard to deflect them. He managed to persuade the Nazis to release a hollow statement affirming that they would allow "competitors of all races."[86] Diem weighed in with his own illogical claim that "people of all countries and all races are welcome in Germany."[87]

Even the frequently deferential IOC was, at first, skeptical that the Nazis could make for satisfactory Olympic hosts. The committee's president, Henri de Baillet-Latour, wrote to Lewald and Karl Ritter von Halt, reminding them that he would not allow the Olympics to be rooted in Nazi ideology.[88] Hitler raged against Baillet-Latour's "impertinent" remarks, but Lewald and von Halt knew they had to respond tactfully. At the IOC conference that June, Lewald and von Halt delivered a statement affirming that Jewish people would "not be excluded from membership in German teams."[89] Their claim didn't come with any practical guarantees, but it was enough to convince Charles Sherrill, one of the leading American officials on the IOC, to declare an end to the burgeoning boycott movement. "I do not know how they did it," Sherrill said, referring to Lewald and von Halt, "but they did it."[90]

They didn't actually do it. Hitler had not signed off on the statement, and anyone paying attention would have realized it did not reflect the official Nazi view. In early May, Hans von Tschammer, who at that point controlled the entirety of Germany's sports apparatus, bluntly said in a speech that "German sports are for Aryans."[91] Political calculations were the only reason the Germans didn't go further in outright barring Jewish athletes from all sports. In a confidential memo, von Tschammer wrote that he was allowing two Jewish sports organizations to continue to practice in Germany only "to gag the Jewish agitation from abroad" in the lead-up to the Olympics. He wanted to create the illusion of fair play, he said. But he assured his fellow Nazis that it wouldn't last: "A general regulation for Jewish sports will come out after the end of the Olympics."[92]

Satisfied that the Nazis would hold up their end of the bargain, Baillet-Latour grew worried about America. He wrote a concerned letter to Brundage in the fall of 1933, having heard about the "nervousness created in America by the Jewish question in Germany," and he wanted to assure Brundage that the German authorities would not discriminate against any athlete.[93] Baillet-Latour also had a favor to ask: he needed a cover to justify his, and the IOC's, support of the Berlin Games. He told Brundage that the Americans should issue a statement requiring the Germans to adopt a policy of nondiscrimination. "This would strengthen enormously my personal position," he noted.[94] That way, when he campaigned in support of the Berlin Olympics, he would not "be suspected of having a false or prejudiced opinion."

Brundage obliged. At that point, his power was regional. He was head of the American Olympic Committee and a member of the IAAF, but he was not a member of the IOC itself. He had his sights set on joining the IOC one day, and he knew Baillet-Latour was a powerful ally. In November 1933, Brundage flew to New York for the annual meeting of the Amateur Athletic Union, the American track-and-field organization of which Brundage was

president. There, officials approved a measure hinging US participation on the requirement that the Nazis "permit and encourage
German athletes of Jewish faith or heritage to train, prepare for,
and participate" in the Olympics.[95] The press interpreted the statement as a broadside against the Germans. The subsequent *New
York Times* headline dutifully called it a "boycott" of the Olympics.[96] No one knew that Brundage had actually engineered the resolution in order to justify sending Americans to Berlin.

The IOC's deference to the Nazis was not out of naivete. Plenty
of IOC officials were openly antisemitic, and they cared about the
plight of Jewish people in Germany only insofar as it impacted op-
tics. The feeling went all the way to the top. Baillet-Latour had little
sympathy for the boycott movement, and he didn't take the systemic
discrimination and violence against Jewish people in Nazi Germany
seriously. "I am not personally fond of Jews and of Jewish influence," he confided in Brundage. He suggested that news about the
violence against Jewish people in Germany amounted to "propaganda."[97] Edström also had a soft spot for the Nazis, implying in one
letter that Jewish people had amassed too much influence in Germany. "In some of the more important trades the Jews governed the
majority and stopped all others from coming in," he wrote.[98] "An
alteration of these conditions [was] absolutely necessary if Germany
should remain a 'white' nation," he wrote in another letter. Ultimately, "it is too bad that the American Jews are so active and cause
us so much trouble."[99]

Brundage was immediately sympathetic to their viewpoint. He
announced that he, too, was frustrated by the "anti-German propaganda which floods the newspapers" in the United States. News
about Nazi violence and discrimination, he thought, had little basis
in reality. He had no doubt that Nazi sports officials "will do their
utmost to carry out the wishes" of the IOC.[100]

CHAPTER 8

SOON AFTER HITLER TOOK POWER, Nazi leaders launched a campaign to crush Germany's queer community. Beginning in March 1933, under the code name Campaign for a Clean Reich,[1] Nazi brownshirts ransacked over a dozen queer bars, forced three major queer advocacy groups to disband, and stripped literature about gender and sexuality from bookstore shelves. *The Third Sex*, a magazine for trans people that had published since 1930, was quickly shut down.[2] On the streets of Berlin, Düsseldorf, and Cologne, new forms of social surveillance emerged. Women who looked too masculine—especially those with short haircuts—were labeled "un-German," and trans and intersex people were judged to be "asocial."[3] People on the margins of gender and sexuality were arrested, imprisoned, and, at times, dispatched to their deaths. When one artist, Ossi Gades, was twice caught cross-dressing in women's clothes, the Gestapo decided to send her to a concentration camp. She died by suicide in Plötzensee Prison before they could take her away.[4]

Sensing the changing tide, some prominent gay Germans issued statements in support of the Nazis. Ahead of Hitler's takeover, the gay publisher Friedrich Radszuweit wrote that he did "not believe that even the National Socialists will proceed so rigorously against homosexuals."[5] Radszuweit evidently thought he could buy himself goodwill with Hitler. The Nazis raided, and shut down, his publishing house anyway.

The gay activist Adolf Brand fared little better. Brand, whose magazine *Der Eigene* (*His own man*) had published continuously since 1896 and was one of the oldest and most influential gay publications in the world, found himself a frequent target of Nazi raids. Police showed up at his suburban home five different times throughout 1933.[6] On November 29, 1933, he finally gave up. "I feel obliged to give you a detailed report on the complete futility of continuing my life work in the new National Socialist Germany," Brand told his readers in the farewell edition of the magazine.[7]

Among Nazi leadership, no queer figure inspired more contempt than Magnus Hirschfeld, who had committed the dual crimes of being both gay and Jewish. On May 6, 1933, a little over two months after Hitler suspended democracy, a Nazi student group raided Hirschfeld's Institute for Sexual Science. Dressed in brown military uniforms, the students chanted, "Burn Hirschfeld!," beating up staff members and destroying bookshelves.[8] Four days later, in a public square, they set fire to thousands of books held by Hirschfeld's institute.[9] Hirschfeld, who was out of the country on a speaking tour, never returned to Germany. He died of a heart attack two years later in Nice, France.[10]

Between 1918 and 1933, before Hitler seized power, German authorities had convicted nearly eight thousand men of "unnatural indecency."[11] Those numbers ballooned under the Nazi regime. In June 1935, Nazi leaders expanded the definition of sodomy to include not just sex acts but also "mutual masturbation," "debauched intention," and even "erotic glances,"[12] categories so broad that police could justify the mass incarceration of anyone they so much as suspected of queerness. In the subsequent years, some estimates suggest the Nazis arrested as many as one hundred thousand homosexuals.[13]

To hear Heinrich Himmler, the leader of the Nazi paramilitary group the SS, tell it, the Nazi hostility toward queer communities stemmed out of a preoccupation with the national birth rate. In the Nazi eugenics state, anyone who underwent a sex-change surgery, or who slept predominantly with people of the same sex, was one fewer reproducer. "All things which take place in the sexual sphere are not the private affair of the individual, but signify the life and death of the nation," Himmler told his SS soldiers.[14] Homosexuality and transsexuality were soon conflated with abortion, all being enemies of natalism. Tellingly, one Nazi official gave a 1937 speech with the title "The Combating of Homosexuality and Abortion as a Political Task."[15]

For all their militarism, the Nazis could not entirely extinguish queer life in Germany. Many queer people resisted, holding secret meetings in personal apartments or in the tucked-away corners of bars. To give it the appearance of a sports organization, the activist Lotte Hahm switched the name of her lesbian nightclub from Violetta to Sportklub Sonne and continued catering to gay clientele until the summer of 1935.[16] Elsewhere, queer people met under the guise of fictional organizations, with names like "Charlottenburg Rowing Club."[17] A bar called the Pauli continued to host lesbian meetups in a secret room, behind a "Private Party" sign, until 1938, around the same time Hitler invaded Poland. "It was terrible, but it was ours," a regular attendee remembered.[18] Whenever the police discovered one secret meeting space, another inevitably popped up to take its place. Queer Germans proved so chameleonic that Gestapo officials once complained they could not "sever the lifeline" of the community.[19]

What the Nazis did crush, at least within the borders of Germany, was the sense that gender and sexuality had become limitless. Only a few years prior, people at the margins of gender and sexuality were celebrities in Berlin; in America, the drag queen Julian Eltinge starred in several early Hollywood films; the French artist Claude Cahun, in their book *Disavowals*, wrote in 1930 that "neuter is the only gender that always suits me."[20] It was a time of unimaginable queer potential. By the end of 1933, however, that sense of possibility was eroding. The global hub of sex research had collapsed, and the country scheduled to host the forthcoming Olympics was now equating gender expression with criminality. It foreshadowed a dark future in sports. The Nazis, who had the ear of prominent members of the IOC, could translate this anti-queer hostility into IOC policy. If Avery Brundage and Sigfrid Edström didn't blink at Jewish discrimination, then likely they wouldn't push back against the Nazi repulsion toward queer people.

The impacts of Nazi rule were playing out on the other side of the German border, in Zdeněk Koubek's home of Czechoslovakia. Even a decade after the war, ethnic skirmishes continued to shake the fledgling country. Street violence over German monuments and Czech-language posters proliferated in the early 1930s; the country's president was not far off the mark when he said that the central problem of the new Czech state was of nationalities.[21]

The numbers there were stacked against the Germans, who made up less than a quarter of the country's population.[22] Despite the Germans' relatively small population, when the Nazis took power, Czech politicians acted quickly to stem Hitler's influence within their borders. In October 1933, just a few months after Hitler suspended democracy in Germany, the Czech state banned the two largest pro-Nazi parties, the Sudeten German National Socialist Party and the German Nationalist Party, from operating in the country. They mobilized police to the Sudetenland, a heavily German region in Czechoslovakia, to suppress any budding resistance movements.[23]

The appearance of armed police only enraged ethnic Germans. On October 3, Konrad Henlein, a calisthenics teacher who had no political background, formed a political movement called the Sudeten German Home Front, which almost immediately became a vector for Nazi sympathy in Czechoslovakia.[24] By the end of the month, 9,500 people registered for the pro-German party, a number that would grow exponentially in the coming months.[25] Czech authorities claimed that the party amounted to "camouflaged Nazism."[26] The liberal establishment feared that giving Henlein access to the levers of power would legitimize him in the eyes of the public, so when Henlein's candidates began winning elections, Czech leaders refused to let them join a coalition government.[27]

That turned out to be a grave mistake.

ooo

By the opening months of 1934, American anti-fascists were embracing the Olympic boycott movement in droves. Brundage's carefully engineered statement about nondiscrimination, which he issued through the Amateur Athletic Union to give himself—and his friends on the IOC—cover, did not win many converts. Activists wanted the American sports establishment to go further. One Jewish sports leader, Charles Ornstein, urged the American Olympic Committee to outright reject Germany's invitation to the Olympics, sending a clear signal that Nazi violence would not be tolerated.[28]

Other activists weren't buying it, either. The leftist newspaper *The Daily Worker* called Brundage's statement about nondiscrimination, correctly, a "stunt."[29] Opposing the Olympics became a rallying cry on the left. At anti-Nazi rallies at New York City's Madison Square Garden, it wasn't uncommon for groups like the American Civil Liberties Union and the American Federation of Labor to specifically invoke the Olympics and call for a boycott.[30]

Theodor Lewald was worried about the escalating movement.

Should the boycotters force the United States to back out of the Berlin Olympics entirely, he knew, the entire enterprise would collapse. Without American participation, "we are sure that the IOC will choose a different city," he wrote in a private letter.[31] He decided to double down. When the next IOC meeting rolled around that May, Lewald and his colleague Karl Ritter von Halt once again played the part of dutiful IOC servants. They affirmed to the committee that they would "loyally" follow their declarations of non-discrimination.[32] More dubiously, they claimed they had the political leverage to do so.

The two men were upholding a fiction that they could act independently of the Nazi state. Lewald often pointed to the fact that the Organizing Committee was independently registered under his name, as if that insulated him from the political pressures of a fascist state. In reality, the Nazis controlled all facets of the German sports bureaucracy. Lewald reported directly to Hans von Tschammer, the Nazi sports czar. When it came to the Olympics, von Tschammer could essentially do whatever he wanted.

Many IOC members still understood that Hitler, not Lewald, was the ultimate decision maker. A US diplomat went as far as to warn the American Olympic Committee in 1933 that Lewald was "no longer a free agent."[33] Hitler had allowed him to stay on only to "give an impression to foreign countries" that the Olympics were not an entirely Nazi-controlled affair, the diplomat wrote. The American Olympic Committee, headed by Avery Brundage, either didn't get the message or chose to ignore it.

By the summer, despite Brundage's efforts to reassure activists, the boycott movement continued to pick up steam. Samuel Untermyer, a prominent politician and anti-Nazi campaigner, began calling on Jewish-American athletes to take a stand against the games, insisting they reject "the hospitality of a country that persists in so insulting, degrading and persecuting our people." His comments grabbed the attention of a *New York Daily Mirror* columnist, who agreed that "the boycott is the only weapon left [for] a harried and persecuted race, torn at from all sides."[34]

The pro-Berlin factions of the American Olympic Committee knew they needed to do something dramatic to quiet the activists. If they wanted to win back public opinion, American sports officials realized they needed to present proof that the Nazis were not going to bar Jewish athletes from the Olympics.[35] Eventually, Avery Brundage came up with an idea: he would make a trip to Germany. If he could investigate the conditions of Jewish athletes up close, then maybe he could determine, once and for all, whether the Nazis were telling the truth. The timing worked well. Brundage was already planning to travel through Europe that July for the next IAAF meeting, and it wouldn't be hard to make a quick stop in Berlin. The American Olympic Committee agreed, giving Brundage "full and complete authority" to reject or accept their invitation to the Berlin Olympics based on his findings.[36]

That summer, Brundage arrived with his wife, Elizabeth Dunlap,[37] in a downtown Berlin that, he mused in letters, had little in common with the city he had visited years earlier. Nazi flags festooned nearly every porch. Jewish businesses had their windows smashed and their roofs crushed. Nazi supporters marched down the streets, chanting, "The Republic Is Shit" and "Jews, Drop Dead!"[38] Posters demanding "Germans, Defend Yourself! Do Not Buy from Jews" blanketed telephone poles and advertising boards.[39] In the summertime heat, the sounds of Nazi speeches on the radio echoed out of shops and apartment buildings; Joseph Goebbels, the Nazi propaganda minister, encouraged supporters to open their windows so that everyone would hear Hitler's voice.[40]

The overwhelming presence of fascism did not leave a lasting impression on Brundage. From the start, the American had little doubt in his mind about what he would decide. During his six-day trip across Berlin, Brundage spent all his time alongside Karl Ritter von Halt. Brundage barely spoke German, so von Halt did all the translating for him.[41] The trip culminated at the Kaiserhof, a swanky Berlin hotel frequented by Nazi leadership. There, Brundage, along with Sigfrid Edström and von Halt, met with three representatives from a Jewish sports league in Germany.[42] Inside the meeting room, a Nazi sports official dressed in black SS clothing stood before the Jewish officials, observing. It wasn't the ideal venue for honest dialogue about anti-Jewish violence, but Brundage voiced no objection.[43]

In the hotel, Brundage leafed through a thick folder of newspaper reports he'd compiled about the expulsion of Jewish athletes from German sports. He quizzed the Jewish sports leaders about their experiences. When Brundage asked, "Can Jews be members of a German sports club?" the officials informed him they were allowed only in Jewish clubs.[44] Brundage seemed unbothered. "In my club in Chicago, Jews are not permitted, either," he told the group.[45]

Robert Atlasz, one of the Jewish sports officials who attended the meeting, was afraid to refute Brundage. He distrusted the American's motivations. Unnerved by the SS official, he stuck solely to answers about sports that could not get him in trouble with the Nazis. He wrote later that he could not "freely and truthfully" answer Brundage's questions,[46] a fact that should have been more than obvious to the American.

Unsurprisingly, Brundage gave a glowing report upon his return. On September 26, at Brundage's recommendation, the American Olympic Committee officially accepted their invitation to the Berlin Olympics.[47] It was welcome news to Theodor Lewald, Carl Diem, and Karl Ritter von Halt, but it didn't sway many of the boycotters. One congressman from New York spoke openly of his belief that "the Reich Sports Commissars have snared and deluded" Brundage.[48]

IN JUNE 1933, as stories of Nazi street violence were making head-lines across Europe, Zdeněk Koubek walked up to a hotel in down-town Prague to meet one of the most famous female athletes in Europe.[1] Before arriving, Koubek called the hotel's front desk to make sure she was there. He was terrified and took a deep breath before knocking on Stella Walsh's door. A voice called for him to come in.

Koubek found Walsh lying on the floor of her hotel room, prac-ticing scissor kicks. A stopwatch lay by her side. Her dark curly hair spilled onto her eyebrows. Walsh had lived much of her life in Cleveland, Ohio, but she was in Prague to compete on behalf of Poland, where she was born. Her career straddled national borders: the year prior, when she won gold at the Los Angeles Olympics, she had chosen to compete for Poland. She hadn't had much of a choice; the United States had been too slow to approve her American citizenship.[2]

Koubek and Walsh had a lot in common. For both of them, their bodies were a source of public fixation. After losing to Walsh, one American relay runner complained that she was stuck "competing against this manly woman." Walsh, she said, "seemed so big and aggressive, and didn't know her place."[3] These were characteristic comments, but Walsh, who was twenty-two, almost three years older than Koubek, had learned to brush them aside. After winning gold, she began to live more and more like a celebrity. She wore extravagant outfits—a racoon coat, a blue tam cap, multiple rings[4]—to emphasize how little the comments bothered her.

When Koubek stepped into her hotel room, Walsh looked up from the floor and smiled at him.[5] She pointed at an ottoman and told him to have a seat. The two sat together and gossiped about other top runners for half an hour. Koubek was overjoyed. Only as he was leaving did he notice Walsh's nightstand: on it, prominently displayed, lay a shaving kit. He turned back to Walsh and noticed the outlines of facial hair just above her lips. Instinctively, Koubek touched his own face, which he had shaved a few hours earlier. Years later, Koubek would remember that moment as a relief. He was "not alone" in his "suffering," he wrote. "Even the most famous track star in the world had to shave."

When Koubek and Walsh faced off the next day, almost no one thought Koubek would prevail. Walsh was an Olympian at the top of her game; Koubek, though he'd notched a handful of impressive victories, was a scrawny nineteen-year-old, still new to the professional sporting world. At the start of the hundred-meter race, Koubek estimated that Walsh was favored to win "by a margin of 99%." But to everyone's shock, Koubek eked out a victory against the gold medalist. He crossed the finish line just milliseconds before Walsh. The crowd was ecstatic. A group of photographers encircled Koubek, and hundreds of spectators lined up to shake his hand.

Two months later, a letter arrived at Koubek's house in Brno from VS Praha, a Czech sports league based in Prague. Enclosed were 100 Czech crowns, plus a personal note: the club wanted him to join its team. Koubek said yes. Prague was the bigger city, with more opportunities for work and athletic growth. And his life in Brno was reaching a dead end. His job at the haberdashery had little prospect for advancement, and he didn't have many friends. That fall, he said goodbye to Boženka, his longtime coworker, and packed his bags for the capital.

In Prague, Koubek secured a job working as an assistant to a university professor. It paid 499 Czech crowns a month, which would have been frustratingly little money were the job not so easy. Koubek essentially worked as a receptionist, answering only the occasional phone call. He had plenty of free time, and he spent it training for his next big athletic challenge: the Women's World Games, scheduled to be held in London the following August, in 1934.

The job also came with free accommodations in a university dorm room on Black Street, a tiny cobblestone street lined with Renaissance-style buildings. Koubek decorated his room with postcards of Mount Vesuvius and Germany's Black Forest, which he dreamed of one day visiting. He didn't have a very active social life, preferring to run laps around the track over a trip to the movies. From the narrative essay he published later, he seemed to be naturally shy, and more than a little bit timid. Friends were never a goal—he was used to spending his free time on his own. In the morning, he woke up to the toll of the clock tower, rolled out of bed, and took a crowded city bus to the VS Praha field.

Living in the big city also meant heightened scrutiny. The more track meets Koubek won, the more he felt watched. In VS Praha, his new club, the women became suspicious of him first; not long after, the men followed. Koubek began receiving anonymous letters that contained thinly veiled accusations that he was hiding something. "Why don't you undress in the communal women's changing room at training and matches?" one anonymous writer asked. Koubek always threw out the letters. He tried to forget they existed at all. They were "drops of poison," he thought, sent by people who only wanted to take him down. But he'd be lying if he said the accusations didn't un-nerve him. Deep down, he knew they weren't far off from the truth.

Soon after arriving in Prague, Koubek received a letter from a man he didn't know. He opened it, bracing for another accusation of cheating. Instead, he found himself thumbing through a long hand-written note. "You will certainly be surprised that I am writing to you," the boy, named Karel Ryska, wrote. "Even I am confused and surprised that I worked up the courage at all." Ryska went on to explain that he was a member of VS Praha. He had seen Koubek practicing on the women's team and had taken a liking to him. "I offer you my heartfelt friendship," he said, "but, you know, separate from sports and in a different way than you are used to from the other boys." Ryska had a request: he wanted to know if the two of them could go on a date. Perhaps, Ryska said, they could meet at a bus station that Sunday and travel down to his family's summer cot-tage in Zbraslav, a town along the Vltava River, just south of Prague.

Koubek surprised himself by saying yes. In those days, he barely trusted anyone. Still, it was a distraction, a person he could talk to about something other than the forthcoming Women's World Games. That Sunday, he caught a bus packed with people dressed for a hike, backpacks and guitars slung across their backs. Koubek wore a gray skirt, which he instantly regretted. When he reached the stop, he found Ryska standing awkwardly, a book in hand, waiting for him. Koubek recognized Ryska immediately from practice. They had played scrimmages against each other, Koubek realized. Kou-bek had always liked him. "You look more like a poet than a hiker," Koubek told him, gesturing to Ryska's book.

After saying hello, they started walking along the river, through a patch of woods lined with chestnut trees. Koubek listened as a group of hikers up ahead sang to themselves:

> *Each boy has his girl,*
> *the girl that he loves . . .*

Koubek apologized to Ryska for walking so slowly. "If I were wearing pants, no doubt I'd be able to overtake those hikers," he said. "You cannot imagine what suffering it is for a runner with the reputation of being the fastest woman on the continent to wear a stupid skirt." Ryska grinned at him and said, "We don't have to rush; it's so beautiful here. We aren't missing anything."

On their way into the forest, the pair stopped at a rock, and Koubek gazed out at the countryside. At first, he didn't notice the cold touch of Ryska's finger on his. Then he felt something wet and warm, and he turned and realized Ryska was kissing his hand. Koubek's heart started racing. Ryska pulled him closer, wrapping his arms around Koubek's waist. "I have been in love with you even before I first saw you," he whispered. He had read about Koubek in the newspapers, he explained, and had known who Koubek was when he joined VS Praha. Getting the chance to compete against each other in scrimmages was just a happy coincidence. "I love you for your beautiful eyes, your clear and honest eyes," he said. "I know that you are truly the girl for me."

Something about that word, "girl"—or perhaps just Ryska's forthrightness—made Koubek jump. He pulled away, tears in his eyes. "You are mistaken, Karel," he said. "I am not the girl for you. Listen to me, I'm not a girl at all."

Koubek didn't know what had possessed him to say that out loud. He realized right away that he'd said too much. He turned and ran in the other direction, back to the bus stop, back to Prague, back to his dorm room. He tried not to listen as his words ricocheted around the woods: *I'm not a girl at all.*

○○○

The next day, Ryska called Koubek and assured him he wouldn't breathe a word of what had happened. He understood that Koubek wasn't interested in him romantically. He wanted, at least, to be-come friends. Koubek was relieved, but knowing his secret was safe didn't stop him from replaying the interaction again and again the following days. He thought about those words, that slip of truth. *I'm not a girl at all*. Why did it feel like he meant it?

As the weeks passed, Koubek grew more self-conscious of strangers' stares, paranoid that the secret of his true identity was on the verge of spilling out. Koubek thought he had finally been ex-posed when, as a part of an April Fool's joke, a Prague newspaper ran a story on him. He was sitting in a café in downtown Prague when he saw the headline. He read it, confused. The paper noted that Koubek was training with male runners on VS Praha as he prepared for the Women's World Games in London. It had a pro-posal. Because Koubek "has no equal rival in Czechoslovakia and soon anywhere in the world, a circle of experts have considered whether it wouldn't be better if she competed in the men's division." When he read that line, Koubek's heart nearly stopped. To compose himself, he had to gulp down a glass of water. It was satire, he re-minded himself. Just satire.

His identity consumed his thoughts. After the satirical article, the anonymous letters, and the interactions with Walsh and Ryska, the idea of traveling to London for the Women's World Games felt increasingly unsafe. The games would be his highest-profile event yet—and if people were this suspicious of him now, he could only imagine what people would say about him there.

After turning it over in his head all week, Koubek resolved to drop out. He told a fellow athlete that he couldn't go to London because he was afraid of how the press would characterize him. The athlete scoffed. "Madame Milliat would have a stroke if she learned the reason you didn't want to run," the athlete said. "Don't pay attention to what people say. Answer with your actions. Who cares even if the whole town is talking about it?"

It was the arrival of a new student, Jarmila Žaková, the wealthy daughter of an industrialist, that changed Koubek's mind. Jarmila was beautiful: rosy cheeks, blue eyes, dark hair. She seemed to understand him instinctively. When Koubek would panic about his future, Jarmila knew how to calm him down. Together, they went out to the movies and inhaled films starring Greta Garbo, Audrey Hepburn, and Marlene Dietrich. They met at cafés, braving the winter rain to gossip about sports or celebrities. With Jarmila's support, Koubek cut his hair shorter, so that it looked more like a boy's. Koubek noticed his confidence returning.

In his subsequent writings, Koubek never clarified the nature of his relationship with Jarmila. Outsiders still assumed Koubek was a woman at the time, and any romantic relationship they may have had would have been coded as queer—a dangerous prospect. But there was undeniably something special about what the two of them shared.

○○○

By the spring of 1934, anticipation around Koubek was building. The Women's World Games in London were mere weeks away, and Czech sports fans were abuzz with the possibility that their hometown hero might bring home gold.

Athletes from seventeen countries were planning to attend—almost all of them European, aside from small delegations sent by Palestine, Japan, Canada, the United States, and British-colonial South Africa.[6] Koubek was all but certain to qualify, but he faced difficult odds at the tournament itself. Czech athletes had long lagged behind their Polish and German counterparts in women's track and field, mainly because of funding. Poland and Germany had made a point of training women athletes and building facilities for women's sports; Czechoslovakia had not. On the field, that differential in investment became clear. Four years prior, when Prague hosted the Women's World Games, not a single Czech athlete won a medal.[7] Koubek was the country's sole chance this time, and Czech sports fans knew it. National celebrities started to back him. In June, a Czech film star, Anny Ondra, heard about Koubek's successes on the track and contributed 3,000 Czech crowns to cover the cost of the Czech women's team's expedition to London.

On August 7, 1934, it was time to leave. Koubek said goodbye to Jarmila at the train station in Prague.[8] Alongside three other track-and-field athletes and several members of the Czech handball team, Koubek crammed into a third-class train car bound for Nuremberg, Germany. The trip was long, punctuated only by ambient conversation and the occasional musical interlude. (One of the players had brought a saxophone to pass the time.) Though in his later writings Koubek did not dwell on it, signs of creeping fascism were everywhere. Koubek brought with him a stack of Czech newspapers to read on the train, but when he reached the German border, Nazi officials forced him to turn them over. Only Nazi-approved literature was allowed inside the country, they said.

Instead, Koubek, who knew little English, began leafing through a dictionary workbook called *One Thousand Words in English*, to prepare for his arrival in London. As he looked out at the farmlands blurring by, Koubek whispered a single English sentence to himself: "I have a new suit, you have a new suit."

The next morning, the train stopped on the coast of Belgium, where Koubek boarded a boat to England. Most of his teammates huddled on deck chairs, exhausted and seasick, trying desperately not to throw up. Koubek looked out, awed, as they crossed the English Channel. It was the first time he'd ever been at sea.

By the time the team arrived at Victoria Station in downtown London, Koubek's nerves had intensified. London was bigger and more cramped than any city he had ever visited. Every street corner seemed to lurch toward chaos. Metros, double-decker buses, luxury cars, sprawling palaces, and traffic cops shouting directions at throngs of pedestrians all might pack a single block. Koubek discovered he hated British food, which left him feeling nauseated after most meals. He relied on broken English, gleaned from the workbooks he'd read on the train, to navigate the city. Most of all, he worried constantly that officials from the Women's World Games would somehow be able to discern his secret: that, increasingly, he was feeling more and more like a man.

ooo

The White City Stadium opened in a former orchard above Notting Hill in April 1908, just ahead of that year's London Olympics.[9] At the time, it was the largest sports stadium in the world, so big that the planners fit a swimming pool in the middle of the track-and-field course. In the years since, it had lost its sheen. Instead of big track-and-field events, after the war, White City mostly hosted greyhound racing, car racing, and occasionally soccer. The Women's World Games was its biggest event in years.[10] On the morning of August 9, standing in front of an enormous crowd at the White City, Lord Desborough, a British aristocrat who contributed funding to Alice Milliat's organization, declared the Women's World Games open. He reminded the crowd that the games were played "for the honor of women's athletics and for the glory of sport."[11] Then he released a dove into the air. Alice Milliat, even though she had organized the event, did not speak.

The track-and-field competitions began that afternoon. Koubek sat in the stadium, scribbling notes. The Czech newspaper *Star* had tasked him with writing dispatches about each game,[12] since the paper couldn't afford to send a real journalist to London on its behalf. There wasn't much to report. The Germans swept every competition—the high jump, the discus, the shot put—and only the

Nazi flag was displayed on the flagstaff.[13] From the stands, Koubek heard the Nazi national anthem blast over the loudspeakers so many times that he memorized the words.

The next day, Koubek turned out for his signature event: the eight-hundred-meter dash.[14] At the track, he lined up alongside a half-dozen athletes, including Britain's Gladys Lunn and Sweden's Märtha Wretman. Koubek bent down and took a breath. The crowd fell to a hush, waiting for the start. When the referee fired a pistol, the athletes were off.

Koubek missed the jump, and Wretman and Lunn leapt out ahead of him. The first lap around the track, he trailed in third place, while Wretman sprinted ahead in first.

Koubek saw his window closing. He pushed himself faster, faster.[15] Suddenly he was in a full-body sprint. Koubek sensed the audience around him going quiet, waiting to see how long he could keep up this speed. "In astonishingly quick time," the papers reported later,[16] Koubek edged out Lunn, and he was within a few feet of Wretman. On the third and final lap, Koubek pushed past the Swede. He didn't slow, not for a second. He barreled across the tape.

When a megaphone declared Koubek the victor, the Czech team erupted into cheers. Koubek was still at the finish line, gasping for breath, when he heard the first notes of the Czech national anthem. Someone raised the Czech flag. Koubek was flooded with emotion. Watching his teammates rush to embrace him was an "unforgettable moment," he wrote later.

At some point, a teammate or a coach or an official told him that he'd broken a world record. His time was 2 minutes and 12.4 seconds, over four seconds ahead of the previous best. Koubek had won gold at the Women's World Games, and in the process he'd bought himself a spot in history. Koubek, though, didn't let himself savor it. In the evening, in a dispatch he wrote for *Star*, the gold medalist sounded oddly dismal. He lamented that if he'd given himself a better start, his record-setting time "might have been even better."[17]

○ ○ ○

The Germans continued to dominate the second day of the Women's World Games. By the close of the event, they claimed nine of the twelve available gold medals, with Poland and Czechoslovakia taking the other three. In the newspaper dispatches from the games, the German sweep was second only to one story: the rise of Zdeněk Koubek. Attendees seemed to be taken with the young sprinter. One report noted that he was "irresistible" to watch, and he "looked and ran just like a splendid male athlete."[18] Another called his eight-hundred-meter dash "the performance to command most admiration" at the Women's World Games.[19] Unspoken was the possibility that, in two years, Koubek might make it all the way to the Berlin Olympics.

Sports executives were eager to meet the new world record holder. That night, Koubek was meant to attend a banquet for the winning athletes alongside members of the European press.[20] In his hotel room, Koubek, dressed in a green suit, stared at himself in the mirror. He couldn't believe how sad the person staring back at him seemed. He knew this wasn't what winning was supposed to feel like. He'd spent years training for this moment. He'd achieved his dreams, shattered a world record. There was no reason to be despondent.

In truth, he felt like a fraud. Tears glistened in his eyes. Why had he traveled to London? he asked himself. Now everyone was going to identify him as a winner of a *women's* competition, a word that seemed to fit him less and less by the day. He glanced down at the gold medal in his hand, which suddenly felt unbearably heavy. He thought about hurling it out the window and onto the streets of London.

Or maybe, he wrote later, he would go back to the White City

Stadium and shout: "Keep your golden reward, I don't want it! It doesn't belong to me! It is intended for the winner of a women's contest. And I . . . !" He thought back to that conversation with Karel Ryska, the boy who had tried to kiss him months earlier. *I'm not a girl at all!*

A phone call interrupted his spiral. Numb, Koubek picked up the receiver and listened as a Czech official urged him to hurry over to the celebrations. "I hope you are already dressed," the voice said. "We'll be there in half an hour! The banquet is right at eight!" Koubek said that he'd be there soon. When he hung up, he thought again about the medal. Yes, he decided, he could return it—he could drop out of the games, and Alice Milliat could just pass his award on to the second-place finisher. Then he'd be free.

He reached for his keys. That was it: he would go to the banquet and give the medal to Wretman, the second-place finisher, "even at the cost of an international scandal," he later wrote in a personal essay.

He was on his way out of the hotel room when he heard a knock. He opened the door, expecting to see his coach. Instead, Jarmila was standing outside. He couldn't believe it. She hadn't told him she was coming. He'd left her at the train station in Prague just a few days earlier. Now there she was, in his hotel room in London, surprising him.

Koubek quickly confessed his plan. When he told her he was going to attend the banquet and return his medal, Jarmila stopped him. He needed some air, some time to think, she said. She took him to a café on the bottom floor of the hotel.

Minutes later, as dusk settled over the streets of London, Koubek was sitting at a table across from Jarmila, sipping lemonade through a straw. He thought about the banquet, which he knew had already started. "I shouldn't have listened to you," he told Jarmila. "I should have gone there. Everyone will be there and I could have returned the medal in front of everyone."

Jarmila laughed at him. "Don't speak nonsense. You don't really mean that." When Koubek tried to protest that he didn't feel comfortable receiving the award, Jarmila shook her head. "We didn't come here to argue."

"But I can't bear this anymore," Koubek said into his drink. "Come what may, at least I will be able to get rid of the hated title of record woman."

Jarmila squeezed his hand. "I understand you," she told him. "I am all for you returning the medal, but do it in such a way that there won't be the slightest doubt of the rightness and legitimacy of your actions. Until then, think of the medal as a kind of deposit." In other words: don't jettison your career, not until you are sure about your gender.

As the streets of London emptied for the night, the two sat and talked in the café for another hour. At some point, Koubek asked Jarmila how she'd gotten to London in the first place, and why she hadn't told him she was here. Jarmila admitted it was a last-minute plan—she'd sweet-talked her father into paying for her trip, which she pitched as a three-month excursion to improve her English. She had made it in time to watch Koubek win gold at the White City Stadium earlier that day.

"I arranged it specifically so that I could see your international triumph," she told him proudly. "It was really hard for me to hold myself back and not rush the field with the other fans and congratulate you right there after your victory."

○○○

What Koubek didn't know then was that at the banquet he had skipped, a mutiny was brewing. Camera bulbs flashed; athletic officials clinked champagne glasses; the winners sat together at a long white-cloth dining table. There was one empty chair. Throughout the night, Koubek's coach kept staring at it. Where was his team's star athlete?

A rumor began floating around the room. Koubek, some people whispered, looked a little bit too masculine on the field that day. Koubek's subsequent account identified the origin of the rumors as a British journalist named "Mr. Simpson," but it's unclear that a sports journalist by that name even existed. Koubek was likely referring to Bertie C. Sims, a white South African sports official who had served as the coach of the South African women's team.[21] Sims was convinced that his team had been cheated. Many of their competitors, he believed, were not nearly feminine enough to be women. He had wanted to confront Koubek at the banquet, at least according to a later essay written by Koubek himself—and when Koubek refused to show up, it only confirmed the South African leader's suspicions.[22]

The day Koubek left London, a thick fog blanketed the city. Jarmila stayed behind. Her father had already committed money to let her study in the city for three months, and she wanted to make the most of it. Koubek watched her through the train window. As he pulled out of the station in London, she waved at him, her fingers curled around a white handkerchief. Then, when the train hurtled forward, she melted into the haze.

For a few weeks, they kept in touch. Jarmila sent a steady stream of letters, including updates on how the British press was covering the aftermath of the Women's World Games. A month or so after the games, Koubek opened a letter from Jarmila that left him devastated. His closest friend in the world had fallen in love. "I have met up with Dr. K. here who is great company. Once you see us together in Prague it will be no wonder to you that I got engaged to him so fast like some romantic little girl," Jarmila wrote. "Don't be mad at me about it. Even if I won't have as much time for you, I remain your good friend."

Jarmila was married by the spring. After that August, Koubek saw her only one more time, sitting in the window of a Prague café. Then, like so many others in his life, she was gone.

○○○

In the days after the Women's World Games, Koubek arrived back in Prague; Alice Milliat returned to Paris; the sports press moved on. But Bertie C. Sims could not let go of his suspicions. A week and a half later, in his report to the British Empire Games Association, he made a surprise plea.[23] He wanted his country, British-colonial South Africa, to withdraw from the Women's World Games. His reason was simple: the Women's World Games were permitting sex fraud.

"I am very much against our taking part in these events," he told the members. "The class of person representing foreign countries in these games is, to say the least, most peculiar, and one heard remarks on all sides that they were not women." Sims didn't have any actual evidence outside his own gut feeling. "From my personal observations I must say I am very much in agreement with these opinions," he told the committee, "as quite a number of the outstanding foreign athletes were shaved, and had very deep voices, and gave the impression of being of the masculine sex."[24]

For the first few weeks after Sims made his recommendation, nothing came of it. He had suggested that South Africa abandon the Women's World Games in a closed-door meeting. Only a select group of sports officials heard him, and for all anyone knew, they may have dismissed the comments as ludicrous and Sims as a conspiracy theorist. Then, on September 20, the British press got their hands on his remarks. They must have known right away that it was a sensational story. Newspapers across the country carried excerpts of Sims's speech, affixed with headlines like "World Games

'Women' Really Men, Says Track Coach"[25] and "Claims Men Posed as Girls in Sport Events at London."[26]

When a Canadian coach and newspaper columnist named Alexandrine Gibb read about Sims's comments, she felt a surge of relief. That August, she had traveled to London to coach the Canadian track-and-field team. Gibb had watched her athletes shuffle into their dressing room, dejected. Some athletes started "asking what chance they had when they were forced to run against 'men' in the women's world games," Gibb wrote in a newspaper op-ed.[27] She didn't know how to respond—she thought it wasn't right: "I had a dressing-room full of Canadian girls weeping because they had to toe the mark against girls who shaved and spoke in mannish tones."[28]

In the first half of the twentieth century, aside from Alice Milliat, few people had done more to shape the development of women's sports than Gibb. In 1925, she founded the Women's Amateur Athletic Union, which soon became one of the premier athletic organizations in Canada.[29] From there, she worked her way up the ranks of international governance. Beginning in 1932, the IAAF, that international track-and-field federation, offered her a spot on its Committee for Women's Sports, alongside Avery Brundage, making her one of the few women to receive such a position.[30]

Gibb, though, was becoming concerned about the femininity—or lack thereof—of top female athletes. In a column in the *Toronto Daily Star* days after the Women's World Games, Gibb lamented that while her Canadian team members were paragons of femininity, "a number of the English girls are extremely mannish."[31] These physical differences between women, she said, made the competitions unfair; the worst part was that everyone could see it. At the White City Stadium, she said, a massage therapist had told her that the Canadians needed more "husky girls" if they ever wanted to win. "These frail lilies of Canadians are so different to the others," the therapist had apparently said to Gibb.

Reading about Sims only seemed to harden Gibb's convictions. When a reporter dismissed the Sims comments as ridiculous, Gibb punched back. "It wasn't so amusing," she wrote at the end of September, "not when you were there and saw real feminine Canadian girls forced to compete against that sort of a mannish athlete in track and field events."[32]

The Sims story created a firestorm in the sports press—though in truth, most reporters didn't know what to make of it. Despite the fervor, the idea that many competitors were not women most likely seemed ludicrous. Many journalists called up other athletes who had competed in the Women's World Games to get their perspectives. A South African field athlete named Eileen Crockart told the press that though many women athletes had facial hair and "we often thought they were men athletes when we saw them on the track," these were only aesthetic discrepancies. "There was no doubt, however, that they were women," she said.[33]

Hilda Strike, a Montreal sprinter, laughed when a journalist asked her about men competing in the Women's World Games. "They seemed feminine enough to me," Strike said. Yes, "one or two of these athletes had a little hair on their faces and had to shave," she said, but many women—athletes or not—"had the same difficulty." According to another athlete, "Some of the girls looked mannish and they were certainly very big, but the statement that they were men is absurd."[34]

Yet for all the skepticism it inspired, the Sims story marked a departure for the sporting world, the opening salvo, in many ways, in what would become a regime of surveilling femininity. While whispers about masculine women dated back to the start of the Women's World Games, never had a prominent official so directly accused opponents of challenging a normative understanding of womanhood—and worse, of *cheating*, by way of gender fraud.

Neither Sims nor Gibb mentioned any athlete by name, but many in women's sports knew who they were describing. Between his avoidance of the women's locker rooms, his boyish new haircut, and the traces of stubble on his chin, Koubek had become a focal point of suspicion. Rumors soon trickled out that during the Women's World Games, a medical group testing to see how strenuous exercise impacted women had asked to examine Koubek for their study. Without explanation, Koubek had refused. While it should not have been suspicious for an athlete to want privacy, Koubek's unwillingness to sit for the examination "gave rise to rumors that there was some mystery about [him]," a Prague newspaper reported.[35]

When Koubek first read the comments by Sims, he felt his face get hot. For a time he thought about using the story as a chance to come forward. It would be so easy to just tell the press that Sims, while misguided, was at least directionally correct—that, yes, Koubek wanted to live as a man. Eventually, though, he thought better of it. When his friends asked him about the article, he told them that it was "nothing new under the sun. They are just good old Czech gossip, dressed in English clothes."[36]

○○○

Alice Milliat did not comment on the Bertie C. Sims report publicly, but according to Koubek, she was furious. The report hit the Women's World Games "like lightning," Koubek wrote later, and Milliat placed urgent calls to Sims, threatening to dismiss him from the FSFI, the organization that oversaw the Women's World Games, if he didn't retract his statement.[37]

The allegations could not have come at a worse time. Milliat could feel the influence of the Women's World Games waning. Her back-and-forth with Sigfrid Edström, the head of the IAAF, was getting more contentious. Edström was plowing ahead with his plan to wrest control of women's athletics from the FSFI, having decided that Milliat was "completely impossible" to negotiate with.[38] Milliat was insistent that she would not give up organizing the Women's World Games. The IAAF "had done nothing for women's sport and was not interested in it," she told the membership of the FSFI.[39]

Still, she could see the writing on the wall. Women's sports were not a particularly profitable enterprise, and putting on the Women's World Games every four years had sunk her deeper into debt. She started taking out newspaper ads that made overtures to social conservatives, claiming that women's sports could extinguish "social evils" and cut infant mortality rates, and urging readers to buy a subscription to the FSFI for as little as 3 francs.[40]

By September, the FSFI's coffers were so empty that Milliat grasped at increasingly implausible solutions. She wrote a letter to Avery Brundage, noting that the group was 1,500 francs in debt, and asked for help.[41] When Brundage shared the letter with Edström, the Swede admitted that Milliat's question "caused me to smile." Milliat's organization had been such a burden on the IAAF, Edström said, that "we certainly have no interest at all to support it."[42] Perhaps if the Women's World Games ran out of money, Milliat would finally disappear.

○○○

FSFI or not, the regulation of amateur sports for both women and men remained a consistent source of controversy. One day in the spring of 1935, a Czech official opened up a copy of *Sport*, a popular German-language newspaper published out of Zurich.[43] Flipping through its pages, he stumbled across an ad for Ovaltine, a milk-flavoring product that marketed itself as an energy booster. The ad featured the brand's slogan, "A daily cup of Ovaltine keeps the body in shape," alongside a photo of a familiar athlete: Zdeněk Koubek.

The official was furious. Koubek, as an amateur athlete, was not allowed to collect any money from his sport *or* from his associated celebrity. This ad looked a lot like a product endorsement, which was illegal under the rules of amateur sport. The official reported the ad to the Czechoslovak Amateur Athletic Union, the organization that governed track-and-field sports in Czechoslovakia. The group threatened to classify Koubek as a professional, which would make him ineligible for the upcoming Berlin Olympics.

Koubek denied the charge that he'd participated in the ad. The newspaper, he maintained, had simply used his photo out of context, without his permission. Though he did like Ovaltine and drank it regularly before his sprints, he hadn't actually agreed for his image to be used in the ad. In a letter to the press, Koubek insisted, "I cannot keep track of all the things that people write about me."

The Czechoslovak Amateur Athletic Union didn't believe him. That June, the sports organization sent a blue slip to his dorm in Prague, informing him that he no longer had a place in amateur sports. The fallout was swift: VS Praha expelled Koubek from its team. No matter, Koubek thought. He would continue to play sports, just on his own. But when Koubek tried to sign up to run an eight-hundred-meter race independently, officials turned him away, telling him only members of a club were allowed to join. Defeated, Koubek watched the race from the stands. Only two runners participated, and they both ran so slowly, he thought, "that they might have been walking."

Koubek could have fought back. But he was exhausted and annoyed, and he hadn't had a vacation in years. Politically, his country seemed to be backsliding: just a month earlier, the country's pro-Nazi party, the Sudeten German Home Front, had won nearly 1.25 million votes, more than any other.[44]

There was also the matter of his gender. If the Ovaltine ad had truly run without his consent or participation, the Czechoslovak

Amateur Athletic Union most likely wouldn't have banned him. His unceremonious expulsion from amateur sports had the hallmarks of an ulterior motive. Perhaps officials were so quick to cut ties with Koubek because they had heard the rumors about him, and, worse, believed them. Koubek made the only decision he could. On June 23, he told *The Czech Evening Word* that he was retiring indefinitely from sports.[45]

The news sent shock waves through Czechoslovakia. Here was one of the country's top athletes, exiting the spotlight before he had even reached his prime. *The Czech Evening Word* wrote up a glowing obituary to Koubek's sporting career, heralding him as "our most popular runner" and "the most photographed woman in Czechoslovakia." But the *Word* alluded to the possibility that more opaque motives had influenced Koubek's sudden decision to quit. "The reasons for this genuinely surprising decision are of a distinctly private nature," the paper wrote.

In the months after his resignation, Koubek returned home to Brno with hardly a penny to his name. He visited the bonfires where he had first learned to sprint. He thought about how unhappy he had been as a child, how out of place he felt. At some point, everything clicked. For as much as the Ovaltine scandal infuriated him, he knew, deep down, that it wasn't the real reason he'd chosen to step away from sports. There was something else he needed to reckon with first, something he'd been pushing off for his entire life.

Ⓞ N OCTOBER 5, 1933, four men stepped out of an armored Mercedes-Benz and onto the field surrounding the German Stadium. Adolf Hitler followed Theodor Lewald and Wilhelm Frick, the Nazi interior minister, onto the scrubby surface where Germany's original Olympic stadium stood.[1]

Twenty years earlier, the German Stadium was Berlin's crown jewel, the embodiment of its global sporting ambitions. By now, it looked out of date, and Hitler was visibly unimpressed. When Lewald and Werner March, the thirty-nine-year-old architect who was tasked with revamping the site, explained the planned upgrades, the dictator shook them off. Their vision wasn't ambitious enough. "German sport needs something gigantic," Hitler told the men.[2] He demanded a stadium that could host over a hundred thousand people.[3] Then he climbed back into his Mercedes-Benz and zipped back to the city center.

Werner March submitted an alternative stadium idea four days later.[4] Hitler was still unsatisfied. He didn't want only a new stadium, he decided—he wanted an entire sports field, something that could capture the imagination of the world. Eventually, he and March settled on a concept they called the Reich Sports Field, a sprawling, gated campus that would include lecture halls; interlocking athletic fields for hockey, tennis, swimming, and track and field; and, at its center, the Olympic Stadium.[5]

Construction on the Reich Sports Field began in the spring of 1934.[6] By the end of the year, it was on track to go hopelessly over budget.[7] The Nazis found the money, but the new subsidy came with strings attached. Hitler wanted to do away, at least privately, with the fallacy that the Organizing Committee, led by Theodor Lewald, was an independent operator. Lewald had little choice but to comply. On October 15, 1934, Lewald and Carl Diem met in secret to sign a document formally rejecting the independence of the Organizing Committee.[8] The Nazi Party would now have full control over organizing the Olympics. It was Lewald's last glimmer of leverage, and he signed it away.

None of this was telegraphed abroad—not that international sports officials were particularly eager to probe for the truth. By the end of 1934, Avery Brundage, for one, assumed he'd extinguished the controversy around the Olympics once and for all. Shoring up his confidence was a poll in March 1935, which found a healthy skepticism of the boycott movement, with 57 percent of Americans saying they were against a boycott and 43 percent saying they were in favor.[9] The American Olympic Committee had already accepted the invitation of the Organizing Committee, which meant Brundage had one last obstacle to clear. In its final meeting, slated for December 1935, the Amateur Athletic Union still needed to certify its athletes for the Olympics. Certification was typically a bureaucratic process, little noticed by the public, and Brundage had no doubt that it would sail through, as it always had.

That sense of stability lasted for only the first few months of

1935. On the evening of July 15, 1935, two hundred Nazi partisans dressed in military boots poured into the streets of Berlin's posh Kurfürstendamm neighborhood, chanting, "Out with Jews!"[10] The Nazis chased, attacked, and beat Jewish citizens. They affixed signs with slogans like "The Jew is the cause of all our troubles" to shop windows. When cars drove past, they forced open the doors and dragged out anyone they thought looked Jewish. Bystanders placed urgent calls to the police, but it was useless: the police were on the same side as the rioters.[11]

It became one of the most violent bursts of antisemitism since Hitler's ascension, and it also almost didn't make the news. In Hitler's Germany, Nazis exerted full control over the press, and they could typically suppress stories they didn't like. The news of the massacre might not have reached America if a reporter for the magazine *The Living Age* hadn't been there to witness it. His subsequent report confirmed what many already knew: Hitler's regime was lurching toward a violent extermination of Jewish residents.[12]

Days later, the American Jewish Committee repeated its call for America to boycott the Berlin Olympics. This time, the boycotters won a key convert. Jeremiah Mahoney, Brundage's successor as president of the Amateur Athletic Union, pledged after the attacks that he intended to block the United States from joining the Berlin Olympics.[13] Brundage was outraged. Mahoney had his sights on the New York City mayoralty, Brundage knew, and Brundage claimed that his sudden opposition to the Olympics was nothing more than a gambit to win political support.[14] The possibility that Mahoney, or any other official, might have been genuinely horrified by escalating Nazi violence did not seem to occur to him.

Brundage, if he had ever felt sympathy for the boycotters, had by then lost it. The naked fascism on display in the Kurfürstendamm neighborhood bothered him far less than the resurgence of the boycott movement. In fiery letters to sports officials, he parroted antisemitic talking points, insisting that New York newspapers were "largely controlled" by Jewish people and that Jewish people "have been clever enough to realize the publicity value of sport and are bending every effort to involve the American Olympic Committee."[15] Brundage raged against "Jewish merchant advertisers" who "may have something to do with" the onslaught of negative press about the Olympics.[16]

IOC officials were equally willing to downplay the Nazis' escalating violence. Charles Sherrill, an American member of the IOC, decided that a PR blitz would be enough to contain the boycotters.[17] On August 24, 1935, as tensions flared, he visited Hitler in Munich. If he could get Hitler to say on record that the Nazis would not bar Jewish athletes from the Olympics, he thought, then the American public would come back around. It wasn't supposed to be a contentious visit—Sherrill assumed he and the dictator would be in agreement. But when Sherrill brought up the idea that Germany should allow Jewish athletes to compete, Hitler scoffed. If the IOC forced his hand, Hitler informed the American, Hitler would stage a "purely German Olympics" instead.[18]

Sherrill wrote a frantic letter to IOC president Henri de Baillet-Latour immediately after the meeting, warning him that he would be "in for the greatest shock of [his] life."[19] Sherrill decided to withhold the details of his trip from the press, but he still didn't withdraw his support of the Olympics. Despite Sherrill's professed commitment to "fair play," Hitler's blunt refusal to allow Jewish athletes at the Olympics wasn't enough to convince Sherrill to back out.

More severe warning signs soon followed, though they, too, could not puncture the delusional aura of credulity that had captured top IOC officials. That September, the Nazis passed the Nuremberg Race Laws, a set of violently racist rules that stripped Jewish people of citizenship and made it illegal for them to marry "Aryan" Germans.[20] (On November 26, 1935, the Nazis broadened

the scope of the Nuremberg Race Laws to exclude Black and Romani people from citizenship.) Anyone could have deduced that the
laws foreshadowed a devastatingly dark future for Germany. Many
boycotters said as much: one Los Angeles sports leader warned that
the "German public may successfully present, outwardly, the appearance of Olympic hospitality," but "the Hitler government has
violated the true Olympic doctrine."[21] Even so, to the IOC, the laws
looked less like a step toward genocide and more like another public relations headache.

Brundage and Edström begged their friend Karl Ritter von Halt,
the IAAF member who had registered as a Nazi, for a credible explanation of the Nuremberg laws. Typically nonchalant, von Halt
wrote back that "on his word of honour Jewish athletes would be
treated just as the other German athletes," as Edström explained to
Brundage.[22] It was, nearly to the word, the same tenuous commitment that Nazi officials had been making since Hitler first took
power. World events had long since revealed von Halt's platitudes
to be rooted in lies, but again that didn't matter to Edström or to
Brundage. They refused to see what was plainly in front of them.
Without further protest, the pair chose to believe him.

In October 1935, less than a year before the start of the Olympics, Baillet-Latour admitted he was "terribly worried" about the
American boycott movement, a feeling he shared with Theodor Lewald, with whom he was in frequent communication.[23] They began
pitching increasingly ridiculous stunts that they hoped would win
back the public. Lewald suggested that he board the famous airship
Hindenburg and fly to America, where he could act as an ambassador of Olympic peace.[24] When Brundage was let in on the plan, he
blocked it. Baillet-Latour then offered to fly to America himself.
Brundage again turned him down,[25] worrying it would be seen as a
sign of weakness if the IOC leader spoke to the American people on
Brundage's behalf.[26]

Though Brundage insisted to both men that he had the situation in America under control, privately he was nervous. By the fall, thousands of anti-Nazi demonstrators were regularly pouring into Madison Square Garden to protest the Berlin Olympics. A group of 138 Protestant clergymen had just issued a joint statement urging the United States to back out of the games.[27] Even some of Brundage's longtime supporters were "beginning to waver," Brundage admitted to Edström.[28] If he was being honest, he had no idea how to stop the movement.

Brundage's saving grace arrived in the form of a carefully planned Nazi publicity stunt. In the days following the passage of the Nuremberg Race Laws, the German propaganda machine revved into action. In late September, the Nazi sports czar Hans von Tschammer leaked to Charles Sherrill, the IOC official, a letter that he'd written to a Jewish-German athlete, Helene Mayer, asking her to join the German Olympic team.[29] Mayer, who had won a gold medal at the Amsterdam Olympics in 1928, was already a well-established star. "I beg you to consider yourself as member of the pre-selected German team," Tschammer had told her. Tschammer explained to Sherrill that he hoped the letter would "support considerably" the American's fight against the boycott movement. "You will find from this that we work entirely in the spirit of the Olympic Statutes," Tschammer said.

The letters did not come with a response from Helene Mayer, or a guarantee that she would participate in the Olympics at all; Mayer was now living in the United States,[30] and the Nazis had, in fact, just stripped her of her German citizenship rights, owing to her Jewish heritage. But Sherrill took the letters at face value and dutifully leaked them to the US press. That fall, citing Sherrill, US newspapers reported that Jewish athletes were receiving invitations to join the German Olympic team,[31] obfuscating the very real violence on the ground in Germany. The idea that he might be propping up a violent regime by leaking the letter did not seem to occur to Sherrill.

○ ○ ○

Despite the leak of the Mayer letter, Brundage soon suffered a significant blow from within the IOC. Ernest Lee Jahncke, a New Orleans–born shipbuilding magnate,[32] was one of three American members on the committee, though undoubtedly the least powerful and least memorable. In truth, except in title, Jahncke was barely part of the IOC. He almost never attended meetings. He was nominated in 1927, at a meeting in Monte Carlo that he did not attend.[33] He also skipped the IOC meeting in Amsterdam the next year, citing business demands. Then, in 1929, the new US president, Herbert Hoover, appointed him to be assistant secretary of the navy, a role that kept him from taking any extended European excursions.[34] He skipped the 1930 and 1931 IOC meetings, making an appearance only in 1932, when the Olympics were staged in nearby Los Angeles. Despite a colleague telling him that it would be "most unwise" if he skipped the 1933 session as well,[35] Jahncke did it anyway.

If Jahncke had fully removed himself from his IOC duties before, the Berlin Olympics brought him back. The more he learned about the state-sponsored violence in Germany, the more infuriated he became.[36] In November 1935, Jahncke broke eight years of near silence when he sent an open letter to Baillet-Latour decrying the IOC's continued defense of Nazi Germany. In the letter, Jahncke urged the Olympics to abandon Berlin as the host. By exacting violence against racial and ethnic minorities, he said, the Nazis had ensured that a truly open and fair Olympics would not be possible.[37] "It is my opinion that under the domination of the Nazi Government the German sports authorities have violated and are continuing to violate every requirement of fair play," he wrote to Baillet-Latour. The pledges from Nazi authorities that all athletes had a chance to compete, he said, were worthless. By repeating these claims, the IOC's top brass were repeating "an argument used by propagandists."

When Baillet-Latour read the letter, he was furious. He called it "discourteous" and "one-sided" and speculated that Jahncke hadn't even written it himself.[38] When asked for his response to Jahncke's comments, William May Garland, the third American member of the IOC, told *The New York Times* that Jahncke "never attended" an IOC meeting "except for about fifteen minutes here in Los Angeles in 1932."[39] The timing of Jahncke's public rebuke of the IOC wasn't a coincidence. With the Berlin Olympics now only months away, members of the boycott movement felt they had one final chance to keep the United States out of the games—the Amateur Athletic Union's typically mundane December meeting. If they could convince the AAU not to certify any athletes for the Olympics, they thought, the United States might not be able to send a team.

For Brundage, the stakes were dire. The international sports world was watching. On December 5, two days before the AAU meeting, Baillet-Latour told Brundage he was "anxious to hear the result."[40] Brundage's career at the Olympics—and the Olympics themselves—was riding on how he handled the meeting. But secretly, Brundage felt sure that his side would win.[41] As usual, he had a plan.

○○○

In the months after he quit sports, Zdeněk Koubek felt like a pariah whenever he walked down the street.[42] People with whom he had once exchanged smiles now looked the other way, fixated on something down the block. It was, he thought, like he'd fled from a leper colony. He began to despair about his future.

Sometime in the fall of 1935, he received a letter that turned his life around. Josef Burda, the owner of a sports betting agency, asked Koubek to come to Prague for a job interview. The next day, Koubek found himself in a fifth-floor office in downtown Prague, listening as Burda, a balding, round-faced man, offered him a salary to work for him. Burda doubled as a sports manager, and he gave Koubek a tantalizing proposition: under Burda's watch, he said, the young athlete could reenter track-and-field sports—not as an amateur this time, but as a professional. It would mean he couldn't qualify for the Olympics, thanks to the IOC's amateur rules, but at least he could compete again. In truth, Koubek missed sports—missed the rush of lining up in front of a track, the tense anticipation, the cacophony of cheers when he crossed the finish line. He said yes.

The first step was for Burda to find a sports club that would accept Koubek into its ranks. The two tried Moravian Slavia, a local track-and-field club, but the officials said they would permit Koubek to compete on only one condition: He first needed to submit to a medical exam. If he wanted to return to women's sports, he needed to "prove" that his body aligned with what they perceived as a normative woman's body. Koubek refused. Instead, he found a spot on AC Sparta, a budding soccer club. But the experience rattled him. Though he knew the Czech sports community had been whispering about him, he could not believe that anyone, much less the upper management of a sports club, would take the rumors so seriously.

On a gray October day, Koubek slipped into a doctor's office in Prague and asked for a consultation. Living outwardly as a woman had become untenable, and he wanted to know whether a gender transition was possible. The doctor told him she wasn't the right person to help, but she provided him the name of a different doctor, whom Koubek later only ever referred to as "Professor H." Koubek agreed to meet with him. Over the next two months, Professor H. gave Koubek a series of exams that Koubek described as "painstaking." He felt like a "guinea pig" at the clinic, the most personal parts of his body turned, uncomfortably, into a subject of study. But that was the cost of getting access to medical care in 1935. What sustained him through the humiliation was the thought of a future in which he could live as his true self. Koubek could not stop imagining his "subsequent transfer to that dreamt-of place—the other shore." By the end of November, Professor H. certified him as "an individual of predominantly male characteristics" and recommended that Koubek have surgery. The doctor said that Koubek should prepare to live publicly as a man.

Around this time, rumors of Koubek's gender transition reached a reporter with *The Czech Word*. A journalist whom Koubek identified only as "Hlava" reached out to Koubek, asking whether it was true that the former track star was going to transition gender. Koubek realized it was only a matter of time before the news became public. He told his new boss, Josef Burda, that soon he would show up to the office with new clothes and a new name. To Koubek's relief, Burda assured him there would still be a place for him. With the guarantee of employment secured, Koubek responded to Hlava. If she wanted, he said, he would do an interview.

On that Sunday, November 30, Koubek was sitting in a café in Prague when a waiter placed a stack of newspapers by his table. Among them was *The Czech Word*. Koubek flipped to the sports section, where a headline featuring the feminized version of his last name—"Koubková Is Undergoing Surgery"—splashed across the page.[43] He smiled as he read it. It felt, he explained later, "not as though reading [my] own obituary but rather the news of the birth of a new person."[44]

The report was contained within two simple paragraphs:

For some time, sports fans have been familiar with the rumors surrounding our popular runner Zdeňka Koubková, who, as it is well-known, is a world record holder. Previously we reported the news that the career of our best female runner had concluded in its current form. According to the information we have now, Koubková has decided to end even her short sporting episode with AC Sparta, where after an extended pause she was to compete. Koubková has now told the [Czech Amateur Athletic] Union that she has left the organization.

We have learned that she will soon undergo an operation, after
which it will be possible to continue to engage in sport, but not in
the capacity of women's track and field.

When Koubek put down the paper, he met the eyes of the other
customers in the café, who blushed and looked away, pretending
they hadn't just been gawking at him. He realized he wasn't embarrassed.[45] At least everyone knows now, he thought. Within a few
weeks, he would undergo surgery, and he would live full-time—
finally—as a man.

Koubek's time in the limelight could have ended there, with a
few reports in Czech daily newspapers. Koubek probably assumed
as much. There was no reason for anyone outside Czechoslovakia
to care about his gender transition. The times he had been covered
internationally, it was almost never in a stand-alone news story; a
line about his achievements might appear in a larger article in *The
New York Times*,[46] but he wasn't the subject of full-scale profiles
outside his home country.

Things changed when the story in *The Czech Word* caught the
eye of a Prague-based reporter from the news service Reuters, who
likely noticed the article's cryptic wording—implying, but not outright saying, that Koubek was no longer identifying as a woman—
and decided it might have legs. Within a few days, Reuters published
its own report on Koubek's transition, stating that the young athlete was planning to live as a man. It was immediately picked up by
newspapers across Europe and the United States.[47] It happened fast.
Neither Koubek nor the IOC would ever be the same.

○○○

The news reached the United States on December 3, when a photo
of Koubek in his sleeveless track-and-field jersey graced many of
the country's biggest newspapers. American editors knew they had

something special on their hands, and they slapped on sensational headlines to entice readers: "Girl Athlete's Sex to Be Changed" (*New York Daily News*), "Champion Girl Athlete Will Become 'Man'" (*San Francisco Examiner*), "Girl Athlete Changes Sex and Legal Status" (*Los Angeles Times*).[48] Koubek, the reporters noted, had consulted multiple doctors about his gender. They all recommended that he pursue a surgery to become a man, and, the papers noted, he'd decided they were right.

It was an unprecedented, shocking story, less owing to Koubek's stature in the sports world than to the idea of transitioning gender at all, which still had the ring of science fiction. Tellingly, the reports couldn't agree on how, exactly, to explain Koubek's identity. Some called his transition a "metamorphosis,"[49] implying that his physical body had somehow spontaneously changed to mirror that of a man's; others noted that Koubek had long lived "on the border line between masculinity and femininity,"[50] suggesting that he would fit a contemporary definition of intersex. (This was probably the only logical way to explain a gender transition in an era when gender as a psychological concept disentangled from biological sex did not exist.) Koubek "has the choice of either sex, and she has decided to become a man," one outlet reasoned.[51] The *San Francisco Examiner* wrote that "Koubek was born a bi-sexual,"[52] a term that, at the time, roughly corresponded to "intersex" today. Other newspapers tried to establish for their readers that there was precedent for Koubek's transition. "Such instance of 'women into man' are not rare in medical history," a British wire service, whose article on Koubek was widely carried in the United States, claimed.[53]

The coverage was bombastic, but not all that negative. To *London Life*, a British magazine with a penchant for covering stories that challenged popular understandings of sex and sexuality, Koubek's transition was a "marvellous story" that "definitively proved" that gender transition was possible in humans: "Within the last five years there have been at least six authenticated cases in this country of women becoming men, and men becoming women."[54] *London Life* hailed the power of medical science to allow people like Koubek to medically transition. "Surgery is coming to the aid of those who in the past have been dismissed as freaks of nature," the paper declared.[55]

American and British readers didn't actually hear from Koubek directly until December 16, when he gave a lengthy interview to the International News Service.[56] He told the outlet that he first began suspecting he was a man in early 1935, which was what led him to quit women's sports. He was happy that his secret was out, he said, but he wanted privacy. Speculation about his physical body was blanketing every major newspaper in the world. "I feel as if suddenly the world had caught me in the nude," he told reporters. The attention felt like "oppressive shackles." He couldn't go anywhere, couldn't even enter a coffee shop, without someone recognizing him. Ultimately, "my other wishes are to lead a normal life and to get away from the world's curiosity, so that I can live like anybody else and devote myself to sports."[57]

With the Berlin Olympics rapidly approaching, Koubek's participation became an inevitable question. He was no longer registered as an amateur, so his presence seemed like a distant possibility, but Koubek, oddly, didn't rule it out. If his forthcoming surgeries were "unsuccessful," he said, then he might attempt to run in the Berlin Olympics on the women's team.[58] Certainly, he wouldn't give up his love of sports. After his transition, he planned to join a men's sports team and continue competing.

The first hurdle was his legal status. Koubek began seeing a lawyer, whom he called "Dr. Č," about correcting the sex marker on his government-issued documents.[59] On December 19,[60] three days after Koubek sat for the International News Service interview, Dr. Č filed a petition to the provincial office in Brno, the city where Koubek had grown up, to change his name and sex on his birth certificate. As he waited on the decision, Koubek continued to show up at his office job in traditionally feminine clothing.[61] It captured the peculiar limbo of gender minorities in 1935: everyone now knew that Koubek planned to live as a man, but because cross-dressing was a crime in Czechoslovakia, Koubek worried he would be arrested if he wore men's clothes before his birth certificate was amended.

When he walked from his house to the train station, he couldn't escape the comments: "Why is that Koubek still wearing a skirt when everyone knows he's a boy?" It was humiliating. The Czech government, Koubek wrote in his personal essay in a national magazine several months later, "has sovereign domain over all the skirts and pants." He lamented, "Without the permission of the authorities not even a single skirt is allowed to come off the registers unauthorized."[62]

The day before Christmas, Koubek trudged into work, dejected. He still hadn't heard anything from his lawyer. He had recently started dating a girl, and he was supposed to meet her parents the next day, but he couldn't possibly show up dressed in a skirt. Then, around 11:00 a.m., a clerk delivered a letter to Koubek's desk. It was from his lawyer. Dr. Č had good news—though the bureaucrats had yet to respond to the petition, Dr. Č was "convinced" that Koubek would be "entitled to wear men's clothing from today onward," without interference from authorities. He included a doctor's note attesting to the fact and told Koubek to keep it with him at all times. "Forthwith, this letter provides you with that legitimization until the day of an affirmative official settlement of your application," his lawyer said.[63]

Koubek was ecstatic. The letter was "the most beautiful Christmas present" he had ever gotten. After work that day, the first thing he did was go out and buy a pair of pants.

A few days later, Koubek returned to his office clad in a knee-length men's coat, a blue tie, his new pressed pants, and a brimmed hat. His blond hair was cut short, parted slightly to the left. It was his first time presenting as a man to his colleagues. "Is that you?" one coworker exclaimed. "How chic you are!"[64]

The news that Koubek was officially dressing as a man spread swiftly. "Czech Athlete Now a Man," *The New York Times* declared on December 29,[65] as if a mere change of clothes was the deciding factor in validating his gender. For journalists, Koubek's new presentation introduced some novel linguistic difficulties: How should they refer to someone who, in their eyes, had just crossed the boundaries between man and woman? While most reporters switched off between male and female pronouns to describe Koubek, others simply dubbed him "the changed person," seemingly torn on what to make of Koubek's current gender status.[66] Another split the difference: "Ex-Woman Makes Debut as Man."[67] Though they didn't always apply the most sensitive language to describe him, most newspapers remained largely unalarmed by Koubek's transition. To the public, it seemed, it was intriguing to consider that the boundaries of sex were so permeable.

It didn't take long for the public fascination with Koubek to trickle down into his day-to-day life. Shortly after Christmas, Koubek took his new girlfriend out on a dinner date. The sight of Koubek kissing the young woman on the hand and locking arms with her as they walked across the street caused a "sensation" among onlookers, according to one newspaper.[68] Just a few weeks earlier, when the world understood Koubek to be a woman, a public display of affection for a girlfriend would have been illegal. As a man, he could kiss her in public without fear. Columnists joked about what would happen if others followed Koubek's lead and transitioned. "Certainly if we must be prepared to find our men friends suddenly become women, and our women men, a new terror has been added to life," a British writer quipped. "For—well, think of the things men say exclusively to men!"[69]

By January, Koubek had figured out how to parlay his newfound fame into a business. Koubek's doctors weren't charging him for his surgeries, citing their scientific interest in understanding sex-change procedures.[70] But the other aspects of transitioning, like hiring a lawyer to correct his sex marker, weren't cheap. To pay the bills, he started charging for photographs and interviews. Paparazzi pictures of him were "commanding high prices," and Koubek hired an "ex-professional boxer" to serve as his manager, according to one report.[71] Whenever the press tried to take a picture of Koubek without permission, the boxer threw himself in the way. It turned out that journalists were more than happy to pay for the chance to interview him, a practice that was not uncommon among tabloids at the time. Koubek asked for $500 from a US wire service in exchange for an exclusive interview.[72] An unnamed French newspaper, likely *Paris-soir*, paid 1,000 francs for a sit-down with him.[73] In just a few weeks, Koubek had become an international media sensation.

ooo

The Koubek news put Alice Milliat in a bind. The founder of the Women's World Games had spent years trying to prove that sports could socialize women into models of normative femininity. A prominent athlete within her federation coming out as a man seemed to provide all the ammunition her enemies needed to finally take her down. Within days of Koubek's announcement that he would live as a man, reporters began peppering Milliat with a single question: Would she take away Koubek's gold medal from the Women's World Games?

Why this would even be a controversy is complicated and speaks largely to the era's understanding of how sex worked. There was no concept of gender as a personal and psychological experience distinct from biology. If Koubek had decided to undergo surgery, read-

ers assumed, it must have been because he already possessed more
of the physical traits typically associated with maleness than with
femaleness. This wasn't necessarily the case—in the 1930s, people
we would consider trans today often had to pretend to be intersex
in order to receive medical care—but it didn't stop reporters from
making assumptions about Koubek's body.

Milliat didn't want to succumb to panic. She valued her athletes,
and she didn't see any reason to abandon Koubek because he wanted
to live as a man. It was simple, she thought: Koubek identified as a
woman when he was part of the Women's World Games. Now he
was identifying as a man. There was no deception at work. She decided to stick by him. "If it is proved that Koubková has become a
man, it is logical to consider that previously she was a woman," Milliat said in an interview on December 13, less than two weeks after
the Koubek news broke. "In that case it would be necessary, in my
opinion, to maintain the name of Koubková and that of her country
in our records."[74]

Central to Milliat's argument was her belief that Koubek was an
isolated case. "I do not share the opinion, held by many athletic
agencies, that other women athletes will follow Koubková's example and let themselves be operated on in order to become men,"
Milliat said in another interview in early January.[75]

It was cold comfort to the male-dominated sporting apparatus.
Rumors that sports officials were looking at ways to block masculine-
presenting athletes spread almost immediately after Koubek's announcement. On January 2, 1936, Prague officials reportedly floated
a requirement that would force any athlete in a women's sports
league to undergo a medical exam "if their sex is doubted."[76] It
wasn't clear what this meant. Was "doubted" sex a specific reference to, say, reproductive organs, or could any woman with traits
associated with masculinity, such as a deep voice, be pushed out of
competition? Few reporters seemed to press this question. Such a
policy, one newspaper speculated, would cut at least two more

prominent athletes from competition, though the paper didn't name the competitors whose sex it "doubted." The *New York Daily News*, in turn, reported that rumors in Europe suggested all women might need to submit to medical exams "in order to remove any doubts as to their femininity" at the Berlin Olympics in the summer.[77] Again, the *Daily News* did not clarify what would lead an athlete to be disqualified under these rules. What did it look like to have "doubts" about an athlete's "femininity"?

As the Koubek news continued to radiate out across international tabloids, calls to regulate women's sports grew. The Canadian sports columnist Alexandrine Gibb again raised the alarm. Koubek's transition, she thought, vindicated what she'd been saying for years: it wasn't fair for some women to "pit their slight feminine frames"[78] against athletes whom she characterized as more muscular and masculine. Though she didn't make clear exactly why this was such a problem—wouldn't different athletes of the same assigned sex inevitably have different body types?—she insisted that other athletes would soon transition gender. "My own guess is that half a dozen more of the girl athletes who competed in those world games last year, could make a choice of sex," Gibb wrote.

She found a prominent ally in Wilhelm Knoll, the head of the International Federation of Sports Physicians, an influential group of sports doctors who advised the IOC and IAAF on medical matters.[79] Knoll was incredibly well-connected and equally focused on a murky definition of "fairness." He was friendly with Carl Diem and Sigfrid Edström, among other powerful officials. When he first read about Koubek that December, he was disgusted that the American, British, and French press were largely championing the Czech athlete. Knoll reached out to *Sport*, the German-language magazine printed out of Zurich, with an idea. He wanted to change the tenor of the coverage of Koubek—to discourage anyone like Koubek from ever coming forward again. If more athletes like Koubek transitioned, Knoll thought, it would mark a dark new future for sports.

Knoll was born in Frauenfeld, Switzerland, in 1876, with the given name Willi.[80] After graduating from school, he became interested in the science behind competitive skiing and eventually studied the impacts of track-and-field sports on the body.[81] Sports medicine was a budding field, and Knoll attracted a following quickly. At the 1928 Olympics, when a group of doctors decided to form the International Federation of Sports Physicians, Knoll was selected to be its president.[82] A year later, when the University of Hamburg announced it was hiring its first sports medicine professor, Knoll sent in his name. His application emphasized his emotional connection to the German people. Knoll wrote that he had long been "an outspoken representative of the German idea in Switzerland."[83] Knoll wasn't the university's first choice, but when other candidates said no to the job, the University of Hamburg settled on him. He was granted German citizenship; to celebrate, he changed his first name to Wilhelm.[84]

Knoll's title as head of the International Federation of Sports Physicians belied his extremist beliefs. He joined the Nazi Party on May 1, 1933, shortly after Hitler took power. He registered as a supporter of the SS, the Nazis' paramilitary arm, on October 1.[85] At the University of Hamburg, Knoll gave lectures dressed in a Nazi brownshirt uniform, a swastika pinned to his shirt.[86] He was known for his frequent antisemitic rants and for his praise of National Socialism. That ideology inevitably trickled down into how he thought about sports. Knoll wrote of his desire to remove "unsuitable elements" from competitive sports,[87] a group that seemed to refer variously to Jewish people, racial minorities, and gender minorities like Koubek.

In early January, Knoll published his op-ed in *Sport*, accusing Koubek of "deliberately fooling" sports officials about his biological sex.[88] "I feel obliged to discuss the affair publicly in order to prevent a repetition in the future," Knoll wrote. He called on the IAAF to ban Koubek from all international sports competitions and to strip him of his world records. Koubek, Knoll said, "has seriously damaged women's athletics because henceforth everybody will gravely doubt women's outstanding feats." By competing in the Women's World Games, Koubek "unfairly makes use of superior physique, as a man, against frail women."[89] The only way to prevent a repeat in the future, Knoll wrote, was to introduce physical examinations of all women competitors in order to keep anyone whose body did not match a rigid understanding of womanhood out of sports. Knoll did not specify what he expected a standard woman's body to look like; he seemed to treat it as self-evident that a universal standard was already in place. Even as a sports doctor, he did not consider that people's bodies naturally existed on a spectrum or that he would need to define womanhood itself if he wanted to impose these medical exams. Was he talking about genitalia? What about body hair or muscle mass? At what point would a woman's body become a "superior physique," as he called it—and thus something to be regulated?

Also unaddressed was the fact that Koubek no longer wanted to participate in women's sports. In interviews, Koubek made clear his desire to play with other men; he only left open the possibility of returning to women's sports should officials block him from joining the men's team. Knoll was minting panic about cheaters in women's sports, even though his main example—Koubek—was actually trying to leave the women's category behind.

Yet Knoll's position as a sports doctor gave his statements, however unfounded, a degree of cachet. Several American newspapers republished excerpts from the *Sport* op-ed, identifying its author only as a "doctor" named "W. Knoll." Knoll's fellow Nazis quickly embraced his talking points, too. On January 11, 1936, the newspaper *Der Führer*, a longtime organ of the Nazi Party, circulated Knoll's comments about Koubek. *Der Führer* thanked Knoll for getting right to the point: Koubek's story was "nothing but cheating," the paper wrote, and proved that female athletes needed to be medically examined before each competition.[90] Neither the Nazi Party nor Knoll himself pointed out that standardized medical exams to determine womanhood were truly novel: no major institution, governmental or otherwise, had imposed such tests on a widespread basis before. Knoll was fashioning the idea of mandatory medical exams to determine sex more or less out of thin air.

The calls for examination trickled back into the borders of Czechoslovakia. When the commissioner of the Czechoslovak Amateur Athletic Union, Czechoslovakia's top track-and-field organization, first read about Koubek in the daily press, he was so "mystified" by the story that he assumed it was false.[91] But as the story continued to spread, he realized there might in fact be some truth behind it. He decided to find out from the source. He repeatedly sent letters to Koubek, asking for an explanation of the athlete's transition. The Czechoslovak Amateur Athletic Union, he said, wasn't interested in sanctioning Koubek. They simply wanted to know whether he was now legally a man so they could figure out which league—men's sports or women's sports—to register him under.

When Koubek didn't respond, the commissioner tried reaching out to the medical clinics that treated him. He got no reply from the medical establishment, either. Frustrated, the commissioner wrote on March 5 to the police director of Prague. He wanted to know where Koubek stood with the law: Had he officially been declared a man? If so, could he wear men's clothes without the police deeming him a criminal? "If this change were true," the CAAU leader told the police director, "and the athlete had sent us a valid application, or an official confirmation of this change, this matter would be settled for us."[92] The police had little information to offer. Yes, they replied, Koubek was now presenting as a man, but they had no idea if Czech authorities had officially approved a change to the athlete's identity documents.[93]

Though Koubek's transition might not have directly perturbed the CAAU, the organization's commissioner needed an explanation, fast. He claimed that pressure was bearing down on him from the IAAF. The commissioner wrote that the international track-and-field group had accused the Czech sports establishment of "having consciously sent a man in disguise to races, which made it much easier to achieve success in women's disciplines." That meant the IAAF believed one of Czechoslovakia's top athletic accomplishments—Koubek's world record from the Women's World Games—was won by cheating. According to the CAAU, "this is what we are blamed for the most."[94]

Defending itself against fraud accusations was not going to be easy for the CAAU, especially because the IAAF, too, seemed confused about the nature of Koubek's transition. To sports officials not well-versed in the nuances of sex science—and the vast majority were not—the idea that Czech officials had conspired to register a man to play in women's sports might have seemed like the only logical explanation. It probably isn't a coincidence, either, that these charges so closely mirrored the accusations that Wilhelm Knoll, and then the Nazis, had leveled a few weeks prior. Most of the IAAF correspondence from this period is unavailable, but it seems plausible that Knoll, who was well-connected in the IAAF, had successfully turned Edström's organization against Koubek.

After Koubek's transition, there was a "shadow cast" on women's sports in the country, Czech sports leaders explained in a subsequent report.[95] One Czech track-and-field official tried to explain to his colleagues that Koubek's story was not cause for alarm, but his efforts failed. "I found only misunderstanding in Prague itself," he said.

CHAPTER 11

AS THE WORLD GRAPPLED WITH THE NEWS that a star athlete was in the midst of transitioning gender, Avery Brundage was fighting to contain the resistance within the Amateur Athletic Union, America's top track-and-field organization. On December 6—a frigid Friday morning—hundreds of delegates from across the country jostled their way through midtown Manhattan and filed into the lobby of the Commodore Hotel, where they planned to settle the question of US participation in the Olympics once and for all.[1] Christmas was in the air. Tourists crowded into popular stores like Woolworth's, searching for last-minute gifts. For the third year in a row, city officials lit up a massive Norwegian spruce in Rockefeller Center.

Brundage walked in with a swagger. He scoffed at the possibility, much discussed in the press, that the AAU could reverse course and, at the last minute, pull the United States out of the Olympics. "If anyone expects bombs to burst during the convention, he is sadly mistaken," Brundage said.[2] He claimed that most executives favored participation, as did most athletes. He said he'd received letters on the topic from 139 Olympic athletes, of which 138 urged him to allow the United States to participate.

For all the chaos of recent weeks, Brundage felt sure he had a winning hand. After over a decade working for the AAU, he had an intimate familiarity with the structure of the organization. In the lead-up to the annual meeting, he'd worked the phones to ensure that his allies, including those AAU members who were not closely involved with the Olympics, were present. That morning, delegates from the antisemitic group the American Turnerbund and the easily persuaded National Cycling Association showed up to support Brundage, even though they had rarely been involved with the AAU in the years prior.[3]

The fight was dirty from the start. Before the full meeting of the AAU, a small group of high-ranking AAU executives gathered for the group's executive committee.[4] Once he called the meeting to order, Jeremiah T. Mahoney, the new president of the AAU, having replaced Brundage in the role, asked that the AAU "give no support or encouragement to the formation of an American team to compete in the Games" and "take no part in the Games either as spectators or competitors, if they are held in Germany." When the votes came in, the delegates rejected Mahoney's proposal, 7–6. But Mahoney wouldn't accept defeat that easily. He decided to cast a vote of his own, splitting the vote 7–7.[5] A group of Brundage supporters accused him of corruption, but they couldn't stop the process.

The following afternoon, when the full committee gathered, Brundage outmaneuvered Mahoney. As soon as Mahoney presented his recommendation to the full AAU, Brundage's allies moved to table it. One delegate asked that the resolution be removed; another quickly seconded. Mahoney was furious, but it became clear that Brundage had the majority, thanks to another backroom deal, negotiated ahead of the meeting. Brundage had informed delegates that if they swatted down the boycott resolution, he would introduce a compromise measure. The choreography played out perfectly. A sports official named Gustavus Kirby, a Brundage ally, stepped forward to introduce a resolution that affirmed US participation in the Olympics.[6] Kirby urged the IOC and the IAAF "to continue their vigilant investigations" of the German treatment of Jewish athletes but concluded, "It is the hope and desire of the AAU that America be represented in all Olympic contests."

When Kirby began to lay out the claim that conditions in Germany had improved since 1933, Mahoney interrupted.[7] Nazi Germany, he reminded those assembled, remained a vile, oppressive country, wholly incapable of upholding any tenets of equality. "It is a question of the conditions that are there, so horrible and unbearably contrary to our concept of the kind of an atmosphere that should exist in that country to which we want our boys and our girls to go," Mahoney told the delegates. "Can the Olympic pledge be kept by any representative of the Nazi administration? I say no."[8]

Brundage spoke next. "I am going to present the facts in this situation, if you will bear with me."[9] He held up an article claiming that 260 Jewish sports clubs remained active in Germany, which he positioned as proof of Jews' equal access to sports. "I know of two Jewish lads from New York attending the Berlin University who are on the basketball team in their spare time," he informed the group. He also pointed to his trip to Berlin the prior summer: "When I was in Germany a year ago, many German Jews told me that they deplored this activity in the United States. They thought it was wrong."[10]

Brundage closed with his most potent rebuke. This entire discussion, he told the members, was entirely symbolic. Even if the AAU refused to certify the athletes for the Olympic Games, the IOC was prepared to accept American athletes anyway. "The only thing that would be accomplished would be to wreck the AAU," Brundage said.[11] He turned to the Jewish delegates in the room. "There are many Jewish citizens whom I have talked to that are opposed to the boycott." Ultimately, "what would be gained if we stayed home?" he said. "The games would go on, Hitler would go on, the Nazis would go on. We can't stop them."[12]

The next day of debate was no less bitter. Delegates in favor of the boycott took aim at Theodor Lewald, whose position as a man of Jewish ancestry on the Organizing Committee amounted to "window dressing"[13] to make the Nazi regime seem less antisemitic. Another delegate enumerated Brundage's Nazi ties and cast him as a double agent. Brundage, the delegate said, "did not talk for our great country, the United States, but evidently was here as a representative of the German Government."[14]

New compromise proposals were introduced, then appended with so many amendments they lost their original intent. One delegate wanted to defer the AAU's decision and appoint an independent commission, comprised of prominent figures like Franklin Delano Roosevelt, to again investigate the treatment of Jewish athletes in Germany.[15] Another suggested that the AAU approve its athletes for the Winter Olympics, to be held in February, and then decide later whether to green-light the more consequential Summer Olympics.[16]

Yet by the time a vote was called in the early evening, Brundage's careful maneuvers had worked. He wasn't particularly charismatic, but his ability to wheel and deal—such as convincing Nazi-sympathetic sports leaders to fly out to New York to support his cause—made it easy to whip up a majority within the AAU. His allies narrowly rejected the proposal to appoint an independent commission and approved the proposal to go forward with the Olympics. Brundage was elated and became even more so when Mahoney, his rival, announced his intention to resign as president of the AAU. Mahoney told the room that he couldn't support the Olympics as they currently stood. "I did not agree with it, I do not agree with it, as President of this organization I cannot in good conscience carry it out," he said. "I want to beg of you not to consider my name in any respect as any officer of this Association."[17]

Minutes later, the coup was sealed. A delegate nominated Brundage to return as president of the AAU. It was quickly seconded, then thirded. Applause erupted as Brundage was escorted to the president's chair at the front of the ballroom.[18] Brundage thanked the body for choosing to support the US entry into the Olympics. "The games belong to the athletes and to them alone," he declared.

With the boycott movement at last defeated, Brundage had won the biggest battle of his career. Yet instead of forging a truce with members of the boycott movement, Brundage, in victory, called for an expulsion of his critics. He told the AAU that he would make sure all members held views "in accord with the ideals of the AAU," and that they were not subject to pressure from "organized minorities"[19]—a thinly veiled reference, it seemed, to Jewish groups.

As the US boycott movement disintegrated, so, too, did similar efforts in European countries. In November, France witnessed what the publication *Sport* called a "wave of protests"[20] against the Olympics, which led three hundred ex-athletes to create the Committee Against the Hitlerian Games in early December.[21] *Sport* ran a separate editorial demanding "not a penny, not a man for Berlin."[22] A prominent Socialist politician brought the issue to the French parliament, declaring that Nazi Germany had "applied its despicable ideas to sport" and that France's attendance at the Olympics amounted to an endorsement of Nazism.[23] But despite galvanizing the French left, his proposal to pull the French team out of the Olympics failed by a vote of 410–161.

Britain's boycott effort was flagging as well. Though some prominent newspapers, including the *Manchester Guardian*, had agitated for a boycott for years, a full-scale movement never took off.[24] Lord Aberdare, the British representative on the IOC, had called for an end to the "uncivilized" behavior of the Nazis,[25] but in a letter to Theodor Lewald that December, he lodged only a meek request. "It would be a splendid thing, if you could give me proof of the re-Appointment of some eminent Jew who has been displaced" in the sports field, Aberdare wrote.[26] When Lewald supplied it, Aberdare issued a statement of support for the Olympics.

Lewald had won, sort of. The Berlin Olympics that he and Carl Diem had fantasized about for two and a half decades now seemed assured, yet the whole business tasted bitter. When a US diplomat confronted Lewald on his claims that Germany was free of discrimination, Lewald had "tears in his eyes," according to the diplomat.[27] The diplomat asked Lewald, as a friend, what had made him do it. "He replied that I must know what the consequences would be to him if he had made any other reply."

Not everyone had the same moral conflict about promoting a Nazi-hosted Olympic Games. Having survived his challenge within the AAU, Brundage was seeing his stock on the International Olympic Committee rise. On December 12, just a few days after the close of the AAU meeting, IOC president Henri de Baillet-Latour congratulated Brundage on his victory. "You have fighted [sic] like a lion and deserve great praise for your achievement."[28]

Brundage's fate was sealed. Sigfrid Edström had raised the possibility of installing Brundage on the IOC as far back as April 1934.[29] Now it seemed like a given that Brundage would claim a seat. He was the talk of the committee—and with Baillet-Latour's endorsement, Brundage's future looked bright indeed. Thanks to him, the Americans were heading to Berlin.

○○○

On the morning of February 6, 1936, Theodor Lewald, Carl Diem, and Karl Ritter von Halt woke up in the southern German town of Garmisch-Partenkirchen relieved to find snow.[30] For weeks leading up to the kickoff of the Winter Olympics, a series of warm winds and rain had turned the mountain slopes into muddied brown slush.

All three men had worried that Germany wouldn't be ready for the competitions to come. The snowstorm had saved them.

Later that day, as Adolf Hitler declared the Winter Olympics open, the sounds of thousands of onlookers chanting *"Sieg Heil!"* echoed across the stadium through the biting wind. A gun went off; despite the heavy snow, a band started playing. It was the opening salvo of Germany's tenure as an Olympic host, and all eyes were on the US team. Because of the intensity of the American boycott movement, some feared that the American team might still find a reason not to come. A British ambassador quipped that everyone felt "considerable anxiety and relief" when "it was heard that the American team had actually arrived in Garmisch-Partenkirchen for the Winter Games."[31]

The ceremony—and really, the Winter Olympics itself—had the air of a dress rehearsal. Though the Nazis invested heavily in the event, constructing an artificial ice rink and a set of ski-jumping hills for the occasion,[32] the world mostly tuned out the Winter Olympics. The Winter Games had always been the lesser sibling, wielding only a small fraction of the clout of its summer counterpart. Many prominent officials, including Brundage himself, thought the Winter Games should not exist at all.[33] Perhaps it was no surprise, then, when only 4,400 visitors from outside Germany showed up,[34] or when organizational snafus—delayed food shipments, hour-long waits for meals, hotel space so overbooked that one American speed skating official had to sleep in a bathtub[35]—dominated the early days.

The Nazis in turn used the games as an opportunity to perfect their propaganda strategy. How could a fascist nation sanitize its image to the rest of the world? Garmisch-Partenkirchen was the testing ground. It was a true Nazi town, and in the months leading up to the Winter Games, it was riddled with antisemitic propaganda. Signs that announced "Jews Not Wanted Here" blanketed the town; hotel owners informed the Nazis they would not host any Jewish guests during the Winter Olympics; copies of the anti-semitic newspaper *Der Stürmer* were sold on many street corners.[36]

IOC president Henri de Baillet-Latour was concerned. He told Hitler, tepidly, that "the signs that greet visitors to the Games are not in conformity with Olympic principles."[37] Hitler was unmoved— "When you are invited to a friend's house you don't tell him how to operate, do you?" he replied—but on December 3, 1935, the same day that Zdeněk Koubek's gender transition ricocheted across the sports world, the order went out to scrub all evidence of anti-semitism from Garmisch-Partenkirchen. A Nazi official asked the city to remove "all signs and posters relating to the Jewish ques-tion" until the end of the Olympics.[38] The gambit worked, and many of the foreign guests left with a sanitized vision of Nazism. A *New York Times* reporter who visited declared in early February that "not the slightest evidence of religious, political or racial prej-udice" could be found at the Winter Olympics.[39]

Those US journalists who had less positive impressions of the Olympics, meanwhile, were shunted to the side. When a *Chicago Daily News* writer complained about the "strong-arm authority" of the Nazi soldiers, who were a constant presence, Karl Ritter von Halt expressed his displeasure to the American Olympic Commit-tee, led by Avery Brundage. Von Halt urged the Americans not to give a press pass for the Summer Olympics to the journalist who wrote "in such a hateful way" about Germany.[40] By the time August rolled around, the German embassy refused to approve the journal-ist's visa.

○○○

On March 7, Hitler sent troops to the Rhineland, a contested strip of land between the borders of France and Germany.[41] The Treaty of Versailles, signed after World War I, had made the Rhineland an officially demilitarized zone. Hitler didn't care. The move sent shock waves through a Europe still less than two decades removed from world war.

In the following days, the future of the Berlin Olympics once again looked imperiled. France's foreign minister suggested on March 10 that the country pull out of the Olympics as a rebuke to Hitler.[42] Three other countries—Czechoslovakia, Romania, and Yugoslavia—all publicly flirted with the possibility of abandoning the Olympics,[43] perhaps sensing that the Nazis would turn to invading them next.

The news irritated Brundage, who assumed the boycott had been finished once and for all. When asked about the potential that some countries would pull out of the Olympics, he replied that it didn't matter what any individual country chose: the only thing that would stop the Berlin Olympics from happening was all-out war.[44] German officials were more concerned. Lewald wrote a letter to Pierre de Coubertin, the French aristocrat who founded the Olympics, at the end of March, begging him to respond to the most recent wave of boycott demands.[45]

In the end, the only country with a legitimate risk of boycotting was France. There, the International Committee for the Defense of the Olympic Idea—a pro-boycott group founded in 1935 that had members in Britain, France, Switzerland, the Netherlands, and Czechoslovakia—made a last pitch for a boycott in June,[46] shortly after the election of a new leftist government. At the conference, the novelist Heinrich Mann, the brother of the more famous Thomas Mann, gave a keynote speech. "People know what the Nazi state is, and yet they are still going to the Olympics," Mann told the crowd. France had a simple choice, he insisted: "He who goes to Berlin deserts the Popular Front! Anti-Fascists, stand up and act! World public, protect the Olympic ideal!"[47]

The group had a further mechanism in mind to jettison the Olympics: France still hadn't approved the final round of funding,[48] equal to 1.8 million francs, to dispatch its Olympic team to Berlin. If the boycott group could block parliament from releasing the money, French athletes might not make it to the Olympics. But garnering a majority was complicated. While he supported the boycott attempt in theory, France's new leftist prime minister, Léon Blum, feared that resisting the Olympics would alienate moderates in his country. On June 19, Blum expressed support for allocating most—but not all—of the necessary funds to send the French team abroad,[49] a half measure that disappointed both sides. He budgeted 1.1 million francs, significantly less than the French Olympic Committee wanted[50] but still enough to pay for the team's travel. When Blum sent the budget to parliament, politicians fought over it for three weeks.[51] In the end, on July 9, parliament approved the funds.

It was the last in a series of close calls for the Germans. Somehow, despite violating a global treaty, stripping Jewish people of citizenship, and expelling racial minorities from top sports organizations, the Nazis would be allowed to proceed as Olympics hosts. Even in victory, Germany's allies couldn't let go of their frustration with the boycott movement. Brundage complained often that "Radicals and Communists" had used the boycott as a pretense to try to derail his career. They needed to "keep their hands off American sport."[52] One colleague on the American Olympic Committee grew weary of the continued screeds. "I take it that the fundamental difference between you and me is that you are a Jew hater and Jew baiter and I am neither," the colleague told Brundage.[53] Brundage bristled at the accusation. "I am too busy to hate anyone and I certainly do not enjoy being hated," he replied.[54] But it was hard to deny the fundamental truth behind the claim.

CHAPTER 12

I **FEEL MYSELF POSITIVELY** and completely a man," Zdeněk Koubek told the *New York Daily News* on February 23, 1936, exactly a week after the close of the Winter Olympics.[1] He had just finished his first surgical operation, a process that he did not detail, except to say that it "did not hurt me at all." He planned to restart his athletic training—this time, in the men's category. His heart was set on winning a men's track-and-field championship, which, he thought, would "prove my athletic prowess to the world."[2]

Some Czech sports officials wanted Koubek to return immediately—in the women's category. A year earlier, the Czechoslovak Amateur Athletic Union had hired a new track-and-field coach for the Berlin Olympics: the American sprinter Ted Meredith. After learning about Koubek's plans, Meredith tried to convince the athlete to delay his new life as a man until after the end of the Olympics.[3] Meredith apparently did not consider the emotional or spiritual importance of Koubek's decision to transition gender. "I argued with her, but lost the decision," Meredith lamented later. "She was the best woman athlete I had," he said, but "she is now a male athlete."[4]

Koubek returned to the clinic in Prague for a plastic surgery operation less than a month later, on March 21. At the time, the technology for female-to-male surgeries was limited. The first phalloplasty wasn't performed until that fall, in Russia.[5] Koubek again didn't discuss the specifics of his operation, but Czech bureaucrats later remarked that his plastic surgeries had removed "all the characteristics of the female sex."[6]

After it was finished, a nurse led him to the men's ward, where he found a hospital bed waiting for him with his new, masculinized first and last names scrawled across: Zdeněk Koubek, as he is known today. Sun poured in through his bedside window. He watched as blackbirds flitted around the garden. Koubek realized it was the first day after spring.[7] Life soon changed for the better. As the press around his transition faded, Koubek felt, for the first time, a glimmer of peace. He grew closer to his new girlfriend. In April, after another one of his surgeries, she visited him in the hospital. Some reports suggested that the two planned to marry.[8]

By that point, Koubek had become one of the highest-profile people in the world to publicly transition gender. The last time a gender transition made international news had been in 1930, when a Danish painter named Lili Elbe received one of the first publicized sex-reassignment surgeries at Magnus Hirschfeld's clinic in Berlin. When Elbe's memoir was published posthumously in 1933, American media covered it under the headline "The Astounding Case of the Man Who Was Changed into a Woman."[9]

What made Elbe and Koubek stand out was not the fact of their transitions but the publicity they received. It was not unheard of for people in the early twentieth century to live as a gender different from the one they had been assigned—they just tended to do so privately. As far back as 1836, a New York court asked Mary Jones, a Black woman who had been assigned male at birth, to explain why she wore women's clothes. Jones replied, "I always dressed in this way."[10] As historians like Jen Manion have documented,[11] local newspapers regularly covered stories of gender bending throughout the nineteenth and early twentieth centuries, but rarely did these stories transcend a particular region. By the start of the twentieth century, people with access to wealth and connections could find a fractured network of trans healthcare services if they looked hard enough. Ewan Forbes, the child of an aristocratic Scottish family with claims to a baronetcy, was assigned female at birth, but at a young age he expressed a desire to live as a boy. When he was fifteen, around 1927, he and his mother traveled to Vienna, Prague, and Budapest to meet with doctors who could help him transition.[12]

Without a concept of sex as independent of gender, many people who transitioned claimed that their physical bodies had spontaneously changed, thus requiring them to reject the identity they'd been assigned at birth. A mysterious illness was sometimes presented as a catalyst for a gender transition. In 1935, newspapers published the story of a seventeen-year-old assigned female at birth who had "always wanted to be a boy." The teenager fell mysteriously ill for weeks, after which he began to exhibit increasingly masculine traits. Physicians reported that the teenager was experiencing "a mild war of the sexes."[13] By the time he left the hospital, he had experienced a "metamorphosis" into a boy named Mac. A year earlier, doctors marveled at a twenty-three-year-old whose gender presentation began changing without warning. "Two years ago, they said, 'Miss X' was pretty and wholly feminine in manner, action and physical being," the *Los Angeles Times* explained. "Today," they declared, "she has luxuriant sideburns, a mustache, her muscles have hardened and developed the characteristics of the male and her hands have taken on a distinctly masculine appearance."[14] Noting the recent proliferation of people who transitioned, one British columnist suggested creating a Ministry of Sex Determination that could approve sex-change applications.[15]

The reason that trans people relayed dubious tales of illness and spontaneous bodily transformations was that their access to healthcare depended on it. Social acceptance necessitated retrofitting their lives into simple narratives that the public could understand. Often, that meant focusing on biology—explaining not that they felt psychologically like a certain gender, but rather that their physical body had shifted in some consequential way. Especially within the medical field, contempt was rampant for those who rejected a neat gender paradigm. In 1892, an anonymous doctor took to the New York–based journal *Medical Record* to warn medical professionals that "the hermaphrodite belongs to the dangerous classes."[16]

Even sympathetic doctors were poorly equipped to prioritize the needs of their patients. Doctors agreed to perform surgeries—or, later, prescribe hormones—only in certain cases, and only when a patient was prepared to lead a life that would look, on the outside, normal. These medical professionals were less concerned with evaluating a person's psychological gender than with preserving a notion of heterosexuality. A typical doctor's note looked like one that Houston-based J. Mark O'Farrell wrote in 1935, attesting that a patient was "clean minded and there is no suspicion of perversion," meaning that the person, if they transitioned, would then be attracted to the opposite sex.[17] Another doctor once described encountering a patient whom he perceived as "a homosexual female." He decided to conduct the surgery because "by making the patient male, the perversion socially ceases to exist. This, of course, is desirable from the standpoint of the community."[18] Some doctors went as far as to recommended surgeries that clashed with the will of their patients. In 1925, doctors at Johns Hopkins Hospital examined a seven-year-old child who had been assigned male at birth but whom the doctors concluded, based on the child's internal organs, was in fact a female. Two years later, physicians surgically removed genitalia that they considered nonnormative for a female. The child grew up feeling like a man anyway, and when he was sixteen, he announced that his name was John and that he wanted to wear men's clothes.[19]

Among the team of doctors who eventually operated on Zdeněk Koubek was František Burian,[20] a prominent Czech plastic surgeon who'd made his name during the first Balkan War in 1912. Burian, who was part of a delegation of Czech doctors providing humanitarian aid to wounded soldiers, performed reconstructive plastic surgeries on soldiers with damaged hands and disfigured faces.[21] He learned to graft skin into place, ultimately making his patients feel more secure in how they looked. In 1921, he established what would eventually be known as the Plastic Surgery Institute at the Jedlička Institute.[22] It was one of the first plastic surgery clinics in the world, equipped with thirty-six beds and, by the 1930s, the site of nearly one thousand annual operations. Burian was not an expert in gender-affirmation surgeries—or "sex change" surgeries, in the parlance of the time—but neither was anyone else. His knowledge of plastic surgery was enough to make him a top candidate to operate on Koubek.

Koubek didn't complain about his experience with Burian, and in fact did not discuss it in much detail at all, but his interest in dating women almost certainly helped him receive a surgery. His whiteness also lent him an air of credibility, especially given the pervasiveness of eugenics in the medical field at the time. Even in Koubek's autobiographical writings, glimmers of this understanding surface. To the press, Koubek repeatedly emphasized his physical strength as a child and his early battles with regulating his facial hair, as well as his repulsion toward other boys, as if to drive home the point: *I was always a masculine heterosexual.* These details might all have been true. But it is also undeniable that both Koubek's medical care and his social standing depended on convincing the public that he had always been masculine, that he was only ever interested in women—in other words, that he was not a threat to the era's sex paradigm.

It is this tension—this struggle to survive in a medical system set up to discount his humanity—that makes it so hard to retroactively apply a label like "trans" or "intersex" to Koubek today. It is also perhaps what made athletic officials fixate on Koubek so much in the first place. They understood him to have always possessed physical characteristics they attributed to masculinity. That, they assumed, meant he had cheated. Any psychological explanation for his transition was beside the point.

○○○

By the end of spring, Koubek realized he had a problem. The worldwide coverage of his transition had drawn the attention of theater producers in New York and Paris, and they had invited him to appear on Broadway. The bookers offered him an eye-popping salary, more than anything that Koubek had ever earned.[23] He agreed to make the trip.

It was all good news—except that Koubek's identity documents no longer matched his masculine public presentation. His Czech passport, which had been issued in 1934, featured a photo of him prior to his transition—his hair in a bob, a fur coat draped over his shoulders[24]—and listed him as female. He feared that when immigration authorities saw the discrepancy, he would be prohibited from leaving the country. Meanwhile, Czech bureaucrats were still stonewalling Koubek's application to change his official name and sex marker. His request was on appeal at the Ministry of the Interior, and it could be many months before they reached a decision.

Koubek wrote a letter to Prague's chief of police on May 23, begging him to help. Experts, he told the police chief, had confirmed that "male characteristics prevail in me," and he had already done the due diligence of requesting a modification of his identity documents. He couldn't wait any longer for the Czech government to validate what he and his doctors knew to be true about himself. "Since I urgently need to go on a tour in America and have applied for a passport, please include a note in my passport that I may cross the border in men's clothing," Koubek wrote.[25]

The police were surprisingly helpful. They assured Koubek that authorities at the border would not give him a hard time about wearing men's clothing. They agreed to add a formal note in his passport in case anyone questioned the discrepancy between the female sex marker in his passport and his status as a man.[26]

At the same time that Koubek was preparing to go to America, the former track star also started writing a series of personal essays. The *Prague Illustrated Reporter* (*Pražský ilustrovaný zpravodaj*), a popular magazine founded in 1920,[27] had commissioned him to tell his full life story. Koubek spared no detail in compiling it, narrating his life from his birth in Paskov until his first surgery.

The *Prague Illustrated Reporter* unspooled Koubek's narrative essay serially, with a new section publishing every Thursday. The first article, which was published on the magazine's third page on February 13, 1936, opened with an introduction from Koubek. The athlete explained his experience living in the international spotlight. He had to endure months of press reports that, he wrote, teemed with "a load of conjectures and largely false deductions." By distilling his life story into an article, he wanted to clear up the misunderstandings. But there was one caveat: he would not turn his life into further gossip fodder. "I will not fight sensation with sensation," he wrote. "If that is what you are expecting, you will be disappointed."[28]

Ultimately, Koubek hoped the Czech public would receive his story—and the stories of others like him—with compassion:

> Do not look upon me as a person who wants to be shown for effect at the entrance to a zoo. Not that. Look at me as a citizen, who after a brief, unpleasant delay wants to get on the right track and

ultimately reach the intended destination via a peaceful path of progress.

Each has their own aim.

And I also have mine: I want to be a lawful and legitimate citizen of the republic and moving forward, continue with my great love: for sport.

Taken together, Koubek's narrative essay spanned nineteen long pages. The *Illustrated Reporter* continued to publish installments from it every week, with the final edition dropping on July 2,[29] just a month before the start of the Berlin Olympics.

CHAPTER 13

FOR MOST OF HIS CAREER, Mark Weston, the shot-putter from Plymouth, England, rarely questioned the gender that had been assigned to him.[1] Sure, in school he mostly hung out with boys,[2] and since he had turned eighteen he had a desire to wear men's clothes[3]—but, he claimed later, he never read too deeply into any of it. Something changed on his trip to the Women's World Games in 1930. Weston never explained why, preferring to maintain his own privacy, but he called the following years "a sort of twilight zone where I doubted my own sex."[4]

The same year, Weston started studying anatomy as a part of his massage work. The more he learned about the natural diversity of human bodies, the more he began to contemplate living as a man. He tried to bottle up his feelings—there was no one to share them with—but he knew he no longer felt safe in women's sports.[5] Without explanation, he started to withdraw from competitions. In the years following 1930, when Weston did compete, he did so only for short stints, and only when British sports executives begged him.

Eventually Weston had enough. In February 1932, he announced he was retiring. He wanted to work full-time as a physical trainer instead.[6]

By the early 1930s, Weston also realized he was attracted to women.[7] He began spending more time with Alberta Bray, a childhood friend. Bray frequently attended Weston's matches; when Weston took the midnight train to London in 1931, for instance, Bray accompanied him there and back.[8] In public, they called themselves best friends. Secretly, the two of them began a love affair.[9]

The beginning of 1936 proved to be a period of whiplash for Weston. His father, Stephen, fell ill and died in January.[10] Around the same time, Weston decided he wanted to seek out answers about his gender. He wrote to Lennox Broster, a prominent London surgeon who had been operating predominantly on intersex patients for several years. Broster agreed to meet, and on April 15, 1936, Weston was admitted for surgery at Charing Cross Hospital.[11]

Broster, a white, South Africa–born physician, had developed a focus on people whom the world perceived as female but who felt an affinity toward masculinity—a condition that Broster dubbed "virilism." A graduate of Oxford,[12] he first operated on a patient in 1927, at the request of a fellow physician.[13] Five years later, he made headlines for performing masculinizing surgeries on three people, which British newspapers erroneously hailed as "the first of their kind."[14] By 1938, he claimed to have operated on twenty-four British patients who wanted to live as men.[15]

Unfortunately for Weston, Broster tended to have a low opinion of his patients. He wrote that he'd noticed a "high percentage" of "mental illness" among the men he operated on. Often, he claimed, they were "pitiably conscious" of their bodies, which Broster referred to as "their disabilities."[16] In one interview, Broster said his role was to make sure an intersex person "reverts to normal,"[17] by which he meant changing their physical anatomy to match normative understandings of what a male body looked like. He also saw surgical operations as a way to codify heterosexuality. For gay patients, a surgical operation might be enough to remove their "perverted sex psychology."[18]

Broster was a eugenicist. He believed that the proportion of people who were born intersex was on the rise, and without surgical intervention, humanity would start "drifting towards a neuter state."[19] Broster lay part of the blame for this "neuter" future on two familiar foes: feminism and interracial relationships. "The emancipation of women has been a big change; there is overpopulation in many parts of the world; there are many factors in our social lives leading to race deterioration," he said in a speech, "and they must react on the individual,"[20] in the form of creating intersex traits. This idea that intersexuality was disseminated as a kind of social contagion anticipated the rhetoric that transphobic doctors used to refuse healthcare to young trans people nearly a century later.

That the doctor who gave medical advice to Weston was more concerned with enforcing heterosexuality and normative understandings of sex than with the autonomy of his patients underscores how difficult it was for Weston, or someone like him, to get real, affirming healthcare in 1936. Broster would have come into his meeting with Weston assuming, from the start, that Weston was broken and in need of fixing. Weston was probably lucky: he was white, which made him seem less suspect to Broster, and dating a woman. Broster also dealt exclusively with people who wanted to live as men; a trans woman, for example, probably would have had far more difficulty receiving care from him.

Weston's meeting with Broster seemed to go well, at least as far as the doctor was concerned. Broster wrote that the young man was a "triumph of instinctual development"[21] and praised the fact that Weston had never harbored romantic or sexual feelings for men. Even though his family had raised him assuming he was a girl,

Weston claimed to Broster that he had never been with a man, and therefore, to Broster's delight, "no trace of homosexuality was to be found" in him.

Broster had no problem recommending a surgical operation. "In his personality, his psychosexual life and in every way he was a complete male—it was only the misfortune of his environment which prevented him from showing it," Broster wrote after his meeting with Weston.[22] He recommended a minor urethral surgery; Weston, he decided, didn't need to undergo what today we would call top surgery. Then Broster got to work. First in April, then in May, he performed two operations on Weston.[23] While Weston recovered, Broster looked after him.

ooo

The tip seemed to reach the offices of the *Western Morning News*, the newspaper covering the Plymouth area, that same May. Weston was now living quietly as a man. When a reporter from the newspaper showed up at Weston's mother's cottage, Weston opened the door.[24] The former athlete, dressed in trousers, a tie, and brown shoes, agreed to an interview. He brought the reporter into the sitting room, where he handed over a certificate that Broster had signed for him. "This is to certify that Mr. Mark Weston, who has always been brought up as a female, is a male, and should continue life as such," the certificate read. Weston explained that he was planning to petition the British government to get his name formally changed, but for now, this was the closest he had to an accurate identity document.

At the reporter's prompting, Weston began to recount his story. He said he had known he was different from most girls but had never questioned his sex until the late 1920s, at which point he began to feel "abnormal." He considered that he might be a man, but he "did not have the nerve" to see a doctor, he said. He finally gave in, thanks to the prodding of his girlfriend, Alberta Bray, whom he was still portraying as a best friend. The surgeries were not without their risks—at one point, Weston said the operation triggered a fever that hit 104 degrees—but they had succeeded. Broster, Weston said, changed his life. After a seven-week stint in an all-male ward of the hospital, Weston said, "I realize I am now in my true element. Before I was going about abashed, but now I can keep my head up and look everyone in the face."

Weston had finally returned to his mother's house a week earlier, following his second operation. He spent his time in isolation drafting letters to his friends and family, informing them that he was now a man. He wrote to his closest friends and his loyal massage clients, explaining that he was named Mark and would dress in men's clothes. To his relief, they embraced him. "Your letter came as a great surprise," one massage client wrote back, but "if by chance you are still carrying on your profession as before, you know you will be just as valuable to us as formerly."

The *Western Morning News* story first ran on May 28 under the headline "Devon Woman Athlete Who Has Become a Man" (a reference to Devonshire, the region where Plymouth is located).[25] A day later, the paper published a follow-up story featuring a photograph of Weston wearing white trousers, a tie, and a sweater vest, standing in the back garden of his mother's cottage.[26]

This time, the *Morning News* fixated on just how "strange" it was going to be for Weston to live publicly as a man.[27] He had a new set of mannerisms to learn, according to the paper. He would have to remember to hold open doors for women, give up his seat on the bus, and tip his hat. "You can fool some of the people some of the time, but you cannot fool all the people all the time," Weston told the paper, but he insisted he was up for the challenge. He'd already taught himself to deepen his voice,[28] and he was working through other changes. He admitted, "I sometimes catch myself thinking in terms of a woman rather than of a man," and he had to dismiss thoughts that he considered too feminine.[29] Even in an era before scientists, and the public, made a real distinction between biological sex and gender, Weston was talking about being a man in the socialized, psychological framework used today.

For the most part, Weston told reporters, he was just thankful that his friends had been so accepting.[30] Having not thrown a discus or put a shot seriously in half a decade, he was much more ambivalent about what his transition meant for women's sports generally. When asked about his medals, he insisted that he had "won them in good faith" because, he said, "I honestly believed at the time that I was a woman."[31] Still, he seemed ambivalent about their fate. If Alice Milliat requested that he return any of his awards, he said, "I shall do so without hesitation."

In the days after the *Western Morning News* article, Weston's neighbors reached out to express their support.[32] Even members of the local sports world embraced him. A male Plymouth official named J. B. Cousins, who also owned a department store, asked Weston to begin serving as a sports executive in Plymouth.[33] "I feel I must write and congratulate you on becoming one of us," Cousins told Weston. He was acknowledging Weston's status as a man— though his letter also betrayed the possibility that a trans woman would not have had the same warm reception. "Has it ever occurred to you how much worse you would have felt had the change been the reverse way?" Cousins wrote. "Though possibly I should have had another customer for a wig."

Despite the reception, Weston was leery of becoming a media spectacle. After first explaining himself to the *Western Morning News*, he gave only a handful of subsequent interviews. He dodged questions he deemed too personal. When the reporter Milton Bronner, an American literary critic who traveled to Plymouth to meet Weston, asked about his gender transition, Weston replied, "I suppose it would be interesting to students of mentality if I attempted to set down my various states of mind during the different phases of my existence, but I don't want to do it." Instead, "I want to get away from publicity and be allowed to live my own life." Bronner was impressed by him. The critic wrote that Weston "has a man's grip when he shakes your hand." Were an onlooker not to know his history, "he would best be described as a good-looking young man" with "little trace of femininity."[34]

○○○

As a teenager in Newcastle, Wyoming, in the 1930s, far away from the bustle of cosmopolitan Europe, the future gay activist Elver Barker often drove into town with his friend to buy the queerest thing around: a pulp publication called *Sexology*.[35] *Sexology* was, ostensibly, a magazine of science. It took the reams of medical research on sex and sexuality and distilled them down so that regular people could understand. In an era in which mainstream newspapers referred to homosexuality only through euphemisms, *Sexology* was the one place many readers could encounter frank discussions about queer issues. For being a magazine of science, *Sexology* had a complicated relationship to evidence, at times letting sensationalism guide its editorial strategy. But its pop-science ethos also helped it push boundaries. In the early 1930s, it published articles about whether homosexuals could conduct happy lives or about women who lived together in pseudo-marriages.[36]

Queer people flocked to it. The United States didn't have a publication catering openly to the queer community and hadn't since Chicago police shut down the short-lived gay newsletter *Friendship and Freedom* in 1924.[37] *Sexology* was, in 1936, the closest analog to a gay magazine. Readers wrote into the Q&A section, offering a rare glimpse into the fabric of queer experience in 1930s America. One reader asked whether it was possible for a surgeon to construct an artificial vagina; the magazine responded that yes, it was.[38] Another wrote concerned that she was attracted to both sexes; *Sexology* counseled her not to worry, though it suggested that she focus on dating men.[39]

When *Sexology* first reported on Koubek and Weston in August 1936, it noted that their gender transitions had proven "intriguing to the general public," but it wanted to correct some misinformation. "Here we are undoubtedly dealing with an intersexual case," *Sexology* wrote of Weston and Koubek. "Nature was uncertain as to her intentions while a baby was being formed, as to whether it should finally be man or woman."[40]

It would turn into a blockbuster story for the magazine. When *Sexology* published that first article on the two athletes, "a considerable number of readers were much stirred," as the magazine explained in a follow-up article. "Some of them wrote and inquired whether the same could not be done for them"—and if so, how could they go about it? What kind of surgical operation would they need, and who could they go to for more information?[41]

Letters poured in from across the United States, from trans and intersex people of all genders. The stories of Koubek and Weston prompted one person, whom the world perceived as a man, to ask *Sexology*:

> Could I live the balance of my life as a woman, as I have desired to be all my life? It seems to me that it would repay me for the years of suffering I have already put in. As I understand it, female sex hormones will cause the ability to give milk from the male breast. These are conditions which are foremost in my thoughts; I have always desired to be able to nurse a baby.

Another letter that *Sexology* excerpted came from a reader who, despite being perceived publicly as a woman, wrote that "there is nothing feminine about me." They asked, "Would it not be advisable to undergo what operations are necessary to become the male

I wish to be? Can you refer me to a competent surgeon who would be interested in my case?"

The outpouring of responses from readers baffled the editors of *Sexology*, who grasped at an explanation for why so many were interested in transitioning gender themselves. The editors referred at least one reader, a textile worker from Alabama whose story the historian Jules Gill-Peterson has chronicled, directly to a medical expert for care.[42] "Is this mere caprice?" the magazine asked its audience.[43] But the letters captured something else: the news was offering a lifeline to a heavily marginalized queer community, an alternate future with a different, more fluid understanding of gender. Zdeněk Koubek and Mark Weston each lived across the world from the mostly American readers of *Sexology*, but many saw themselves in the two men anyway.

It is in the pages of *Sexology* that glimmers of a queer and trans embrace of Koubek and Weston surface. For people whose genders did not align with the one that had been assigned to them at birth, Koubek and Weston may as well have been folk heroes—proof that transitioning and creating a new life were possible, even on a national stage. The letters written to *Sexology* are one small data point, but they suggest a second dimension to the importance of Koubek and Weston. The two athletes didn't just change the sports world. They also brought new attention, and possibility, to queerness itself. Anyone struggling with their own gender could look to these two athletes and feel a rush of relief. Perhaps they were not alone after all.

One of those queer admirers was an English diplomat living in Tokyo who went variously by the names Thomas Baty and Irene Clyde. If they were alive today, Clyde likely would fit a framework of trans identity. Though they publicly identified only as a man, Clyde wrote in their subsequent memoir that, for many years, they "longed passionately to be a lady—and have continued to do so."[44] They "could not bear" the thought of embracing traditional masculinity.[45] Clyde ran a privately printed journal called *Urania*, which was designed to showcase broader possibilities for gender expression, namely, to celebrate masculine women and feminine men who transgressed gender norms. "There are no 'men' or 'women' in *Urania*," the journal declared. Instead, gender was a spiritual experience, determined internally by the individual: "We do not hold that the physical envelope matters."[46] To prove their point, Clyde often wrote "woman" in scare quotes.

When Clyde learned about Koubek, they were thrilled. In January 1936, under the boldface headline "Authentic Change of Sex," *Urania* hailed the news of Koubek as "a clinching corroboration of our main thesis: that sex is an accident."[47] Six months later, in the issue published that June, *Urania* ran an article titled "Another Extraordinary Triumph": Mark Weston had transitioned, too. Clyde was elated. Koubek's news, they wrote, "seemed so rare" that "it is extraordinary that it should be followed by another equally well-authenticated case."[48]

That invisible queer community stretched all the way to Belgium, where, in the final weeks of 1935, the cyclist Willy de Bruyn was leafing through *De Dag*, a popular newspaper in his home country.[49] De Bruyn was a rising star in women's cycling competitions across Belgium, but in recent years, he had felt a strong pull toward masculinity. That December day, he was searching for news about the upcoming Berlin Olympics when he stumbled on the article that would change his life. The paper had published a short item stating that Koubek was now living full-time as a man, and that he'd petitioned his government to change his name and sex marker on his identity documents.

To most of the readers of *De Dag*, the Koubek news was an oddity, further proof that nature—and sex—continued to evade their understanding. But when de Bruyn read about Koubek's transition, he said later, his "salvation appeared." De Bruyn and Koubek were linked in more ways than one. Though not as famous in Belgium as Koubek was in Czechoslovakia, de Bruyn was also a minor athletic success. He'd won the women's world cycling championships in 1934, in a competition against athletes from seven other countries. De Bruyn beat out a French racer by just a few feet.[50]

Also like Koubek, he'd spent years agonizing over his gender. Since the summer of 1934, he had researched whether a gender transition could be possible. He was often depressed, but he reminded himself that his gender was not a personal failing. "Should one blame an individual, when he is victimized by the imperfections of medicine and of the legal system?" he wrote later.

Though he'd felt certain he was a man, it wasn't until he read about Koubek that de Bruyn realized he could do something about it. He felt, for the first time, hope. In the early months of 1936, de Bruyn reached out to a doctor in Belgium, who examined him and wrote up a medical certificate verifying that he should begin living as a man.

The doctor's note in hand, de Bruyn traveled to the civil court of Oudenaarde, the Flemish municipality where he lived. He explained that he wanted to change his name and sex on all his identity documents. If the request surprised the clerk, she didn't show it. When de Bruyn announced his desire to register as a man, the clerk gave him a "very friendly reception" and directed him to collect more documentation. De Bruyn met with a second doctor, who also signed off on his desire to present as a man.

His next stop was to hire a lawyer, who helped him file a formal application to change his documents. Then there were more tests and medical exams, the costs of which piled up. De Bruyn applied for jobs in Brussels under his masculine name, Willy. He knew it was risky: the Belgian government was still processing his identity documents, which meant that, on paper, Willy de Bruyn didn't exist. He found a job as a dishwasher at a hotel in Brussels, but shortly after starting, his manager called him into his office and sat him down. "We are working on the necessary administration for your pension card," the manager said. "The city council of Erembodegem claims that there is no Willy de Bruyn registered there. What is the meaning of this?" When de Bruyn confessed his history, the manager told him that because he was still legally considered a woman, he couldn't work there anymore: "Yes, that is all well and good, but I am not authorized to employ women in my kitchen." His hands were tied, he said.

Throughout 1936, de Bruyn ran into the same problem again and again. He was hired as Willy de Bruyn at an array of jobs—delivering bread, operating an elevator, working at a lumber warehouse—only to be discovered, then summarily fired, days or weeks later. Every manager had the same excuse: they couldn't hire him until his sex marker was legally changed. Only in early 1937, around a year after he first filed his application to change his civil status, did he receive a new identity card in the mail. He trembled when he opened it. In broad, round letters, the government of Belgium had affirmed his new name: Willy.

ooo

Weston's story quickly spiraled outside his control. Within two days of the *Western Morning News* article, Weston's face was plastered across newspapers in the United States and Europe. The story by the American journalist Milton Bronner was reprinted by countless outlets.

With the news spreading both underground through publications like *Sexology* and across mainstream outlets throughout the world, it didn't take long for the media to zero in on the curious similarities between Weston's story and Koubek's. If one athlete publicly transitioning could be dismissed as an oddity—the kind of tale of gender subversion that had cropped up in local newspapers off and on for many decades—then two athletes signaled something else entirely: a pattern.

Part III

SURVEILLANCE

CHAPTER 14

IN THE SUMMER OF 1936, the American magazine *Time* tried to make sense of a puzzling phenomenon for its readers. "Such cases of 'sex change' fascinate not only tabloid editors but also serious students of the tremendous complexity and almost infinite variations of human hermaphroditism," *Time* wrote.[1] The magazine had been intrigued by the back-to-back announcements from Zdeněk Koubek and Mark Weston, and it wanted to find an explanation. Gender transitions happened far more frequently than most people realized, it announced, as "nature some times [*sic*] blurs sexual development in men & women."

Time was referring to one of the era's dominant theories of biological sex. Many sexologists believed that in the womb, all embryos began with both male and female traits. Then, shortly before a child was born, the characteristics of one sex started to overtake the other. In this understanding, even people whose bodies corresponded to a normative understanding of male or female always maintained the traits of both sexes. According to one gynecologist in Chicago, "There are few 100 percenters among human beings from this standpoint, there being a bit of the feminine in all men and a corresponding tinge of the masculine in all women."[2]

Time's relatively straightforward, nonjudgmental accounting of Koubek and Weston was hardly exceptional. Amid the deluge of stories that the duo inspired, most tried to promote sympathy for people who transitioned gender. *Physical Culture*, one of the most popular American sports magazines, tasked a sexologist named Donald Furthman Wickets with explaining the transitions to its audience.[3] Wickets said that Koubek and Weston existed on a well-understood spectrum of biology: "Sex is relative. No man is 100 per cent male, no woman 100 per cent female. Every male, even the lustiest, retains certain rudimentary characteristics of the other sex." While Wickets acknowledged that much of the science surrounding biological sex remained in flux, he did feel confident in calling stories like Koubek's and Weston's somewhat normal. Echoing the embryo theory, Wickets said all people were born with their sex "more or less undifferentiated." While in "95 out of 100" cases, people fell into the normative understandings of "man" or "woman," that left 5 percent of people, in Wickets's estimation, who didn't. "It is not surprising that nature should produce 'freaks' who possess both male and female sex organs," Wickets concluded. "It is only surprising that such cases do not occur more frequently!"

That one of the largest sports magazines in the United States would publish an essentially nonjudgmental article about transitioning athletes, minus the use of a word like "freaks," was significant. By coming out as men, Koubek and Weston were inspiring a much wider discussion around the nuances of biological sex. Newspapers ran numerous op-eds in support of the athletes. Dr. Morris Fishbein, the long-serving editor of the *Journal of the American Medical Association*, penned a nationally syndicated op-ed about Koubek and Weston, positioning the men as part of a long history. "Cases like this are repeated again and again in the pages of medical publications," he wrote in his op-ed. If Fishbein had one piece of advice to the average reader, it was to be more understanding. "No doubt in various places in the United States today there are little girls growing up who will eventually turn out to be predominantly male and who will need the type of diagnosis and surgery that has been mentioned," he wrote. Instead of judgment, "what they need most at this time is proper understanding by their parents, by their doctors and by the community in general." Fishbein, like many of his contemporaries, elided discussion of trans women—and of anyone else who might transition from male to female.[4]

As the media continued to embrace Koubek and Weston, sports officials deepened their suspicions of the two athletes. In the weeks following Weston's transition, the top brass of the IOC and the IAAF fired off frantic letters about the need for action ahead of the Summer Olympics, which were now less than two months away. Wilhelm Knoll, the Nazi sports doctor who had first accused Koubek of deception earlier that year, began lobbying officials to act. On June 19, holed up in his office at the University of Hamburg, Knoll wrote a flurry of letters to various international sports federations, which oversaw leagues like track and field, soccer, and swimming.[5] Identifying himself as the secretary-general of the International Federation of Sports Physicians, Knoll urged these officials to take a stance against Weston and Koubek.[6]

One of Knoll's letters ended up in the hands of Carl Diem, the German official who, in addition to his work on the Organizing Committee of the Berlin Olympics, was now a prominent member of the IAAF. "Two bogus cases of hermaphrodites have been in the press lately," Knoll wrote to Diem, citing Koubek and Weston by name, "proving that women's elite sports contain elements that do not belong there and must be eliminated at all costs." If the Organizing Committee wasn't proactive about the threat of "abnormal" athletes playing in women's sports, Knoll warned, then the Nazis risked enduring accusations of cheating at the forthcoming games.

Knoll concluded: "I request that all female participants in the Olympic Games should have their gender checked beforehand by a specially-commissioned doctor." He suggested that these checks be done at the women's dormitories shortly before the start of the Berlin Olympics. Since all the women were going to live together in the same dorm, called the Friesenhaus, implementing a sex test should require "no technical difficulties." Knoll made no mention of testing athletes in men's competitions. In his framing, trans and intersex women, whom he called "hermaphrodites," a common term at the time that in Knoll's writing retained a derisive edge, were the only group worthy of concern. The fact that one of the inspirations for his letter, Koubek, was now preparing to play in men's sports and therefore would not have even been examined under this framework, did not seem to cross his mind. Knoll signed off, "Heil Hitler!"[7]

Knoll still had not developed a clear explanation of how he wanted sports officials to "check" the female athletes or what they should even be looking for: What defined an "abnormal" athlete in the first place? Though he occasionally nodded to the misconception that certain "abnormal" women possessed athletic advantages, he didn't make clear *what* those advantages were. Would he have considered a woman with too much muscle or body hair to be "abnormal," and at an advantage, and therefore worth disqualifying on the grounds of cheating? What about tall women? Didn't they have an advantage in some sports, too? Or was he simply concerned with genitalia—and if he was, what genitalia would he have considered disqualifying?

Reading between the lines of these letters underscores the truth: there was no coherent ideology or intellectual idea behind Knoll's push for sex testing. For as adamant as he was that the Olympics needed to regulate athletes on the basis of their bodies, he seemed to spend shockingly little time considering what those regulations would look like. He simply hadn't thought it through. Instead,

Knoll's push for sex testing could be seen as a reactionary measure, colored almost entirely by his own anxieties about masculinity and femininity—and, perhaps not incidentally, by his commitment to eugenics.

Knoll's campaign for medical exams sounded a lot like his prior statements urging that Nazi leaders purge "unsuitable elements," a group that he included to mean Jewish and non-white people, from sports. To Knoll, regulating women's bodies was probably an extension of that fear of difference. A woman who didn't meet his standards of femininity, whatever those standards were, represented a challenge to the eugenic state. The Nazis associated masculine women with sterility and lesbianism; they were seen as unable to reproduce and, therefore, should be swept to the margins of society.

When Carl Diem received Knoll's letter, he passed it on to Sigfrid Edström, the head of the IAAF, who received it warmly.[8] Edström, himself often sympathetic to the Nazi point of view, didn't seem to notice any of the holes in Knoll's plan. As his years-long skirmish with Alice Milliat had made clear, Edström felt, at best, ambivalent toward women's sports, and he was sympathetic to fears about masculine women entering track and field. "I am extraordinarily happy that you have brought this question [of testing] into discussion," Edström told Knoll a week later. But for now, he lamented, there was not much he could do. With the Berlin Olympics less than two months away, the IAAF didn't have time to make the "investigation" of women athletes obligatory. He promised that the IAAF would address the issue at its board of directors meeting, which was scheduled for Berlin at the end of July, and he underscored how sympathetic he was to the idea of bodily examinations. "In the principle, the matter is perfectly clear," Edström wrote. "Only women shall participate in the competitions for women."

It was an empty statement, meaningless on its surface. Stating that women's competitions would be reserved exclusively for women was intentionally redundant; it made an incredibly complex topic sound simple. Of course, the real work of the IAAF should have been in *defining* what "woman" meant in the first place, but leaning on fearmongering allowed Edström and Knoll to skirt that question altogether. Both men seemed to take the view that they would know a supposed outlier when they saw one. They couldn't have known it then, but their lack of foresight would come to haunt the sporting world for the rest of the century and beyond.

Knoll was thrilled by the IAAF's response, in part because the track-and-field organization was the only international federation that seemed receptive to his proposal. The other federations to whom he had recommended creating a sex testing policy, he lamented later, "decided the question is not worth considering, and do not seek to understand it."[9]

Knoll and the Nazis weren't the only ones campaigning for sex examinations. The need for sex testing became a particular topic of fascination among fascists in Europe, whose embrace of eugenics made them naturally suspicious of trans people, intersex people, and really any woman they deemed too masculine. An Italian fascist newspaper suggested that medical exams could "protect" athletes from "future unpleasant surprises of the kind brought up in this case by the gender switch of a woman." Fixating on Koubek, the paper deployed Knoll's dog whistle about supposed athletic advantage: it noted that after his transition, Koubek's "record performances became understandable and—less imposing. Were they even really world records?"[10]

In Canada, Alexandrine Gibb, the sports columnist who had complained about the masculine women at the Women's World Games in London, dashed off a series of columns about Weston in May and June 1936. Writing that "another Mister has come out of the ranks of the girl athletes," Gibb railed against the warm reception that the public had given to both Weston and Koubek.[11] Sports leaders, she complained, weren't realizing "their responsibilities to the 100 per cent girls" and were instead prioritizing "men-women" like Koubek and Weston. Like Knoll, she had a solution: medical exams. If sports officials were to inspect the bodies of athletes ahead of each international competition, she said, they could begin to weed out the "men-women" who were threatening the "dainty girl runners" who had previously, in her mind, been the norm at the Olympics.

Like Knoll, Gibb did not specifically explain what kinds of athletes should fail medical exams. What was a "man-woman," to use her parlance? A muscular woman? A woman who shaved? She used "man-woman" to refer to Koubek and Weston—but Koubek and Weston had actively transitioned gender, and neither of them wanted to continue to play in women's sports after their transition. Invoking both athletes seemed to be a tactic to whip up panic, creating the impression that an athlete who was now living as a man could still enroll in women's sports.

As the Olympics grew closer, sports officials continued toying with the idea of instituting physical examinations in women's sports. In early June, Avery Brundage received a letter from an anonymous sports fan warning him that a prominent American sprinter was not a "normal" woman.[12] Citing the sprinter's deep voice, the writer demanded that "rules should be made to keep the competitive games for normal feminine girls and not monstrosities." Addressing the complaint to Brundage made sense, given Brundage's position as head of the American Olympic Committee. But Brundage was also uniquely sympathetic to the fear that masculine women were taking over sports. Privately, he'd long harbored concerns that some top women athletes displayed the characteristics of men.[13]

On June 23, Brundage forwarded the letter to two prominent Olympic executives, Henri de Baillet-Latour and Theodor Lewald.[14] He couldn't resist adding his own commentary. "I do not know whether hermaphrodites are as common today as they evidently were two thousand years ago," Brundage wrote, "but I do know that the question of the eligibility of various female (?) athletes has been raised because of apparent characteristics of the opposite sex." He connected the risk of "hermaphrodites" at the Olympics to the recent news about Mark Weston, whom he said had garnered "considerable publicity" in the United States following his transition. "Perhaps some action has already been taken on this subject; if not, it might be well to insist on a medical examination before participation in the Olympic games," Brundage said.

The letter marked a turning point in the history of gender surveillance in sports. Here was a high-profile official asking the head of the IOC to embrace sex testing. Brundage's intentions were most likely not this ambitious, but really what he was requesting was for the IOC—a sports organization made up of wealthy white men with no real medical training—to draw a firm delineation between "male" and "female." What was a woman? The IOC, Brundage was saying, should be the ones to decide.

ooo

That sports officials would endeavor to sort people into a sex binary based on cursory medical exams was, in many ways, bizarre. Human bodies vary so wildly that, in the 1930s, surgeons who worked with intersex patients were still arguing over how to simply define sex. Many medical authorities were coming to terms with the possibility that there might not be a universal distinction between male and female at all.[15] "It used to be thought that a woman was a woman because of her ovaries alone," William Blair-Bell, a high-profile British doctor, wrote two decades earlier. But "there are many individuals with ovaries who are not women in the strict sense of the word, and many with testes who are really feminine in every other respect."[16]

In pushing forward sex testing policies, Brundage was doing something radical—taking a concept of sex that even medical professionals had not resolved, and enshrining it into institutional policy. He was codifying the idea that "male" and "female" were distinct biological categories, ones that not only could be but *should* be identified and measured. Even as doctors around him were struggling to define methods to clearly distinguish men from women, Brundage was reinforcing the misconception that sex distinctions were natural. The stature of the Olympics would, whether he intended it to be or not, become the ideal vector for this kind of fiction. If the biggest sports event in the world decided that it needed to create a stringent definition of "female," then why shouldn't other regulatory bodies, or societies, do the same?

Sports became the platform for sex sorting almost accidentally, driven by a misguided fear of women's sports as inherently delicate. The very same sports executives who had fought to pry the Women's World Games away from Alice Milliat, and who despised the idea of a separate, women-led competition, immediately turned around and litigated which kinds of women could be allowed to participate. Though Brundage didn't state it outright, the idea of sex testing seemed to come from a belief that more masculine women—or intersex women, as his "hermaphrodite" comment seemed to be referring—would have an advantage against traditionally feminine athletes.

That's the most generous read of Brundage, at least. The less charitable understanding is simply that Brundage, along with many of his colleagues, didn't like looking at masculine women. Brundage said as much many times throughout his career. A few years earlier, he had memorably suggested abandoning women's sports entirely. Perhaps, at first, a part of him envisioned sex testing as an excuse to remove women who seemed to challenge patriarchal gender conventions. In this understanding, trans and intersex women would become collateral in a campaign to impose ideals of femininity across the entire women's category at the Olympics.

Decades later, this type of sex sorting would come to be an

expected part of life in a gendered society. Prisons, single-sex colleges, social services agencies, and operators of swimming pools and changing rooms would all construct working definitions of "male" and "female" that present both, wrongly, as binary and stable biological categories. Often, administrators and bureaucrats have wielded those definitions to exclude trans and intersex people, usually out of fear that they would spread some kind of moral or sexual perversion. But in the 1930s, few regulatory bodies had yet taken it upon themselves to build out regimes of gender surveillance. That sports would become the center stage for this attempt to regulate gendered bodies is a strange twist of history.

Take women's prisons during this time. Occasionally, prison officials removed women whom they discovered to be trans or intersex. For instance, Mary Baker, a Brooklyn trans woman, was incarcerated at the Women's House of Detention for two days in 1937 before officials discovered she was trans and moved her to a men's prison.[17] Yet cases like Baker's seemed to be largely one-offs; prison officials there or elsewhere didn't instantly create policy around how to define and measure the meaning of "woman." Even governments often lacked formal definitions of "male" and "female." The United States did not have any laws that governed when to permit people to change the sex on their legal documents. Instead, decisions on when to change sex markers were highly personalized, a byproduct of the whims of local judges.[18] Only in 1955 did Illinois become the first state to codify a pathway for trans and intersex people to amend their birth certificates. The law allowed identity document changes for a "person" who "by reason of [medical] operation" needed "the sex designation on [their] birth record . . . changed."[19]

Perhaps the only organizational body where gender surveillance had become a matter of policy by 1936 was the US Bureau of Immigration, which, since at least 1909, turned away immigrants whom they deemed "degenerates," a broad group that included people we might today categorize as gender nonconforming, intersex, and/or homosexual.[20] As the historian Margot Canaday has documented, border officials, alongside teams of doctors working with the Public Health Service, were trained to weed out potential degenerates at the border, often claiming that they risked becoming "public charges" in need of state support. It was maddeningly circular logic: sexual and gender minorities were not tolerated in America, bureaucrats pointed out; therefore, they would not be able to find economic or personal stability stateside and should be blocked from entering the country in the first place.

A 1918 manual titled *Manual for the Mental Examination of Aliens*, for instance, instructed doctors to watch out for immigrants with bodies where "the characteristics of one sex may approach those of the other,"[21] seemingly a reference to intersex and gender-nonconforming people. Likewise, a Public Health Service inspector told his team to single out immigrants who displayed "an oddity of dress" or "unusual decoration worn on the clothing."[22]

The extent of this gendered border surveillance varied based on the location of the border crossing and on the race of the crosser, according to Canaday. At Ellis Island in New York, where many migrants were arriving from Europe, inspections tended to be far more cursory than those at Angel Island in California or at the Mexican border. Similarly, because notions of degeneracy were heavily racialized, Asian and Latino men were more likely to be strip-searched than their white counterparts.[23] The end result was that people deemed to be gender or sexual minorities were deported because, one official explained, they "present bad economics risks." The official wrote, "It is pretty difficult for these unfortunates to get or retain jobs."[24]

By pushing for the IOC to consider a sex testing policy, in other words, Brundage was taking a leap that only the American immigration system had ever actually institutionalized. Under his watch, the Olympics was on its way to becoming one of the first global institutions to enshrine into practice gender surveillance. And because the Olympics, unlike the immigration system, was so visible to the public, Brundage's policy prescriptions, despite being rooted in forms of hysteria and panic, would inevitably inspire similar efforts far beyond the realm of athletics.

Brundage may have been the loudest proponent of sex testing, but he didn't speak for everyone in the sports world. Some officials did not see the need to make substantial policy changes simply because of Koubek and Weston. Even in the June 10 issue of *Reichssportblatt*, a Nazi-run sports magazine, Heinrich Voss, a German delegate on the IAAF, made the case that the recent news about Koubek and Weston shouldn't result in more regulation of women's sports.[25] While he said that "boyish types" were "always reproachfully cited" by opponents of women's sports, he found this line of argument misleading. Sports didn't *turn* women masculine, he stated. "That one can make a girl boyish by running and jumping and throwing is a claim that cannot be proven and in any case contradicts all experiences," he said. Anyone who understood biology knew that women who had some traditionally masculine features were a fact of life. "These boyish types did not become, but came: as they generally appear in life, so they also came to sports." Voss seemed to shoot down the possibility of implementing a wider regime of physical examination. Referring to the measures suggested by critics of women's sports, Voss said, the "eternal attacks and the extraordinarily clever investigations" suggested by some athletic officials "are pointless."

Brundage and Knoll disagreed, and their voices proved to be the loudest in the room. Within the IOC and the IAAF, the plan to implement medical exams exclusively for female athletes quickly gained traction. In retrospect, it might be easy to assume that these early advocates of sex testing were specifically targeting trans or intersex women, as sports organizations do today. That may be true— but assuming that the past parallels our present elides just how confused and disingenuous this inception of sex testing policy was. Brundage and Knoll discussed sex testing in such vague terms that if, say, a very muscular woman showed up for a medical exam, they may well have been able to call her "abnormal" and disqualify her.

There was no driving ideology behind these early sex testing proposals. Perhaps that was because these officials were too naive to realize that the sex binary did not exist at all. Or perhaps the vagueness was the point. They could eliminate anyone they wanted, just by calling that athlete's femininity into question.

CHAPTER 15

ALICE MILLIAT BELIEVED SHE'D BEEN DUPED. Certainly, she had never trusted Sigfrid Edström. She'd known for years that he and Avery Brundage were angling to get her to give up the Women's World Games.[1] But his sheer lack of shame surprised her. In late June, Edström bluntly informed her that he didn't want any delegate of the FSFI, Milliat's organization, at the IAAF's upcoming session in Berlin.[2] At this point, he told her, "it would be advisable that the [FSFI] give up its work." Milliat replied that his approach, which was to appoint a group of men with little knowledge of gender issues to govern women's athletics, was "quite wrong." Women needed to be involved in the governing of women's sports, she said.[3]

The mechanism by which Edström was planning to push Milliat out was confusing, but it boiled down to this: if the IAAF could convince the IOC to institute more track-and-field events for women, then the Women's World Games would lose its appeal and necessity. The Olympics remained far more influential and, importantly, better-funded than Milliat's project. Surely any diminished interest in the Women's World Games would spell disaster for Milliat. It was a cold calculation, made by a political operator who didn't seem to care about the years of work Milliat had poured into women's sports.

By the summer of 1936, Milliat was staring down the end of her career. Her health was failing, and had been since as far back as 1926.[4] A year earlier, in March 1935, she had announced her plan to retire from the FSFI.[5] Despite her health, she wasn't content to be cut out of her own organization just yet. She pressed for a meeting with the top brass of the IAAF before her departure. Edström agreed to schedule a session for Paris on June 27. When Milliat arrived, she expected to greet three representatives from the IAAF, including Edström.[6] Instead, only a single member, the French official Joseph Genet, showed up. Edström, Genet told her, was too sick to attend. He apparently hadn't bothered to let her know in advance.

Once the conversation began, it became clear that Genet was little more than a conduit for Edström. Milliat noticed that Genet was carrying "a number of telegrams of instructions" from the IAAF leader. He referred back to his bundle of files throughout their discussion, parroting the party line.[7] The IAAF takeover was happening whether she liked it or not, Genet said. He insisted that the IAAF "would do what is necessary for women to have a more substantial program at the Games."[8] His commitments were vague, which was probably intentional. Edström and Genet knew that the IAAF needed the IOC's approval in order to add more athletic competitions for women, so they tried to assuage Milliat without actually committing to anything.

Alone with Genet, Milliat began to despair. The IAAF was better respected than the FSFI would ever be. If Edström was this intent on taking her down, then she couldn't see a way to stop it. "The methods of force" that Edström had used "to keep us far away from the IAAF Congress, away from the jury, far away even from the stadium" had convinced Milliat that she was outgunned. Edström "would not back away from any means of killing the FSFI," she concluded. Defeated, she agreed to Genet's proposal.[9]

Milliat promised she would not resist the IAAF takeover of women's athletics on two conditions. First, she wanted the IAAF to recognize all world records from the Women's World Games. Because the IAAF was a subsidiary of the Olympics, that would automatically turn all the records from the Women's World Games into Olympic records. And second, if the IAAF could not guarantee an expanded slate of women's athletics for the 1940 Olympics, she informed Genet that the FSFI would hold one last Women's World Games—the 1938 Games in Vienna, Austria. As Genet summarized in a letter to Edström, "Mrs. Milliat and her colleagues would agree to disappear" as long as those two conditions were met.[10]

The problem for Milliat was that Edström had the upper hand, and he knew it. Though he insisted he would try to recognize the records from the FSFI, he hated the idea of another Women's World Games. In early July, while still sick in bed, he wrote Milliat a letter rejecting the possibility that a fifth Women's World Games would take place under his watch.[11]

Milliat was out of moves. She seemed to be too ill to travel to Berlin,[12] her organization was bleeding money,[13] and Edström seemed on the verge of destroying her life's work. That July, just a few weeks ahead of the 1936 Olympic Games, the reality finally sank in: her dream of a women's sports competition governed largely by women was dead.

ooo

By the end of June, as the American boycott movement faded from public view, Avery Brundage had one final concern. He needed money. Financially speaking, it wasn't looking great for the American Olympic Committee. Sending teams to the Olympics had never been a particularly lucrative enterprise, but that year in particular, thanks to the combined burdens of the Great Depression and the public fury that a Nazi-hosted Olympics had generated, the Olympic team was short on funds. Few people wanted to donate. On March 17, the secretary of the American Olympic Committee had given a curt assessment of the situation to Brundage: "We are in a hell of a hole financially."[14] The American Olympic Committee had just $9,844 to its name, and it needed to scrounge together $350,000 in order to afford to send its team to Germany.[15]

Brundage hated fundraising. It was undignified, he felt, and it underscored just how little the US government cared about sports. While other countries subsidized their Olympic teams, the United States did not.[16] Even so, Brundage had no choice but to push aside his frustrations and begin a "strenuous campaign" to raise funds before his team's departure on July 15.[17] He courted wealthy Germans, whom he thought would be sympathetic to an Olympics held in Berlin. To rally support, Brundage leaned on red-scare tactics. Communists, he said, were trying to "trick" American athletes into boycotting the Olympics.[18] He needed money to fight back.

Brundage also attempted to court Jewish business owners, though his appeals dripped with antisemitism. In a letter to Albert Lasker, a Jewish advertising entrepreneur, Brundage wrote that donating to the Olympics was the best way to stave off "the great and growing resentment in athletic circles in this country against the Jews."[19] He seemed to position money as a salve for rampant antisemitism. Giving to the American Olympic Committee, according to Brundage, "might be useful in the future" to Jewish leaders.

The appeals didn't work. As the Olympics approached, Brundage was growing desperate. One American official approached the radio news channel NBC and demanded that it pay the American Olympic Committee $100,000 for the right to interview American athletes during the Olympics in Berlin.[20] NBC balked. When the organizers of the Olympics, Carl Diem and Theodor Lewald, found out about the demand, the two men asked the Americans stop. Germany, they insisted, had sole control over broadcasting rights, and it was already planning to offer access, for free, to a radio control room tucked under the Olympic Stadium, a twenty-one-meter-long device called the 40-Nations Switchboard.[21] It didn't need the American Olympic Committee to get in the way.

○○○

Eventually, Brundage scrounged together enough cash to at least get the athletes on the boat. The morning of July 15, a track-and-field athlete named Helen Stephens, along with the rest of the Olympic team, boarded the SS *Manhattan* from a port in New York City. A morass of thousands of radio reporters, sports fans, dockworkers, and at least one movie star—the actress Helen Hayes—gathered at the end of West Twentieth Street for the send-off.[22]

It was a sticky summer day, the tail end of a heat wave that had sparked forest fires and left 375 people dead.[23] Stephens was too ebullient to mind the heat. She was on her way to the Olympics, and for the first time in her life, she felt like a celebrity.[24] Over the past year, she had become, alongside Jesse Owens, one of America's preeminent stars ahead of the Olympics. Many commentators predicted she might come home from Berlin with a gold medal in track and field.[25] As she checked in and boarded the ship, bystanders held out autograph notebooks and shouted questions.[26]

A pair of radio reporters with NBC and CBS were on hand, relaying the scene aboard the *Manhattan* to millions of Americans. They flocked to Stephens and Owens. Asked about her chances of victory, Stephens was humble. "I figure I'm just as good as they are," she said.[27] By 10:30 in the morning, the entire US Olympic team, 384 athletes in total, had crammed onto the ship.[28] The food rations—25,000 apples, oranges, and grapefruits; three tons of beef; eight tons of milk; and 2,400 bottles of Coca-Cola—followed shortly thereafter.

Brundage, fresh off a flight from Chicago, arrived to give the goodbye speech. "We have the best athletes in major and minor sports ever to represent us," he said.[29] Then he pivoted to discussing his financial woes. The American Olympic Committee was still short of its fundraising goal, and the axe was swinging in every direction. Dee Boeckmann, who coached Stephens and the rest of the women's track team, had agreed to forgo her salary in order to travel to Berlin.[30] Many athletes needed to pay for the cost of the trip themselves or else return home.[31] One sprinter on the women's team, who was warned that she might be cut in order to save money, secured her spot on the SS *Manhattan* only when she showed up at the last minute with a check for $500. "I shall not rest content" until the committee managed to bring in another $25,000 of funding, Brundage told the American athletes.[32] The Olympics would go forward either way, but Brundage wanted to keep the American Olympic Committee from slipping into debt.

At the send-off party, little trace of the boycott movement that had consumed the United States for nearly three years remained. To the average attendee, it probably looked just like any other Olympic goodbye. Only if you squinted could you see the cracks. Not a single important federal official had shown up to wish the team luck: President Franklin Delano Roosevelt, whose advisors had warned him not to weigh in on the boycott debate, hadn't even sent the traditional farewell message.[33] A single picketer showed up outside the *Manhattan*, bearing a sign that declared, "Boycott Hitler Germany; fight for tolerance, freedom and liberty."[34]

Soon after the *Manhattan* departed, it became clear that the Olympic boycott movement wasn't dead, exactly—it had just gone underground. Covert messages, aimed at specific athletes, now replaced massive protests at Madison Square Garden. Stephens watched the Statue of Liberty fade into the distance as they left New York Harbor, then headed downstairs. When she settled in her small third-class cabin on the lowest level of the *Manhattan*, she discovered a stack of pamphlets on her bed. Stephens leafed through them and realized they had been left by boycotters. Treating the Berlin Olympics as an ordinary event, one pamphlet warned her, was a mistake. The Nazi regime was too brutal to be normalized. It urged Stephens to take a stand against the Nazis, suggesting that she throw her race as a form of protest.[35] Stephens wasn't swayed. She reported the incident to Brundage, who was furious. He confiscated the pamphlets and threatened anyone on board caught distributing anti-Nazi literature.[36]

Otherwise, Stephens had a "grand" time on board the ship.[37] The *Manhattan* had a movie theater, a putting green, and a dance floor.[38] Lunch was roast beef and baked potatoes, while dinners included chicken with gravy and mashed potatoes, plus some ice cream and candy for dessert.[39] Every morning from 9:00 until noon, Stephens ran drills on deck with the track-and-field team.[40] In between training, she mingled with the other athletes and—still not used to the fact of her own celebrity—asked them for autographs, as if she were a regular spectator, not a star in her own right. Jesse Owens signed her autograph book, wishing her luck at the competition.[41]

Stephens did not know it, but she had been the subject of the letter that Brundage had received in early June, the one that warned him of a suspiciously masculine American sprinter who was soon to attend the Berlin Olympics. The anonymous writer, who had reportedly met Stephens, complained to Brundage about her "deep bass voice" and her "10 ½ inch shoes." She was, according to the writer, "a border-line case if there ever was one."[42] It was a common reaction. When most people met Stephens, they first noticed her voice, which had a deep, raspy timbre because of a childhood accident: while Stephens was a child in Fulton, Missouri, she tripped and fell face-first in the front yard while playing with her dog, Doogie.[43] A wooden arrowhead she was wearing around her neck pierced her larynx. Stephens, unable to speak, rushed into the kitchen, blood oozing onto her clothes. For the rest of her childhood and adolescence, her voice would stay several octaves below that of her peers.

Stephens was never concerned with fitting in. As a child, she rebuffed her mother's requests that she learn to play the piano, opting instead to help her father herd cattle and pitch hay on the family farm. She went to middle school at a one-room building a mile away from her house. Every day, she jogged the distance between home and school. Sometimes she raced her cousin, who traveled on horseback just to keep up with her.[44] In 1931, by the time she was thirteen, she enrolled in Fulton High School. Even at that age, Stephens was taller and more muscular than most of her classmates. It was a blessing and a curse. While the other kids steered clear of her, the school's track coach asked her to try out for the track team, starting with a simple fifty-yard dash. Stephens agreed to give it a shot. After finishing the sprint, she jogged back over to the coach to see how she'd done. The track coach looked at his watch, then at her, "puzzled-like," Stephens said later.[45] He told her he didn't quite get her time and asked her to run it again. When he clocked her the next time, it was nearly the same result—an astonishing 5.8 seconds.

Over the next two years, her high school dispatched Stephens to larger and larger competitions. In the spring of 1935, her coach convinced the school to send her to St. Louis for the Amateur Athletic Union championships, her highest-profile event yet. Money was tight, but the school scrounged just enough to book a hotel room. Stephens's coach drove her across the state in his old Ford,[46] where Stephens faced off against the veritable star of women's track and field, Stella Walsh. Walsh, the onetime Olympic gold medalist who had a few years prior met Zdeněk Koubek in her hotel room in

Prague, usually got along with her competitors. She had been friendly to Koubek, and before him, to the Japanese sprinter Hitomi Kinue.[47] But something about the Fulton star rubbed Walsh the wrong way. Ahead of the race, Walsh dismissed any suggestion that Stephens could beat her. Surely, "that greenie from the sticks,"[48] she said, didn't stand a chance.

To Walsh's shock, Stephens won. Walsh later accused her of cheating. Stephens started running before the gun went off, Walsh said. But losing to a high school student rattled her. For the next year, Walsh repeatedly canceled her scheduled meets against Stephens,[49] pointing to scheduling conflicts. Now, in Berlin, they would finally have a rematch.

The two women were much more alike than either preferred to admit. Most of the sports world regarded them as insufficiently feminine. The columnist Alexandrine Gibb, for instance, suggested that Stephens would have an unfair advantage at the Berlin Olympics because she was "six-footed" and "mannish."[50] Gibb fantasized about creating a separate event for athletes that she thought were too muscular to play in women's sports. "I'd like to see a special 100 metres at the Olympic Games," she wrote. "In it I would put Stella Walsh, Helen Stephens, a couple of special German contestants, at least two English girls, and one or two other Europeans."

o o o

On July 16, while the American team cruised toward Europe, the Nazis wrote a letter to Gretel Bergmann, the most important Jewish athlete planning to compete on the German team. Bergmann, the letter announced, would not be allowed to participate in the Olympics. Her "mediocre performances," combined with the fact that the Jewish sports club to which she belonged was not an official member of Germany's governing track-and-field organization, meant they could no longer offer her a spot on the team.[51] Instead, the Nazis offered to give her a free standing-room-only ticket to attend the Olympics as a spectator.

When Bergmann read the letter, then reread it several times, she did not cry. "A stream of invectives came pouring out of my mouth," she said later.[52] It was a ridiculous excuse to give to a prospective gold medalist—not least because it was the Germans' own policies that kept her Jewish club from being recognized. Just a month earlier, in June, Bergmann had tied the German record in the high jump.[53] She was nearly certain to take home a medal for Germany, if not win outright. But after years of promoting violence against Jewish people, there was no reality in which the Nazis allowed a Jewish woman to win on their home turf, especially not under the banner of Germany.[54]

The timing of the letter, just days after the Americans had already set sail for Berlin, was probably not an accident. The Nazi sports czar Hans von Tschammer, who wrote the letter, knew that expelling Germany's most prominent Jewish athlete—and the only athlete on the slate who had two Jewish parents—from the Olympic Games could reignite the boycott debate. By axing her just a few days before the Olympics itself, von Tschammer wasn't leaving enough time for any international delegation to respond. His plan worked. Although the letter should have caused an international uproar, it barely made a blip in the press. In the United States, the *Jewish Telegraphic Agency* was one of the only papers to cover Bergmann's expulsion from the German team.[55]

The Bergmann news didn't appear to register with Avery Brundage or any of the athletes on board the *Manhattan*, either. On the morning of July 25, the ship finally came to a halt outside Hamburg, Germany. Helen Stephens and the rest of the Olympic team disembarked after breakfast,[56] but not before Brundage offered one last warning to his team. "I hope you will not be outdone in politeness and courtesy any more so than you are on the field," he told the athletes, noting the political sensitivity of the coming games.[57]

With that, the athletes, dizzy from over a week at sea, marched down a ramp leading off the ship. The first thing Stephens saw in Germany was a pair of flags, hung on the edge of the dock. A Nazi flag, featuring a swastika, was nestled alongside the American flag. In the middle, a banner announced, "Welcome to Germany."[58] The athletes tried not to see the port where the *Manhattan* had docked— wharf 13—as an omen of bad luck.[59]

The teams took buses to Hamburg's city hall, where the mayor was waiting to greet them in a massive room stocked with marble statues and oil paintings.[60] Brundage gave a short speech and passed out fruit punch and cigars. Then they were off again, boarding a train to Berlin. Stephens watched through her window as the train blazed across the countryside,[61] farms and forests blurring together in the distance. Arriving at Berlin Central Station floored her. Some of Germany's top athletic officials were waiting for the American team on a platform festooned with flowers and flags, including Theodor Lewald, Henri de Baillet-Latour, Hans von Tschammer, and Carl Diem.[62] Outside the station, at least twenty-four thousand Germans crammed behind street barricades, jockeying to get a look at the American athletes. Some stuck their heads out of apartment windows, while others cheered from balconies or roofs. It was more of a welcome than many of the athletes had ever received. The Americans laughed and waved back before boarding a bus to down-town Berlin.[63]

Eventually, Stephens and the rest of her teammates made the trip out to the edges of the Grunewald Forest, where the old Ger-man Stadium once stood. Twenty years after the canceled 1916 Olympics, it had been converted into a vast lawn featuring assorted sports stadiums, including the new Olympic Stadium. The lawn was called the Reich Sports Field, and also within its bounds were the women's dorms, where Stephens dropped off her bags.[64] While male athletes slept in gleaming new facilities in the Olympic Village—or, in the case of the rowing team, in a castle outside

Berlin—the women's teams settled in a former student military barracks,[65] which the Nazis called the Friesenhaus. Despite the difference in accommodations, the Germans, it seemed, had spared no expense. They hired catering companies that produced separate menus for each national team, tailored to the specific tastes of their countries. The Americans received milkshakes and steaks cooked medium rare, while the French had anchovies, bread, and wine and the Chinese were given soy sauce and fish.[66] The Nazis offered generous helpings of items like butter, which was in short supply throughout the country, to give an illusion of abundance.[67]

Nazi Germany wove its propaganda into all parts of Stephens's stay. At the Friesenhaus, Stephens found her movements heavily restricted. Though in their free time she and the other Olympic women athletes often walked along the Reich Sports Field, they couldn't leave the perimeter, which was surrounded by a fence. If they wanted to go shopping or eat out in Berlin, a personal translator assigned to them by the Nazis needed to join.[68] These translators wore white suits emblazoned with the Olympic rings. Stephens's coach later called the translators "very fine girls," seemingly oblivious to the fact that they had been asked, in part, to spy on each athlete.

Brundage, too, was on top of the world. He was the first to exit the train when the American team arrived in Berlin. Theodor Lewald rushed to embrace him. In the crowded station, the aging former bureaucrat planted a "lusty" kiss on Brundage's cheek,[69] according to news reports. Lewald had reason to be grateful: without Brundage, the American team might not have shown up at all— and without the American team, the entire Olympics might have collapsed.[70]

To Brundage, it felt like a hero's welcome. Officials led him, Lewald, and a group of American athletes into the redbrick Berlin city hall, where Lewald had held the first meeting of the Organizing Committee over three years earlier. There, a Nazi official presented Brundage with a commemorative medal and gave a speech in German, a language few of the athletes—and certainly not Brundage himself—spoke with much fluency. Officials passed out German-language propaganda books about Nazi Germany, which most of the Americans could not read. "They have lovely pictures," one athlete remembered, "but I don't have any idea what they are about."[71] When it was Brundage's turn to talk, he lavished his hosts with praise. "No nation since ancient Greece has captured the true Olympic spirit as has Germany," Brundage told the audience,[72] a puzzling and slightly anti-American statement given that the previous Olympics had been hosted in Los Angeles.

Beneath the surface, it wasn't hard to see that something in Berlin was off. Nearly everyone in the city was dressed in military uniforms: street sweepers, bus drivers, soldiers.[73] Draped over every light post was a Nazi flag, and instead of "hello," locals greeted the athletes with "Heil Hitler."[74] Whenever an athlete met the eye of a Berlin resident, the resident always managed to beam back—a fact that was charming at first but soon turned eerie as it kept happening, again and again, as if scripted. The most unsettling part, though, were the absences. There was no graffiti, no garbage, no dirt in the streets. Every blemish, it seemed, had been expunged.[75]

Before the athletes' arrival, the state had directed the press to whitewash the realities of the regime. A ban on jazz music, which the Nazis had implemented because of the genre's origins in Black America, was briefly lifted, though with the caveat that radio stations could only play jazz performed by all-white orchestras.[76] The Nazi press was also instructed to keep racist rhetoric to a minimum. When one newspaper quoted a racist book on sports, Nazi leaders chastised its editor. Such explicitly hateful remarks, officials said, were certainly not wrong, but journalists needed to bite their tongues until after the Olympics had finished.[77] And occasionally, when foreign visitors tried to talk politics with the locals, they received looks of fear. When one Kansas schoolteacher asked passersby, "Are you a member of the Nazi Party?" she received hushed responses. "I don't want to talk about it," one local whispered.[78]

Though the Nazis worked hard to sanitize their ideology, they continued to enforce prohibitions on racial mixing. Ahead of the games, German Jewish residents were told not to buy concessions out of concern they might strike up a connection with an "Aryan."[79] During the Olympics, the state police censured fifty-two white German women for flirting with "colored foreigners" in "an undignified manner."[80] Ahead of the games, officials deported a group of six hundred Romani residents of Berlin to a concentration camp near the outskirts of the city,[81] where many would be imprisoned and killed. Other members of marginalized groups met a similar fate: state police arrested a number of actual or suspected homosexuals, including one salesman who had allegedly made "advances" on two Argentinian visitors.[82]

The Nazis unsurprisingly built an entire surveillance apparatus around the Olympic Village. Plainclothes officers abounded, and the secret police held daily meetings to discuss potential threats.[83] Any mail that came in and out of the city was read and sometimes censored. A police unit at the Charlottenburg post office reportedly discarded hundreds of letters that included messages critical of the Nazis. On August 8, Nazi officials found a cluster of seventy-four good luck cards from England that, inside, contained anti-fascist writings.[84] One letter asked Jesse Owens to refuse to accept his Olympic medals as a public rebuke against a "government that preaches racial hatred." The Nazis confiscated the letter before Owens could see it.

On a few occasions, these letters slipped past the censors. Their content was, for the visiting athletes, uniformly terrifying. While in Berlin, Dorothy Odam, a British high jumper, remembered opening a letter from someone imprisoned in a concentration camp. It was "about how terrible the camps were," Odam recalled to the author Guy Walters decades later. The letter writer had asked Odam to report the abuses in Nazi-run concentration camps to British authorities. But Odam was fearful of what would happen if the Nazis caught her with the letter. Unsure of what to do, she turned it over to her German chaperone. "I felt that it had nothing to do with me," she remembered. "Who would I have given it to?"[85]

CHAPTER 16

RAINSTORMS BOOKENDED THE FIRST FEW DAYS in Berlin, leaving the athletes holed up in their dorms. An "epidemic" of sore throats, sore muscles, and colds swept through the American team.[1] More than a hundred Americans asked for medical treatment, and journalists began to wonder whether the US contingent would be ready to compete at all. The sick and injured weren't missing much. The Nazis had organized vaudeville shows designed to be legible to audiences that spoke dozens of different languages, which meant they contained almost no dialogue.[2] Most athletes found them incredibly boring. With little else to do, athletes wandered the city instead. The British teams enjoyed responding to the constant greetings of "Heil Hitler" with their own hello: "Heil King Edward!"[3]

Neither the chilly weather nor the wave of ailments could spoil Avery Brundage's mood. This, he knew, was going to be an Olympics he would never forget. In the waning days of July, Brundage gave a few interviews and speeches, but mostly he attended parties. A rotating cast of Nazis, including Joseph Goebbels, Adolf Hitler, and the future foreign affairs minister Joachim von Ribbentrop, hosted a series of swanky banquets throughout Berlin, and Brundage was a fixture at all of them. He attended a dinner for two thousand guests on Peacock Island, a small body of land on the other side of the Grunewald Forest that the Nazis festooned with paper lamps.[4] He also joined a private tour of the Temple of Zeus at the Pergamon Museum.[5] There, in a room overflowing with newly excavated Greek sculptures, Brundage listened to a performance of Beethoven's Ninth Symphony.[6] Lewald passed out gold chains, featuring the Olympic rings, to the gathered executives.[7]

Hermann Göring, the Nazi leader who a few years earlier had created the Gestapo, hosted a grand buffet for hundreds of dignitaries outside his house on Potsdamer Platz.[8] Brundage loved it. Dozens of tables of food had been laid out for the guests, taking up so much space that Brundage estimated it stretched a hundred meters. At the end of the night, a set of curtains parted to reveal a full orchestra. After the performance finished, Göring led his guests to an amusement park he had set up in the backyard. "The evening must have cost well over one hundred thousand dollars," Brundage, awed, wrote later.[9]

To Brundage, Germany felt positively alive. New streets had been paved; everywhere he turned, public works projects were underway. The people, too, seemed happy. Whereas before Hitler, he wrote, the German people had been "discouraged and demoralized," today they were "believing in themselves and in their country again."[10] It was no wonder that Brundage found the Germans to be a "friendly, courteous and obliging people" who, he thought, couldn't be capable of tolerating the kinds of atrocities many American newspapers alleged they supported.

Yet there was something else different about this Olympics, something Brundage may not have noticed, but Helen Stephens certainly did. In the press and in the dorms, a new system of gender surveillance seemed to be taking hold. Neither Zdeněk Koubek nor

Mark Weston was attending the Berlin Olympics, but their stories had begun to inform policy.

If two world-class athletes had transitioned gender in a matter of months, some in the sports world figured, then other stars could soon follow. And everyone was waiting to see who it might be. "The recent multiplicity of these cases of sex transformation has caused sex, for the first time in the age-old history of the Olympic Games, to become a major controversy among competitors," the British magazine *London Life* explained to its readers. "Girl athletes of every nation, particularly Britain, are complaining bitterly about the running athletes whom, rightly or wrongly, they regard more as men than as women."[11]

Athletes who competed at the Berlin Olympics were on high alert. Some became attuned to which women showered and changed with the others and which avoided the locker rooms altogether. Stephens felt these pressures firsthand. Physically, she stood apart from many of her peers. She was nearly six feet tall, and she lacked the classically feminine aesthetics that male sports executives expected of women. It made her a target. On board the *Manhattan*, the American diver Velma Dunn wrote to her mother that Helen Stephens "acts very mannish and talks lower than most men." Meeting her in person, she said, gave her "the surprise of my life."[12]

Under this intensified surveillance, many athletes took Stephens's deep voice as proof of her masculinity. The DNB, Nazi Germany's official press office, reported that "there was always a bit of a panic in the [women's dorms] when Helen Stephens's masculine voice echoed through the corridors."[13] The DNB decided that Stephens, who possessed a "raw cowboy bass voice that sounded as if it came from a deep ravine," had the deepest voice of all the female competitors. A British newspaper insisted that "some women athletes who had arrived in Berlin looked more like men," adding to the urgency for sports leagues to address what the newspaper called the "problem of the 'man-woman.'"[14] Other commentators complained that it was going to be difficult to watch "the English girls compete against freaks."[15]

On newsstands across Berlin, even scientific journals were parroting these talking points. That month, Wilhelm Knoll, that persistent Nazi sports doctor, published an article about sex in Olympic sports in *German Medical Weekly*. Knoll warned that the quest for personal glory was convincing intersex athletes, whom he called "pseudohermaphrodites," to enroll in women's sports, a reality he treated as inherently nefarious. "We also see a strange phenomenon in women's sports that has serious pathological traits and is likely to damage the really good women's sports," he wrote. "It is the appearance of manly pseudohermaphrodites in women's sport, who usually boast good performances."[16]

Knoll directly named Koubek and Weston and informed his medical audience that something needed to be done. Nazism practically guided his viewpoint. Knoll called these athletes a "deviation" and a threat to the "health" of sports. He insisted that sports federations should "thoroughly clean women's sport of such elements." Knoll said he had written letters urging sports leaders to institute mandatory sex testing policies for all women competitors. The same urgency needn't be applied to men, because "of course, men's sport is not at risk in this respect." Knoll hardly gestured to the supposed concerns around "fairness" that some advocates for sex testing would later adopt. Instead, his push for medical exams at the Olympics sounded much more unapologetically like eugenics.

There, in Berlin, in the summer of 1936, the climate around gender and sports had become irreversibly steeped in suspicion and even paranoia. Stephens tried to brush the comments aside and focus on her training, but the insinuations struck close to home. When she arrived in Berlin, she was harboring a secret of her own. Months earlier, she had fallen in love with a woman, and on the boat ride to Germany, she had penned a series of letters to her.[17] Stephens was not open about her attraction to women, nor could she be: openly queer athletes were few and far between, especially in a country as hostile to queer identity as Nazi Germany.[18] None of the whispers about Stephens included a word like "lesbian," but to Stephens, the insinuations about her gender felt dangerously close to the truth. What if someone found out?

○ ○ ○

The fears of masculine women at the Olympics gained new legitimacy on July 28, when a group of eight IAAF members filed into the auditorium of the House of German Sports,[19] a lecture hall located in the former German Stadium, where Carl Diem had once planned to host the 1916 Olympics.

Avery Brundage slunk in from the rain,[20] as did Sigfrid Edström and their mutual friend Karl Ritter von Halt. It was the meeting of the organization's highest-ranking members, who made up the IAAF Council. The group was incredibly powerful. It decided what to present to the full membership of the IAAF, and it tended to have the final say. If the council was behind a measure, the rest of the IAAF usually fell in line.

Inside the meeting hall, which was flanked by rows of spare stone columns, the group ticked through agenda items. The eight men approved the minutes of the previous meeting, analyzed their expenditures, discussed taking over the Women's World Games from Alice Milliat, and debated whether to accept Malta's application to join the organization. Finally, toward the end of the session, the IAAF's secretary, Bo Ekelund, turned the group's attention to Zdeněk Koubek and Mark Weston. In light of the recent news stories, the IAAF, he said, needed to figure out what to do about athletes who transitioned gender. He titled the agenda item "Sex questions in Women's Sport."

Ekelund read aloud the letters that Wilhelm Knoll had written to the IAAF about the need for medical exams over a month earlier.

Knoll's letter was clearly bigoted, calling for "hermaphrodites" to be expelled from sports, but it went over fine with the men in the room. After hearing Knoll's complaints, they "considered that this question was very important and that a paragraph should be inserted in the IAAF Rules" that could give the hosts the right "to order medical inspection," according to the subsequent meeting minutes. Ekelund, the secretary, resolved to write the wording of the new rule, which he would circulate to the IAAF membership in advance of their next meeting. The final decision would be made on August 10, when the full group of IAAF members met.

No one in the room seemed to acknowledge the gravity of what they were proposing, nor did they ask why it was even necessary. Why were a group of eight men in a sports governing body so interested in mediating the differences between "man" and "woman"? What stake did the IAAF really have in delineating who could qualify as a woman? Perhaps these men had become so lost in their suspicion of athletes they regarded as improperly feminine that they didn't stop to consider what would happen when they opened up the floodgates. There was no real plan, just an ambient sense of panic motivated by groupthink and pseudoscience. The critical nuance that Koubek and Weston, the twin inspirations for the proposal, were now living as men, and had no desire to play in the women's category again, was also lost on group members. The IAAF's certainty that Koubek and Weston had committed fraud was their only guiding motivation. They felt something had gone wrong, and they wanted to create regulations to stop it—even if those regulations were so unspecific that they amounted to a "we'll know it when we see it" doctrine.

When the meeting of the IAAF Council adjourned, Edström, Brundage, and the rest of the membership filed out. They disappeared into downtown Berlin, off to attend the high-profile parties that a rotating cast of Nazi officials and European diplomats had planned. The IAAF meeting received no coverage in the press. The public had no sense of how deep the obsession with sex had become—and how consequential that obsession would be.

○○○

July 30 was Avery Brundage's coronation day. Over the past few years, he had proven to be a dutiful foot soldier of the IOC, putting the success of the Olympics above geopolitics. He was ready to be rewarded. That morning, dozens of members of the IOC filed into a large domed hall on the outskirts of the Reich Sports Field, where the German College for Physical Exercise,[21] the sports university Carl Diem had pushed to create, once held lectures. Brundage was not invited to the IOC's opening meeting, since he was not a member, but he stayed close by. He knew what was coming.[22]

After opening the IOC session, Henri de Baillet-Latour ran through the plan that he and Brundage had spent months choreographing: he moved to have Ernest Lee Jahncke, the American representative who had called for a boycott of the Berlin Olympics, expelled from the body on the grounds that he had missed too many meetings.[23] It was the first time that the IOC had ever publicly removed one of its own members, but the gathered delegates seemed to agree that the disruptive Louisianan had to go. Only one committee member, the American representative William May Garland, refused to vote on the issue, though even Garland expressed his "profound disapproval" of Jahncke for his comments in support of the boycott movement. Then came the kicker: in Jahncke's place, William May Garland moved to elect Brundage as the second of three American members on the IOC. The IOC agreed, and in a 49–0 vote, Brundage was chosen to join the board.

Brundage was asked to sit for the rest of the meeting to help the IOC sort through its growing array of agenda items. At 4:00 p.m., the afternoon session opened with a warm welcome.[24] Twenty-four years after competing in the Olympics, Brundage had finally made it into the inner sanctum.

The main order of business was to consider two sharply conflicting visions for the next Olympic Games from dueling prospective hosts: Helsinki, Finland, and Tokyo, Japan. Across three days of IOC meetings, both cities presented their plans to the members. Helsinki, for its part, chided the organizers in Berlin for turning sports competition into a spectacle. The Finnish delegates promised that, if chosen, they would return the Olympic Games to "Spartan simplicity."[25] "We wouldn't attempt to compete with Germany in flags and dinners," the mayor of Helsinki, who had traveled to Berlin for the occasion, told the members of the IOC.[26] It was a curious pitch, given the IOC's appetite for the extravagant, and it paled in comparison to the expensive project that Japan had in mind, which involved a new $4.5 million stadium and half a million dollars in public transit subsidies.

Financial commitments aside, Japan had another advantage, which was that the IOC liked the idea of expanding the Olympics into Asia. In forty years, the Olympics had not chosen a single host outside the United States or Europe. Brundage himself felt that picking Japan would broaden the reach of the Olympics internationally.[27] In the end, in a 36–27 vote, Tokyo won the bid to host the 1940 Summer Olympics. Brundage voted for Japan,[28] and despite his lack of experience on the IOC board, he reportedly managed to persuade many of his colleagues to do the same. What did not appear to get addressed was that a few years prior, Japan had invaded Manchuria; that the IOC was choosing a host country with a distinctly fascist orientation, which was ripe to attract a boycott movement along the lines of the anti-Nazi one, did not seem to cross the mind of anyone present.

The next day, on July 31, Brundage entered the German College for Physical Exercise holding what was likely the letter he had written to Baillet-Latour a month earlier, the one suggesting that the IOC deal with "hermaphrodites" in women's sports.[29] Late that afternoon, after a discussion about whether to allow Ireland to compete under its own flag, the IOC members turned their attention to Brundage, who presented his letter. The discussion topic was listed as "Abnormal Women Athletes."[30] Brundage had a simple question for his new group of colleagues: Should the IOC begin requiring medical examinations for all women's competitions, as a way to screen out these so-called abnormal athletes?

It was a major moment—the first time in the history of the IOC that sex testing was officially discussed. The minutes of the meeting are sparse and offer few glimpses of the back-and-forth conversation between the representatives, but the IOC officials seemed to recognize that they were in over their heads. Determining a definition of "woman" was probably not the most comfortable job for the aging male aristocrats. After some debate, the IOC concluded that it would "forward a letter from the American Olympic Committee on this subject to the international federations of sport in which feminine participation is allowed," including the IAAF. These federations could then make their own decisions on how to evaluate female athletes and therefore take the heat off the IOC itself for any fallout. It seemed the IOC didn't mind the idea of sex testing, but it certainly didn't want to answer for it.

This first sex testing debate at the IOC was surprisingly perfunctory. More than an actual prescriptive policy, Brundage's campaign had the air of covering his bases. The proposal made little effort to engage with the evolving science of biological sex. Brundage didn't specify who, exactly, he thought he would be weeding out with these tests or why those particular athletes represented a threat to the integrity of women's sports. In fact, there is little record of what Brundage was thinking at all, because he hardly discussed sex testing in the copious letters he sent in 1936. Brundage saved nearly all his files from this period, yet few of them contain references to sex testing or gender surveillance. He didn't consult doctors or other sports officials on the merits of sex testing. He seemed to conceive of the idea himself, perhaps influenced by the agitations of Wilhelm Knoll, and pushed it through without real consideration of the impacts.

It probably wasn't a coincidence, either, that the IOC first considered sex testing policy at the same time that the Women's World Games was on the verge of collapse. The IOC was about to become the primary arbiter of women's sports, which meant the all-male committee could do as it pleased. Many members had long expressed repulsion for masculine-presenting women; Brundage, too, found butch women unpleasant to watch. Now, if they wanted, they had the power to simply ban masculine women from competing.

The Associated Press wrote about the IOC debate the next morning, describing Brundage's proposal to make all women undergo "sex examinations."[31] The United Press published a story of its own, which cited Koubek and Weston as the primary motivators for the IOC potentially introducing a sex test.[32] The *New York Daily News* printed a photo of Brundage with the provocative caption "Girls must be girls,"[33] and the *Richmond News Leader* wrote that Olympic officials seemed "somewhat bothered" by the recent high-profile transitions of Koubek and Weston.[34] But beyond those stories, coverage was scattershot. Likely only the most attentive sports news consumer knew the debate around sex testing was happening at all. Amid the frenzy of headlines about Hitler and the boycotts and Jesse Owens, Brundage's amendment at the IOC meeting was a mere blip.[35]

When columnists did weigh in on the sex testing proposal, they were critical. In the days after the IOC meeting, Jimmy Powers, a sportswriter for the *New York Daily News* and a Brundage skeptic, dismissed the push as part of Brundage's long history of antagonism against women. He wrote that Brundage was "fixing to get his ears pinned back" by women sprinters. According to Powers, it wasn't clear what problem sex tests solved. Some of America's most prominent women athletes, including its rising track star Helen Stephens, might have "biceps like cantaloupes," he wrote, but that didn't negate their femininity. In the long run, Powers worried that a campaign to regulate the category of "woman" could hurt sports. He speculated, jokingly, that if Cleopatra and Helen of Troy were alive in the 1930s, the IOC would have singled out them for sex tests. Left to simmer, the "Brundage scepticism [*sic*] is a deadly virus which will affect us all."[36]

In some ways, Brundage had already won. The IOC may have punted the final decision on sex testing to the individual federations, but he had convinced the other executives that medical exams could be a useful tool to deploy against insufficiently feminine women. After the meeting, Brundage told the press that sports executives in Berlin weren't afraid to selectively examine any female athlete who attracted too much scrutiny. In the coming days, "if a specific case arose where there was a definite question of sex, an examination would be made," Brundage said.[37]

It proved to be prophetic.

○○○

At eight o'clock on the morning of August 1, IOC officials staying at Hotel Adlon in downtown Berlin woke up to the sound of a German band playing celebratory music outside their windows.[38] Despite the early hour and the gray skies, the streets swelled with tens of thousands of spectators, who had begun jockeying for spots two hours earlier.[39] It should have been a madhouse. But aside from the band, a strange hush blanketed the crowd. The hundreds of soldiers and Hitler Youth officers who stood by seemed to want it that way. "No one spoke in the street. Not a word," a French athlete remembered later.

The gates to the Olympic Stadium didn't open until noon.

Throngs of tourists, journalists, and sports officials, 110,000 people in all, took the train to the edge of the Grunewald Forest, hurried through the gates of the Reich Sports Field, and poured into the new Olympic Stadium to get their seats. The famous zeppelin *Hindenburg* hovered above the stadium,[40] decorated for the occasion with Nazi swastikas and Olympic rings.

The Nazis bused Helen Stephens, along with the rest of the competitors, to the promenade that led into the Olympic Stadium. The athletes were asked to stand at attention as high-ranking officials from Germany and beyond marched inside. Everyone had their distinctive national outfits: the French in blue berets and white pants, the Canadians in red blazers.[41] The Americans couldn't hold their pose for long. Standing perfectly erect was exhausting. Many sat down and, to the horror of the German organizers, waved at foreign dignitaries from their perch on the grass.[42] When Hitler's Mercedes-Benz crept along the promenade, a group of Americans rushed to the front of a rope barrier to get a better look. At the sight of Hitler, the audience inside the Olympic Stadium erupted into screams that one athlete, who heard it from outside the walls, remembered as "blood-curdling."[43]

A few minutes shy of 4:00 p.m., trumpets cut through the summer air, and the procession of the athletes began. The Greek team marched in first; inside the stadium, the audience roared and held up their arms in the Nazi salute. Around 5:00 p.m., Avery Brundage led a group of 383 American athletes, dressed in blue and white, inside.[44] They stopped in front of Hitler, who wore a brownshirt uniform and a Nazi armband, before taking their spot on the field. Some Americans whispered that the dictator looked like Charlie Chaplin.[45] Theodor Lewald and IOC president Henri de Baillet-Latour stood by as well, dressed in gray clothes and top hats. In a sea of brownshirts, they seemed laughably out of place. Later, the Nazi propaganda chief Joseph Goebbels would sneeringly compare the IOC officials to "flea-circus directors."[46]

The ceremony began after the German team marched into the stadium. The recorded voice of Pierre de Coubertin, the founder of the modern Olympics, boomed over the loudspeakers.[47] "The important thing at the Olympic Games is not to win, but to take part," Coubertin instructed the audience, once again oblivious to the spirit of nationalism that he had allowed to infect the games. Lewald spoke next, in a meandering speech that went on for an astonishing twenty minutes. It was a small miracle when his pronouncements about "harmony and friendliness" finally drew to a close. Hitler then strode up to the podium.

Baillet-Latour had worked hard to downplay Hitler's role in the proceedings as much as he possibly could. He allowed Hitler only to speak a single line, which Baillet-Latour had prewritten. When Baillet-Latour first handed him the canned statement, Hitler promised he'd "take the trouble to learn it by heart."[48] Standing there that evening, in the middle of the stadium he had constructed, Hitler read it aloud. "I announce as opened the Games of Berlin, celebrating the eleventh Olympiad of the modern era," the dictator said. Then the Olympic flag was flown, a flock of pigeons shot into the air, and the audience broke into applause. Germans gave the Nazi salute, perhaps knowing it would be perilous not to; any German citizen who failed to salute was quietly arrested after the ceremony.[49]

Most of the visitors left the Olympic Stadium impressed. Helen Stephens wrote in her diary that it was a "thrilling day" that would "long be remembered."[50] But the tight choreography of the ceremony alarmed others. After the ceremony, the American writer Thomas Wolfe sent home a postcard remarking on the militarism of the German people.[51] "We can never learn to march like these boys," Wolfe wrote, adding an ominous prediction: "And it looks as if they're about ready to go again."

He was not wrong. During the Olympics, even as he played the part of diplomat, Hitler had war on his mind. In early August, the dictator began drafting a secret memo, later called the Four-Year-Plan

Memorandum, that directed his government to prepare for conflict in the next four years. For over a century, the dictator wrote, "the world has been moving with ever increasing speed toward a new conflict," one that would pit Germany against Bolshevism. Germany, he warned, needed to be prepared. "A victory of Bolshevism over Germany would not lead to a Versailles treaty, but to the final destruction, indeed the annihilation of the German people."[52] Hitler, in between glad-handing IOC representatives, was making plans for the next world war.

○○○

On the morning of August 4, Helen Stephens woke up to rain. It was a cold, wet day, and the intermittent downpour was enough to muddy the cinder-and-clay track inside the Olympic Stadium.[53] In the women's locker room, Stephens threw on sweatpants and a tank top emblazoned with an American flag. Over it, she slipped on a navy tracksuit. Nothing could spoil her mood. "At last the great day arrived!" she wrote in her diary.[54]

Stephens had multiple events scheduled for that day. First was the discus. It had never been her best sport, and in this case, it was little more than a warm-up. That morning, she kept looking at the one-hundred-meter track, where she watched her rival, Stella Walsh, prepare for the sprint. "I was really beside myself with anxiety," she said later.[55] Stephens came in tenth place in the discus, then hurried over to the track.

The one-hundred-meter race started soon after she arrived. Stephens's cleats were covered in mud, but she tried not to worry. When she fell in line alongside the other runners—Stella Walsh, Käthe Krauss, Marie Dollinger, and Annette Rogers—she dug her shoes into the clay, creating a starting block for herself.[56] She shook her arms, trying to focus, and leaned forward. The wind was gone. All that remained was a light drizzle. Stephens took a deep breath. It was just a hundred meters, she reminded herself. She'd run it thousands of times before.

As soon as the starting gun went off, Stephens shot forward. Though she later claimed she'd gotten off to a bad start,[57] the ninety-five thousand spectators in the stands hardly noticed. Within thirty paces, she'd taken the lead.[58] Stephens moved so quickly that the parts of her body seemed to blur together. The crowd cheered twice: first when Stephens crossed the finish line in first place, well ahead of Walsh, and again when an announcer declared that, at 11.4 seconds, Stephens had established a new world record.

Officials raised the American flag to celebrate her victory. Stephens described it as a "thrill."[59] As she walked over to the winners' stand, where she was given her gold medal, she was surprised when Walsh warmly congratulated her. The two shook hands, provoking a frenzied reaction from the audience. Bill Henry, the CBS radio reporter, hailed Stephens for accomplishing "the most remarkable performance of all time" for a woman athlete. "I can tell you there are a lot of fellas running for colleges in the United States today who can't run a hundred meters in eleven and four-tenths seconds," Henry told radio listeners back in the United States.[60]

That evening, Stephens shared the spotlight with America's biggest sports celebrity: Jesse Owens. Around the time that Stephens broke the one-hundred-meter record, Jesse Owens had set a new world record in the broad jump, earning him his second gold medal in two days.[61] The two dominated headlines the next day, and Stephens sat for a series of radio interviews. In Stephens's home state of Missouri, residents raised American flags outside their houses.[62] People in St. Louis could be seen with their ears pressed to their radios, waiting for updates about the hometown hero. To Stella Walsh, American reporters were much less kind. After her loss, one newspaper called Walsh a "has-been."[63]

At some point in the evening, the conversation turned. The months of coverage about Zdeněk Koubek, Mark Weston, and the possible IOC sex testing policies reached their inevitable end point—with an accusation of gender fraud. In Poland, Walsh's home country, Stephens's victory was greeted with skepticism, even disgust. Some Polish reporters had heard the whispers about Stephens's deep voice and muscular biceps, and they decided to speak out. Before the day was finished, the Warsaw-based newspaper *Kurier Poranny* sent an inflammatory story to press, insinuating that Stephens was not a woman at all. "It is scandalous that the Americans entered a man in the women's competition," the *Kurier Poranny* wrote, in reference to Stephens. Walsh, the paper reported, "would have gained first place if she had competed only against women."[64]

Another Polish newspaper, *Kurjer Warszawski*, issued a similar claim. The *Warszawski* wrote that "Miss Stephens does not betray any femininity. She has broad shoulders, fully masculine arm muscles and legs, and runs like men."[65] The Polish newspapers were not the only ones to level accusations against Stephens. In a column published in the French newspaper *Petit Parisien* the same day, the writer Roger Mahler speculated about whether Stephens would undergo a surgery to become a man, "as this is the fashion right now."[66]

Exactly what the newspapers were accusing Helen Stephens of was never made clear. Were they claiming that Stephens was intersex? That she was born a cis man and was masquerading as a woman? That she was just too masculine? Perhaps it didn't matter. The mere suggestion of duplicity was enough to send shock waves across the Olympics.

Stephens found out about the comments while appearing before a group of reporters on the morning of August 5. One journalist translated the Polish article aloud for Stephens. Instead of expressing sympathy, the reporter dug in. "Are you really a woman? Are you disguised, a man running in women's races?" the reporter asked her.[67] Stephens was mortified. She could only manage an angry retort: she told them, as she would paraphrase to her biographer decades later, "to check the facts with the Olympic committee physician who sex-tested all athletes prior to competition."[68] Of the rumors, she told the journalists, "It's just sour grapes."[69]

Americans rushed to her defense, accusing the Polish of stirring up "ugly rumors" with "no proof."[70] One writer called it "dirty journalism."[71] *Time* published an article calling the accusations an example of "what is now a routine lack of chivalry toward female Olympic competitors."[72] The publicity continued to fuel speculation. A day later, on August 6, Stephens's mother, who was still at home in Fulton, Missouri, because the family couldn't afford a trip abroad, spoke out. "Helen is absolutely a girl," Stephens's mother said in a telephone call with an American reporter. "No one else in all Helen's life has ever raised such a question." She was horrified that her daughter would face such an accusation in what should have been a moment of triumph. "I had better not say what I think of any one who would charge that she is anything else."[73]

The incident shook Stephens. Even though she kept an extensive diary of her time at the Olympics, she didn't write about the accusations that she was a man. She wanted to put the negativity out of her mind.[74] Yet the story didn't die. In the following days, a number of newspapers published a tantalizing revelation: German officials had apparently already given Stephens a sex test.[75] The officials, according to these reports, had expressed concern about Stephens's biological sex soon after her arrival, and Nazi authorities had asked her to undergo a physical examination to verify her sex before the start of the Olympics. They let her compete only after they felt satisfied that she was a woman, according to the newspapers.

The reports were bombastic. If true, it would mark the first time that an athlete was sex tested at the Olympics. Concern about masculine women had reached such a fever pitch that Nazi authorities had physically inspected the body of a top American sprinter to determine whether she looked, to them, like their understanding of a woman. It was a violation of Stephens's privacy, and a dramatic first lurch into an era of bodily surveillance, one in which athletes, particularly female athletes, would be stripped and studied to satisfy paranoia about so-called gender frauds.

Almost as soon as the reports surfaced, however, Avery Brundage denied them.[76] He told the press that the Nazis didn't administer a sex test on Stephens. No further evidence surfaced, and indeed the story seemed to disappear in the following days, lost in successive news cycles about gold medals and Hitler's antics. Exactly what happened may forever be relegated to speculation. Everyone had a different story: in his book *Farewell to Sport*, which was published in 1938, the sports columnist Paul Gallico suggested that American sports officials, not the German Olympic organizers, had examined Stephens ahead of the Olympics. According to Gallico, after the Poles "accused Miss Stephens of being Mr. Stephens," the Amateur Athletic Union, which oversaw track-and-field sports in the United States, "revealed solemnly" that Stephens had undergone a sex test. Before Stephens even boarded the SS *Manhattan* on her way to Berlin, Gallico wrote, "the Olympic Committee had had La Stephens"—meaning Helen Stephens—"frisked for sex and had checked her in as one hundred per cent female."[77] This exact revelation does not appear in press accounts from 1936, however; whether Gallico had insider knowledge, or whether he'd simply gotten the story confused in the intervening two years, is not clear.

Similarly, Stephens implied to her biographer that "an Olympic committee physician" had "sex-tested all athletes prior to competition."[78] In 1936, doctors were regularly checking American athletes to assess their health, and Stephens likely did sit through a basic physical before the Olympics—but the goal was usually to make sure the athletes were physically well, not to check their sex. Maybe Stephens was misremembering. Or maybe she had been singled out.

MURIEL CORNELL couldn't believe she was dealing with this. Early in the morning on August 6, 1936, the former sports star hurried into the lobby of the Russischer Hof, a hotel in downtown Berlin, several miles from the Reich Sports Field. It was the first meeting in two years of the Fédération Sportive Féminine Internationale (FSFI), the organization that put on the Women's World Games, and with Alice Milliat entering retirement, the future of the organization seemed more tenuous than ever.[1]

Cornell had made her name in England as a long jump champion, though she could never quite secure a gold medal for herself. She finished second to Hitomi Kinue twice in the Women's World Games, in both 1926 and 1930. Then, in 1934, she injured her leg, ending her career.[2] She moved into sports governance, joining the British Olympic Committee.[3]

So far that summer, Cornell's trip to Berlin had been full of disappointments. She vociferously opposed the IAAF's planned takeover of women's sports.[4] She wanted to focus on keeping the

Women's World Games alive—but suddenly, sports officials couldn't stop talking about sex testing. The attacks on Helen Stephens the previous day underscored just how tangled the relationship between sex and sports had become.

Cornell tended to think the insinuations about masculine women were all a little bit ridiculous. Two years earlier, when the South African coach Bertie C. Sims had claimed that men were participating in the Women's World Games, Cornell had called his bluff.[5] Sims, she told the British press, wasn't even there for the final days of competition. How could he possibly know who was a man? But even she could recognize that this story had, at least among the elite sports executives with whom she spent her time, become too big to ignore. The FSFI needed a policy. Though she had her reservations,[6] she seemed to believe that some form of testing would, at least, assuage the critics of women's sports.

Before the full meeting of the FSFI, a six-member, mixed-gender technical commission met in the lobby of the Russischer Hof.[7] Cornell opened the session. She announced that the FSFI should require all athletes to sit for a medical exam before entering the Women's World Games. She suggested that the FSFI appoint a small team of doctors who could oversee the exams. That way, individual countries couldn't be accused of tampering with the results. Cornell explained that these medical commissions could deal with "doubtful cases" of sex,[8] a term she did not define but that likely served as a coded reference to intersex people. Inside the meeting room, the other members were enthusiastic. After some discussion, they agreed to take it to the main FSFI meeting later that day.

A few conversation topics later, before the close of the technical commission meeting, František Bléha, the delegate from Czechoslovakia and a member of the Czech Amateur Athletic Union, brought up the name on the tip of everyone's tongue: Zdeněk Koubek.[9] As a part of the compromise between Sigfrid Edström and Alice Milliat, the FSFI was going to submit its list of world records to the IAAF, so that the records of the Women's World Games would officially become Olympic records. For the FSFI, Bléha explained, the only remaining question was whether Koubek's record-breaking eight-hundred-meter sprint should be submitted.

Some sports executives had floated the possibility of stripping Koubek of his records, but Bléha argued that Koubek's historic sprint should be kept intact. Bléha knew Koubek personally. He had hosted Koubek at his house in Prague back in 1932, when the young athlete traveled to the city for the first time to compete in the national championships.[10] Though the meeting minutes provide no indication of what Bléha said,[11] his speech must have been compelling. After he finished, the group decided to keep Koubek's world record. Later that week, when the FSFI forwarded its records to the IAAF, Koubek's was included.

By 10:30 a.m., the rest of the FSFI delegates arrived for the full congress. W. B. Marchant, a British sports leader and a close colleague of Milliat's, took charge as the new president.[12] He opened the session with an acknowledgment that Milliat, the group's figurehead and the person who brought women's sports mainstream, was retiring. Marchant read aloud from a letter Milliat had mailed in, expressing her gratitude for the work of the committee. The members unanimously adopted a resolution recognizing her work over the past fifteen years and naming her president of honor.

The meeting that followed betrayed few signs of an organization whose very existence was in peril. The FSFI announced a change of address for its offices in France, settled on Austria as the next host of the Women's World Games, and agreed to extend the deadline for the handful of countries that were behind on their membership dues. When it was time for the technical commission to present its conclusions from the morning, Muriel Cornell's proposal on medical exams came first. A member of the commission read the new rule aloud: "To assure the regularity of the competitions, all national federations are requested to admit to athletic events only athletes with a medical certificate."[13]

The idea enthused Mario Tollini, an Italian official. It was critical, Tollini said, to ensure "only women who are really women can participate in the events." Bléha, who had earlier defended Koubek's right to keep his world records, was less thrilled. He reminded the group that it wasn't so easy to come up with an objective definition of "woman." What happened when intersex women enrolled in the Women's World Games? "According to the opinion expressed by doctors," Bléha said, the topic of sex was "in a state of evolution." It would be "very difficult" for even trained medical authorities to make exact judgments on each athlete's sex. Biological sex, he argued, was too complicated to regulate.

It was a rare admission from a sports leader that sex, as a stable idea, did not exist, and it didn't seem to strike a chord with the other committee members. O. L. Shearer, the representative from South Africa, stepped in with what he perceived as a compromise.[14] What if, instead of testing all athletes, the FSFI examined only the record holders? In the end, the group settled on that approach. It would require anyone who won a world record to produce a medical certificate "regarding the physical state and the sex." The policy was seemingly designed to marginalize intersex athletes. As with the IOC and the IAAF, however, the FSFI did not actually specify this intention, nor did it explain what a disqualifying "physical state" meant.

The policy was entirely symbolic. The FSFI had no real power. At the close of the meeting, the members approved a statement that Genet and Milliat had drafted together in Paris in June: "From August 10, 1936, onward, women's athletics will be governed by the IAAF which will recognize the validity of world records approved by the FSFI."[15] The FSFI voted to kneecap itself. Oddly, though, the group's leadership was still planning to host one final Women's

World Games in 1938.[16] Something must have gotten lost in translation. Milliat knew full well that Edström had no intention of letting that happen.

∘∘∘

August 9 marked the conclusion of the Olympic track-and-field events, which, at least for the American visitors, was the spiritual end of the games.[17] Thousands of American fans left the city. That was probably for good reason: the next set of events was not nearly as kind to the United States. Japan swept the swimming competitions, which the United States had historically dominated.[18] Meanwhile, Germany edged out five of seven gold medals in the rowing competitions, losing only to the Americans in the highly watched men's eight competition.[19]

There was one last event that everyone seemed to tune in to: the women's fencing competition, in which Helene Mayer, one of two athletes of Jewish descent to play for the German team, made her first and only appearance. In the months leading up to the Olympics, Theodor Lewald and Carl Diem had repeatedly touted Mayer's participation as proof that the Olympics were open to all. The question remained whether the Nazis would actually let her on the field.

Tensions were high. The Nazi press was under strict orders not to comment on Mayer's "non-Aryan" background.[20] After a half-hour battle, Mayer won the silver medal,[21] a personal triumph that didn't exactly earn her favor with her government. The Germans who watched her performance were nervous to show too much enthusiasm. According to one report, at the announcement of a silver medal for Germany, the audience broke into fervent applause—then, remembering the high stakes of a public display of support for a Jewish woman, fell silent.[22] Mayer understood the risks of alienating Hitler. With the eyes of the world on her, she gave a Nazi salute.[23]

After the Olympics ended, Mayer, whose citizenship had been

revoked by the Nazis on account of her Jewish heritage, was forced to return to the United States. Months later, she wrote in a letter to a group of friends that she felt conflicted about watching her country descend into fascism: "I know only that I'd like to return to Germany, but that there's no place for me there now."[24]

The spectacle of a half-Jewish woman medaling at the Olympics seemed to satisfy Avery Brundage and Sigfrid Edström, who had long chosen to believe the likes of their friend Karl Ritter von Halt when he told them there would be no discrimination in Berlin. On August 10, the three men, along with the rest of the IAAF, reunited for the full-group meeting of the IAAF.[25] They returned to the House of German Sports, the large, ringed lecture hall located off the new Reich Sports Field. At 10:00 a.m., von Halt greeted the IAAF members with a triumphant speech. The Olympics weren't yet over, but the Nazi official already seemed to be claiming victory. Attendance had been tremendous. The previous Olympics, in Los Angeles, had shattered records by bringing in slightly over one million spectators. The Berlin Olympics boasted triple that.[26] By the end of the games, Germany would have accrued the most medals, in large part because of its strength in the women's competitions. Joseph Goebbels, the propaganda minister, wrote in his diary that Germany was now "the premier sports nation in the world."[27]

When Edström, who had recently recovered from his summer illness, took the floor at the lecture hall in the House of German Sports, he praised the Germans for their work in preparing and hosting the Olympics. "We all feel that the Games have been extremely successful," he said, adding that these were "the largest Olympic Games that have ever taken place."[28]

One of the first agenda items centered on women's sports. Edström read aloud a report written by himself, Karl Ritter von Halt, and Joseph Genet, the members of the IAAF's Committee for Women's Sport.[29] The report called the existence of separate organizations for men's and women's sports, meaning the simultaneous existence of the Women's World Games and the Olympics, "expensive and troublesome" and noted that women's sports "has not the same standing" in the IOC as men's sports. Their goal: cut off the Women's World Games at the root. The authors ticked through Alice Milliat's terms—a full athletic program, approval of the women's world records, and a fifth Women's World Games—but quickly editorialized with their own recommendations. Though the commission was willing to approve the FSFI's world records, "the commission is, however, against the 5th Ladies Worlds Games," Edström read aloud. "The commission wishes that the work of the FSFI finish this year."[30] Edström turned it over to the rest of the members, who quickly fell in line. In a 19–5 vote, the IAAF agreed to approve the FSFI world records—but, following Edström's advice, the members rejected the FSFI's request to host a final Women's World Games in 1938.

It was later in the afternoon that Bo Ekelund, the secretary of the IAAF, put forward Avery Brundage's sex testing proposal.[31] The organization claimed to be discussing "questions of a physical nature," but Ekelund was blunt in his characterization of what the organization was referring to. Here, Ekelund told the gathered members, they would be discussing "cases where women competitors were believed to be men."[32] It was one of the first times that a sports official directly spelled out a motivation for sex testing, rather than couching their intentions in innuendo about masculine women or the "natural order." As before, the logic made little sense: no Olympic athlete had ever posed as a woman to compete, and the ability to pull off such a feat seemed impossibly small, if entirely implausible. But, from the limited meeting minutes that survive today, none of the members of the IAAF appeared to have raised an objection.

Brundage had decided to house the sex testing question under the IAAF's protest rules, which allowed an athlete to lodge a complaint against a competitor shortly after each competition. Protests usually involved an accusation of cheating or unfair refereeing, but

Brundage wanted to expand the definition. If anyone believed they had competed against someone who didn't fit a strict understanding of womanhood, Brundage said, then they should be allowed to lodge a protest under the auspice of fair competition.

Ekelund read aloud the proposed amendment to the IAAF rules:

> If a protest concerns questions of a physical nature, the organization responsible for carrying through the meet shall arrange for a physical inspection made by a medical expert. The athlete must submit to the inspections as well as the decision taken on account thereof.[33]

It left a lot to be desired. As before, the official wording didn't actually outline what these "questions of a physical nature" looked like, or whom the IAAF was trying to screen out. Would an intersex woman necessarily be disqualified? Or a woman who had undergone a gender transition and was competing in her new gender category? At what point would IAAF officials, as the organization's secretary put it, believe that a woman was too much like a man?

In light of Koubek and Weston and the controversy surrounding Helen Stephens, the IAAF wanted to look proactive, but none of the gathered men seemed to have a very deep understanding of biological sex or its inherent variations. They also, as the newest stewards of women's track-and-field sports, knew they had the power to ban whomever they wanted.

In the discussion, no one seemed to point out that Koubek and Weston were both living as men; Weston was retired from sports, and Koubek was publicly expressing his desire to play in the men's category in line with his identity. The IAAF had already whipped itself into a frenzy that fraud had been committed or at least *could* be committed. It seemed, to them, wrong that Koubek and Weston had ever played in women's sports at all.

That sports executives fixated on a pair of trans men who did not even want to continue in women's sports to justify a rule that would later be wielded disproportionately against trans women is one of the many ironies of sex testing's origins and history. Sex testing, from the start, was never about an actual threat to women's sports. It was always about the *perception* of a threat; the ambient sense of panic around femininity, masculinity, and gender transition; the *feeling* that something fundamental was shifting in the relationship between gender and sports and that the only way to stop it was to forcibly examine the bodies of anyone deemed suspect. It was policy rooted not in real harm, but in abstract fear. Who was the IAAF really trying to keep out?

During the back-and-forth, IAAF members focused on only one aspect of the proposal. A delegate wanted to know: How much time should an athlete have to lodge a protest? After some debate, the group agreed that protests must be lodged within two hours of the end of a meet.[34] Then it approved the new rule.

By the close of the two-day session, the IAAF had officially taken over control of women's sports. The members voted to make women's athletics its domain, effectively ending the FSFI. While they did not allow the FSFI to host one final Women's World Games in 1938, they did officially recognize the records from the previous Women's World Games. That included Koubek's record-breaking eight-hundred-meter sprint.

Though no one seemed to make the connection at the time, it was a significant, and ironic, moment. The same day that sex testing was further cemented into sports policy, Zdeněk Koubek was, at the end of the August 11 meeting, officially entered into Olympic history.

○○○

Even Koubek probably didn't realize that he had, in a roundabout way, become an Olympic world-record holder. His mind was elsewhere. He had a Broadway tour to attend to.

On August 5,[35] Koubek boarded the *Île de France* on his way to the United States, clutching a years-old passport that still inaccurately listed his sex as "female." Though they had yet to change his sex marker, Czech officials had hastily scrawled across it, "The bearer is now officially a man."[36] Six days later, on August 11, Koubek arrived in New York, where immigration authorities registered him as "Mr. Z Koubkova."[37] Wearing a gray suit and a blue felt hat, he welcomed a throng of reporters with a handshake that one writer described as "unmistakably masculine."[38] "I always felt like a man," he told the journalists, "so I do not feel at all strange now."[39] *The Brooklyn Daily Eagle* printed a photo of Koubek stepping off the ship under the headline "She Was a Girl, Now He's a Man."[40]

Koubek was there to make his Broadway debut. The producer Clifford C. Fischer was crafting a new variety show for the French Casino,[41] a popular nightclub on Fiftieth Street in Manhattan, and he wanted Koubek to appear in it. The gambit was probably a publicity grab on both sides. Koubek's visit brought a significant amount of press to Fischer's in-development show: even the trade press, including *Variety*, referred to the casting of Koubek as an act of "brief but punchy showmanship."[42]

Koubek's growing celebrity was impossible to ignore. Movie producers in Czechoslovakia were asking him to appear in their films, and Koubek claimed that he was in talks to star in a Hollywood movie based on his life.[43] As soon as Koubek arrived in New York, he was flooded with interview requests from the United Press, a nationally syndicated wire service, and the British news agency the Central Press. The flurry of coverage brought extra attention to the Broadway show. The journalist Harry Levin noted with approval that Koubek was "very handsome either as a male or female."[44] Throughout his stay in New York, Koubek carted along his manager, a man variously identified in press reports as William Taussig and Hermann Taussig. Because Koubek spoke limited English, when he sat for newspaper interviews, Taussig acted as his interpreter.

In between sightseeing trips up and down Manhattan, Koubek posed for American photographers. One paparazzo snapped a photo of him in his New York hotel room, shaving his face.[45] The photojournalist seemed awed that Koubek could grow facial hair. During dress rehearsals, newspapers highlighted Koubek's skill at styling his female castmates. After watching Koubek brush one female castmate's hair, a reporter marveled, "He knows all about coiffures from experience, since they were of concern to him when he was the foremost girl athlete of Czechoslovakia."[46]

The story that Koubek told American reporters about his gender "transformation," as it was often nicknamed, was simple, if a little fantastical: he'd spent his life believing he was a woman. Then, in recent years, more masculine physical traits had begun popping up.[47] He started to grow a beard; his voice deepened; his muscles grew very large, very fast. Koubek explained that his "soul" was "always more for being a man,"[48] implying that his psychological experience of gender had inspired his transition. But without a widespread understanding of gender as a psychological reality, Koubek was limited in how he could describe the actual process. Instead, he needed to convince the public that his physical body had changed miraculously before his eyes.

Some observers might've seen a gender "transformation" as a challenge to the norms of American society, but Koubek was quick to position himself as a part of the traditional heterosexual world. The spark for consulting a doctor, he told reporters, was when he met the love of his life, a law student at the University of Prague[49]— a woman he never identified by name. He realized he could be with her only if he transitioned: "It was all because of her that I decided to have the operations. 'How can two girls marry?' she asked me. And so I consulted the surgeon, who promised me that everything would be all right."

Koubek planned to marry her once his identity documents were changed, he said, flashing an engagement ring on his finger. "I am looking forward with much eagerness to a happy marriage and becoming the father of a healthy and large family," he said. He also expressed little sympathy for homosexuality. When asked what he would have done if, prior to his transition, a man had asked to make love to him, Koubek replied, "I would have flattened him with a punch."[50] Koubek seemed happy in the United States, where he was, at least for one month, treated as a celebrity. He insisted that he wanted to come back in a few years and live there permanently with his wife, though much of his future remained up in the air.[51] He needed more surgical operations. Anyway, now that he was seen as a man, he might be asked to serve in the Czech army.[52]

The *Folies d'Amour*, the cabaret show in which Koubek was planning to perform, opened on August 25. Hundreds of people shelled out the $2.50 admission fee[53]—around $55 today—and piled into the French Casino, a massive Art Deco venue in which the city's most glamorous people, including a number of celebrities, sipped cocktails and ate filet mignon in front of a stage.[54] By all accounts, the turnout was significant. According to the *New York Daily News*, audiences were eager to "give up money for a view of a guy who used to be a gal."[55]

The *Folies* contained a disjointed series of skits, many of which had a circus-like flair for the dramatic and sometimes the exploitative.[56] At one point, a trapeze artist dangled forty feet above the crowd, held in place, reportedly, by only a strand of hair. A double-jointed performer tied herself in "bowknots." A seal, which had been trained to dance, made a brief appearance on the stage. Koubek opened the second act, right after the intermission. When the curtains were pulled aside, they revealed the athlete dressed in what would become his signature outfit: tennis shoes, white shorts, and a white sleeveless top that showed off his biceps.[57] His blond hair was slicked back, and he looked into the crowd with bright blue eyes.

Yet if the guests expected a grand performance from Koubek, they might have been disappointed. Onstage, Koubek sprinted on a treadmill, which was hooked to a timing device. The concept, according to reports, was that Koubek "runs against time."[58] In a cabaret show that included knife throwers, trapeze artists, and gyrating seals, Koubek's skit might have seemed out of place, far tamer than, say, a dangling gymnast. But the truth was that Koubek himself was the spectacle. The mere fact of his gender transition was so extraordinary, so radical, that it captivated "Gotham's wonder loving cabaret diners,"[59] according to one news service, for whom just laying eyes on Koubek was delight enough.

○○○

On August 11, the day of Koubek's arrival in New York and of his acceptance into the Olympic record books, the American public received another shock: Mark Weston, the British athlete who had transitioned that spring, was now married.[60] Alberta Bray, Weston's childhood friend, had agreed to tie the knot, and the Plymouth clerk's office had dutifully issued a marriage license.

From the outside, the two must have looked like the picture of heterosexuality. The wedding ceremony had actually happened more than a month earlier, on July 8, but Weston, ever leery of the press, made no effort to publicize it. The *Daily Mirror* discovered the marriage only during an interview with Weston in August. Weston said that in Bray he'd found "a girl in a million." Though he noted that she'd been his "helpmate" since 1928,[61] he was careful not to allude to any sexual or romantic feelings that either of them might have felt prior to his operation. The prospect that the two might have been intimate at a time when they were both outwardly perceived as women could have damaged the tacit acceptance that Weston had found in Plymouth. Bray, he said, had been his confidante in all matters relating to his sex. Over time, "our friendship as girls together changed to a deeper feeling when I found myself a man," he told the *Mirror*. Meanwhile, when the *Mirror* spoke to Bray, whom it described as a "shy blonde," she said cryptically, "Mark had always been the one to whom I turned for help long before he became a man."[62]

A day later, a reporter for the *Western Morning News* showed up at Weston's house and found the former athlete painting the front door.[63] Weston told the reporter that he was thrilled to be married. Even more exciting, he said, was to see his name listed as a husband—a formal recognition that he was a man.[64]

Even though they were in the news concurrently, neither Weston nor Koubek ever seemed to address the topic of the Berlin Olympics—or, for that matter, each other. They were both taking breaks from their athletic careers, and Nazi-controlled Berlin wasn't a safe place for them to visit as spectators. The German crackdown on queer people had intensified in recent years; Koubek and Weston were too visible for authorities to ignore.

In its report on Weston's nuptials, the *Western Morning News* did manage to pose one sports-related question. What, the reporter asked, did Weston think of the decision by the IAAF to institute a sex testing policy at the Olympics? Surprisingly, Weston did not seem put off by the decision. He replied that he "heartily agreed" that women in international sports "should undergo medical inspection to ascertain their sex."[65] It was an intriguing perspective that Weston did not elaborate on any further in subsequent interviews. Perhaps it stemmed from some deeply held belief; perhaps he simply thought that agreeing with the policy would be the easiest way to get the press to leave him alone.

000

In the days after the Olympics drew to a close, the IAAF's decision to formalize a system of sex testing received a blitz of press attention.[66] When the meeting minutes were made public, reporters balked. They noted that the paragraph on sex tests was "gingerly worded,"[67] a fact that they attributed to the IAAF's tentativeness around governing women's sports in general.

Some athletes and experts complained about the inhumanity of the new rule. Ted Meredith, the American sprinter, had been coaching Czechoslovakia's track-and-field team since 1935. In that capacity, he had gotten to know Koubek personally and understood the young athlete's situation well. Meredith wasn't happy about the fact that the IAAF and IOC were now in the business of regulating sex. "When the situation reaches a point where it is necessary to subject athletes to an examination to prove whether they sing bass or soprano, the subject becomes not only ridiculous but nauseous," Meredith told a sports reporter on August 12.[68] It was a rare, unvarnished takedown of sex testing as a policy. Meredith wasn't just critiquing *how* the IAAF was going about regulating sex—he was taking them to task for doing it at all.

Other sports leaders were tired of discussing the issue. In November, a few months after the Olympics, the German track-and-field magazine *Der Leichtathlet* published an interview with Heinrich Voss, the IAAF delegate who also wrote a defense of women's sports that summer. When the magazine brought up Koubek and Weston, Voss seemed annoyed. He couldn't believe that he was still fielding questions about the two athletes. Voss emphasized that the press had given the question of intersex athletes, whom he called "hermaphrodites," "exaggerated importance." *Der Leichtathlet* did not include exact quotes from Voss, instead paraphrasing his comments. Though "it is often claimed that even today some who take part in women's competitions are actually men," the magazine wrote, Voss rejected those ideas outright. He had no reason to think any individual country had been cheating, or that any would try to in the future. "One must not forget that these cases are regrettable exceptions," not worthy of excessive attention, Voss concluded.

Yet for as much as Voss attempted to quell the brewing—and, for the Nazis, politically useful—panic among sports leaders around these athletes, he was firm in his condemnations of Koubek and Weston. According to the magazine, Voss emphasized that "women stand at a competitive disadvantage toward the hermaphrodites." Ultimately, these athletes should be "eliminated so that women's sport can be protected." To get there, he said, medical exams could be expanded to look for biological "irregularities" in women athletes.[69] It was perhaps the most evenhanded perspective that Voss could get away with in a sports magazine run by the Nazi Party— but it further entrenched the unfounded and damaging trope that intersex athletes had inherent athletic advantages over their peers.

It was telling that the IAAF was the only athletic federation to institute sex testing policies following the Berlin Olympics. The IOC had kicked the question back to the individual federations, yet only the track-and-field body—not the swimming federation, not the fencers—was moved to craft a policy. The reason that the IAAF was out in front on sex testing probably stems from the individual anxieties of its leaders, like Brundage and Edström, and perhaps from the fact that both Weston and Koubek were track-and-field athletes. But the IAAF's singular urgency on the issue of sex testing also has deeper roots.

From the start of the Olympics, panic about masculine women always focused on track-and-field sports. In the context of the Olympics, track and field attracted the highest shares of working-class women and women of color, who were deemed less feminine than their rich, white counterparts. Gender surveillance, in other words, felt most imperative in track and field because of the demographic composition of its athletes. Understanding these class dimensions betrays some hint of what the IAAF might have meant when it stated its intention to exclude "abnormal" women from sports, by way of sex testing.

Brundage was too victorious to pay much attention to the response to the IAAF's new policies. When he landed in New York at the end of August, his mood was celebratory: he'd successfully rebuffed efforts to boycott one of the most consequential Olympics in history, and he'd been made the newest member of the IOC. The Berlin Olympics, he told anyone who would listen, were "the most magnificent ever held" and "sports leaders are indebted to the German people" for hosting it.[70]

That didn't mean Brundage was feeling especially generous toward his skeptics. After one Jewish-American athlete criticized the American Olympic Committee for ignoring the racism of the Nazis, Brundage privately told colleagues that he wanted the athlete expelled from sports.[71] Later, when a reporter asked Brundage for his thoughts on the state of women's sports, Brundage couldn't help but dish out criticisms. "I am fed up to the ears with women as track and field competitors," he said following the Olympics. When a woman was running on a track, "her charms sink to something less than zero."[72]

It was a demeaning comment from a man who, as a top executive of the IAAF, would now have an outsize say over the governance of women's sports. It rubbed many former members of Alice Milliat's FSFI the wrong way. "Women's athletics have only been recognized by men during recent years, and it seems a pity that control should follow almost immediately upon recognition," Muriel Cornell, the FSFI member who traveled to Berlin, said in August, in the days following the collapse of the organization.[73] She sounded resigned to the inevitable: that, despite all the work they had put in, the IAAF almost certainly would not make space for her or other FSFI delegates on its committee. Instead, men like Brundage were going to govern women's sports. In keeping with the sentiment, the *Daily Mirror* lamented, "Women athletes all over the world will be under the thumb of men from now on."[74]

On August 20, Helen Stephens finally left Berlin. She took a plane from Germany to France, where she and hundreds of her teammates boarded the SS *Roosevelt* back to New York. Though Stephens hoped the victory celebrations would take her mind off the rumors of her masculinity, the accusations continued to dog her.[75] On August 28, before docking in New York, American officials "inspected" Stephens "with little difficulty," she wrote in her diary.[76] It wasn't exactly clear whether this inspection had targeted her. At a dinner three days later, a reporter asked her about her biological sex, but her coach, Dee Boeckmann, intervened.[77] Next, Stephens took a meeting at the offices of the Amateur Athletic Union, where Boeckmann assured the US sports officials that, as Stephens's biographer put it, "there wasn't a shred of truth" to the rumors that Stephens was a man. The exam she had taken after leaving the ship, Boeckmann said, would ease those concerns. But Stephens feared the damage was already done. She was terrified that the accusations, even if they'd been discredited, would ruin her budding romance with a girl she'd met in Fulton, Missouri, or that they would impact her social life that fall, when she was planning to enroll in college.

Stephens had one moment of true escape. On the night of September 3, at the request of the mayor's office, nearly all members of the US Olympic team showed up at the French Casino to attend a performance of the *Folies d'Amour*.[78] At intermission, members of the American team—which included Stephens and Jesse Owens—reportedly met Koubek.[79] It was a full-circle moment, whether or not either Koubek or Stephens acknowledged it at the time. In the history of the Olympics up until that point, no two people had received more scrutiny for their gender. And now there they were, face-to-face.

○○○

Koubek didn't stay in New York for long. In late October, he boarded the liner *Lafayette*, bound for France. Some newspapers claimed that he cried on the deck, allegedly upon finding out that he needed more surgery to complete his gender transition.[80] On October 31, Koubek docked in Plymouth, England,[81] the town where Mark Weston was living. British reporters interrupted Koubek at a dinner to interview him. Koubek's manager fielded their questions. When a journalist brought up the fact that Weston had a house nearby, the manager said that he knew of Weston's story. The manager even claimed to have met Weston a few years earlier, but there's no record that Koubek and Weston themselves ever met.

A day later, Koubek arrived in Le Havre before traveling on to Paris.[82] He performed in the music hall Folies-Bergère alongside the world-renowned dancer Josephine Baker and partook in track-and-field exercises onstage.[83] The two were top-billed together.[84] French newspapers carried a photo of Koubek bending over to kiss Baker's outstretched hand. One Canadian woman who attended the show remembered Koubek signing autographs at intermission in running shoes, shorts, and a sleeveless top, his manager at his side.[85] But Koubek's stint in Paris lasted only a week.[86] Soon, he was on his way back home to Prague, where he'd never been more famous.

Koubek didn't disclose how much he was paid for his performances in New York and Paris, but he said in a subsequent interview that he made more in a month in America than he would have in half a year in Europe.[87] It was enough to furnish his new apartment in Prague and still have savings left over. In early 1937, soon after his return home, Koubek wrote to thank the French Casino for hosting him and expressed his love for New York: "In all my 24 years—man and girl—I've never seen anything like it."[88]

Part IV

AFTER BERLIN

CHAPTER 18

WILLY DE BRUYN WASN'T HOME when a pair of journalists from *De Dag* showed up on his parents' doorstep in the village of Erembodegem, Belgium, but his mother was.[1]

It was sometime in the early months of 1937. The journalists had just found out that de Bruyn, the Belgian cyclist, was in the process of transitioning gender, and they were eager to speak to "the Flemish Koubek," as they later called him. De Bruyn's mother didn't like the idea. She didn't trust these journalists from Brussels, and she worried that bringing extra publicity to her son's gender transition might only make his new life harder. She agreed, however, to have them back when de Bruyn returned, just as long as they promised to keep the story to themselves until de Bruyn received formal recognition as a man from the Belgian government.

On April 24, 1937, *De Dag* published a personal essay from de Bruyn, mapping out both his sports career and his early relationship to his gender. It was titled "A New Life: How I Changed from a Woman into a Man." The journalists claimed they were looking for more than just lurid sensationalism. But in their introduction, the authors framed de Bruyn as an object of pity, writing that his essay would show the reader "the extent of anguish" that he battled. He "suffered in silence," *De Dag* wrote, but "after so much uncertainty and fear, he is owed this space" to tell his own story.

When they first received the tip about de Bruyn's transition, the reporters were skeptical, "not because we did not believe in the possibility of female-to-male transformations," they said, "but rather because of the delicate nature of the task ahead: to convey to the public the things we learned about this case." *De Dag* noted that de Bruyn's story might sound a lot like Koubek's and Weston's. In fact, all three had given rise to a new myth—that athletes were uniquely primed to transition gender: "Curiously, almost all confirmed cases have been associated with the world of sports."

Koubek, Weston, and de Bruyn were not alone. A few days before de Bruyn's article hit newsstands, another European athlete also came forward about his own transition.[2] That athlete was Witold Smętek, a javelin thrower assigned female at birth who earned national recognition in Poland in 1932, when he won the country's premier javelin-throwing contest at the age of twenty-one in the women's category. He continued to enter a variety of track-and-field competitions after: he finished fourth in a cross-country championship in 1934 and placed highly in a series of handball tournaments.

When Smętek moved from Lodz to Warsaw in 1935, his life changed. There, he began meeting with a surgeon named Henryk Beck, who worked at a gynecology clinic not far from where Smętek's team practiced. At some point, Beck and Smętek agreed that Smętek should begin living as a man. On April 21, 1937, Smętek checked into the Hospital of the Infant Jesus in Warsaw for the first of two surgeries. Smętek, who was an observant Catholic, stopped by a church and received communion. The next day, the Polish press broke the news that Smętek was a man. "I'm happy the operation is behind me and that I can finally start my new life," Smętek told a reporter from his hospital bed, wiping a tear from his eye. "I am very happy to be a boy now and I no longer need to hide my secret from anyone."[3]

Smętek was exhausted, still dealing with the aftereffects of the anesthesia, but he managed to field a series of questions before a nurse ushered out the journalist. He said he chose his new name in honor of a caretaker he had as a child. When asked about his future, he made clear that he didn't plan to stop playing sports. "I'm not getting out of sports, because I love it so much," he said. He wanted to stay at his sports club in Warsaw, this time joining the men's team. He also applied for new identity documents; months later, on September 30, the Polish state would issue him a new birth certificate with little pushback.[4]

After the news broke, people wrote letters to Smętek in the hospital, asking for autographs or, in some cases, professing their love.[5] *Newsweek* declared him "the latest sex switcher" and told readers that he was going to continue to play competitive sports even after his transition. "I can throw the javelin better than any man in Poland, and almost as well as any man in the world," Smętek told *Newsweek* in the lead-up to his surgery. "The doctor said he can change my sex with an operation, and I am ready for his knife."[6]

Reporters, unable to wrap their heads around the fact that now four different athletes had transitioned, sought out explanations. Several doctors clarified to one newspaper that "although such cases" of gender transition "have occurred chiefly among sportswomen, it was no proof that they were due to the influence of sport."[7] There was probably a simple explanation, however, one that few people at the time could articulate. Perhaps sports weren't some special hub of trans or intersex people—it was just that these athletes were watching others like them transition publicly and realizing they no longer had to hide. Perhaps, from across the European continent, the four of them had inspired one another.

Smętek soon cited Koubek as an idol of his. The French newspaper *Paris-soir* reported in April 1937 that Smętek was planning to befriend Koubek and maybe even compete against him in a friendly sports match. The possibility of a collision between two athletes who had transitioned gender seemed to tickle *Paris-soir.* "One wonders if these two athletes," the newspaper wrote, "are not going to join together in an association which will defend the rights and the prerogatives of women-athletes who have become men."[8]

ooo

While the Polish state hastily approved Witold Smętek's petition to change his name and sex on his documents, not every athlete was so lucky. Throughout the latter half of 1936 and into the first months of 1937, Koubek's application to change his identity documents bounced around Czech bureaucracy. Representatives from the Ministry of the Interior, the Ministry of Public Health, the Ministry of Justice, and more fired off letters debating what, exactly, they thought separated "man" and "woman" as distinctive identity categories.

These bureaucrats couldn't decide what traits should define Koubek's sex. The Czech Ministry of Health, for instance, conducted an extensive—and invasive—nude evaluation of Koubek, which it ultimately deemed inconclusive. Koubek's "development did not go unidirectionally in terms of a single sex," the ministry wrote on February 12, 1937. The Ministry of Health decided to take into account Koubek's own psychological sense of himself. His "subjective feeling also corresponds to" an identity as a man, a representative from the agency wrote.[9]

The Ministry of Health ultimately concluded that Koubek's identity documents should be changed. "Since it is presently possible to find in the examined individual many more male characteristics," including in "mental terms," the ministry wrote that "there is no objection from the perspective of medical science for [him] to be registered as a man." Adding texture to its decision was the fact that, if Koubek's identity documents were not changed, he could be prosecuted for homosexuality. Koubek was largely attracted to women, and changing his sex marker to male could "safeguard this person from prosecution in the case of following the male sexual drive," the ministry wrote. An arrest "remains a possibility until she is declared a man."

A second government agency, the Ministry of Justice, also made a small plea in Koubek's favor.[10] It noted that assigned sex at birth "can hardly be considered definitive and absolutely reliable," largely because, the ministry believed, biological sex could change throughout a person's life. "The claim that a once-recorded entry in the birth register about the sex of a child should in such an abnormal case be decisive for the entire duration of such a person's life, seems to us to be too formalistic." In other words, the Ministry of Justice supposed that Czech citizens should have some ability to change their sex markers later in life.

Ultimately, however, the deciding agency, the Ministry of the Interior, opted to reject Koubek's appeal. On May 20, 1937, Koubek received the news that his application had not been approved. The decision was puzzling, given how publicly he had transitioned gender, and Koubek likely found little comfort in the fact that it rested on a technicality. Citing a law from 1844, the Ministry of the Interior informed Koubek that Czech authorities were permitted to amend a birth certificate only if they could prove that there had been a mistake on the original document. Koubek's birth certificate, the bureaucrats said, had been correct at his birth; he did, after all, go on to live as a woman for many years. Because there was no original error, they couldn't rewrite it. "Neither the submitted medical certificates nor the official medical examination showed that the entry in the birth register was incorrect," the Ministry of the Interior informed him.[11] The requirement that the birth certificate contain an error in order for it to be amended made little sense, and it showed just how unprepared bureaucratic systems were for any complication surrounding gender. Koubek was a man—wasn't that proof enough of a mistake?

Hastening the ministry's decision to reject Koubek's application might have been the rising tide of fascism that was seeping into Czechoslovakia, thanks largely to the influence of the Nazis. In 1937, a prominent Nazi newspaper called homosexuals "enemies of the state,"[12] a sentiment that pro-German newspapers in Czechoslovakia were quick to echo. When a moderate leader of Czechoslovakia's Nazi-sympathetic Sudeten German Party (formerly the Sudeten German Home Front) was arrested for homosexuality that summer, far-right members of the party used the news to discredit the party's centrists. One party member suggested that homosexuals should be shot. Another compared homosexuality to a social disease, a "contamination" from which it needed to protect "fellow German citizens" in Czechoslovakia.[13] The Czech left, meanwhile, seized on the stain of homosexuality in a right-wing party as proof that the entire Sudeten German Party reeked of "moral foulness." On both sides of the aisle, scapegoating homosexuals became a convenient way of scoring political points.

Despite not identifying as homosexual, Koubek was not exempt from those threats, and neither were his genderqueer contemporaries. By the end of the 1930s, famed Czech erotic artists like Toyen were going underground. Once the Nazis began encroaching into Czechoslovakia, starting with the annexation of the Sudetenland in 1938 and followed by Hitler's occupation of the entire country in March 1939, Toyen published their work only in private publications.[14]

During World War II, Koubek disappeared from public life. In February 1938, even though his birth certificate remained unamended, he managed to receive a driver's license that identified him as a man.[15] The new license may well have rescued him from

Nazi violence. In 1940, as the Nazis were actively sending queer and trans people to the death camps, Koubek married a woman named Uršulou Škrobačovou. They lived together in Prague, where Koubek worked at the Czech automobile manufacturer Škoda.[16] The couple must have looked like any other: an example of normative, white, non-Jewish heterosexuality. During years of repression in Nazi-occupied Czechoslovakia, the ability to pass probably saved Koubek's life.

CHAPTER 19

A YEAR AFTER the close of the Olympics, the Nazis started to clean house. In 1937, Hans von Tschammer, the Nazi sports czar, pressured Theodor Lewald, who had done so much to make the Nazis' treasured Olympics a success, to resign from the IOC. The Nazis couldn't tolerate a representative of Jewish descent any longer. In his place they installed a military general and former athlete, Walther von Reichenau, who in just two years would lead the Nazi invasions of Poland, Belgium, and France.[1]

If the IOC members were alarmed by the ousting of Lewald, they didn't show it. In 1938, the increasingly isolationist Japanese government denounced the IOC and withdrew as host to the 1940 Olympics. The last-minute shakeup left the IOC reeling, and they found a replacement host, once again, in Adolf Hitler. That June, the IOC chose Garmisch-Partenkirchen, the German city that had hosted the little-noticed Winter Games in 1936, as the next host of the Olympics.[2] Despite their rapidly accelerating violence and brutality, the Nazis were on track to become Olympic hosts for a second time.

Some IOC members, like Avery Brundage, remained defiant in their sympathy for the German government. In 1938, the Nazi-affiliated director Leni Riefenstahl finished *Olympia*, her documentary of the 1936 Olympics, which Brundage ardently supported. The film was blatant propaganda for the Nazis, meant to lionize German athletic achievements for the world. To Brundage's mind, though, it was proof of the glory of the Berlin Olympics, "an artistic masterpiece" whose reception in the United States was in peril because "the Jews, who own all the picture theaters in America, will understandably prevent its being shown here."[3] By November, Riefenstahl traveled to New York to screen the film. A few days after arriving, news of the Kristallnacht massacre reached the United States. Riefenstahl, a steadfast supporter of Hitler, dismissed it as mere "slander" of the Nazi Party.[4] Unperturbed by these comments, Brundage told Riefenstahl to screen her film in Chicago instead. He let her stay at his home, and he gathered together a group of thirty-five people for a private viewing. Brundage then convinced his IOC colleague William May Garland to organize a similar screening of the controversial film in Los Angeles.[5]

Once the Berlin Olympics ended, Carl Diem, that original architect of Berlin's Olympic ambitions, also saw his political fortunes enter a state of limbo. Out of power, Diem managed to become head of the International Olympic Institute in 1938, a mostly inconsequential Berlin-based research organization that was only tacitly associated with the IOC. Diem began grasping for relevance.[6] As war approached, he ignored the escalating crimes of the Nazis in order to advance his political and sporting careers; he became increasingly strident in his conviction that Nazi Germany was now the center of world sports. He declared that "the reorientation of European sport has its geographical and spiritual center in

Germany" and followed that up with his expectation that Germany would become "the crossroads of world sport."[7] In some ways, it was what he'd always wanted. Since he had first begun planning the 1916 Olympics, he had dreamed of turning his country into an athletic superpower. Somewhere along the way, he stopped caring about the blood that his country was shedding.

○○○

Despite the Nazis' best efforts at suppressing the German queer community, their leadership soon had to contend with a gender quandary of their own: in the lead-up to World War II, a top German athlete was outed for transgressing gender lines.

Heinrich "Heinz" Ratjen was born on November 20, 1918, near the city of Bremen, Germany.[8] His father owned a local hotel.[9] He was assigned female at birth, but growing up, he began to question his gender. "I was already beginning to be aware that I was not a girl, but a man," Ratjen said later. "But I never asked my parents why, if I was a man, I had to wear women's clothes."[10]

He first drew the attention of sports leaders in June 1934, when, at age fifteen, he defeated a gold medalist in the high jump in his home city. The Nazis quickly scouted him for their Olympic team. At the national trials in early 1936, Ratjen shared a room with Gretel Bergmann, the Jewish track-and-field athlete who was ultimately barred from the Berlin Olympics. Bergmann thought he was odd. Ratjen had a deep voice, and he never entered the communal showers. "I knew something was weird, but for a Jew to say something about an Aryan, forget it," Bergmann recalled later.[11] Other competitors made fun of Ratjen behind his back. One fellow athlete pointed out that he shaved,[12] although surely they knew that wasn't uncommon: plenty of women waxed and shaved. "No one knew or noticed anything about her different sexuality," a German high jumper said later.[13]

For Ratjen, coming of age under a Nazi regime that persecuted queer people, including people who didn't conform to its strict gender conventions, must have been terrifying. He didn't dare share his secret. At the Berlin Olympics, Ratjen was not a top-place competitor, tying for sixth in the high jump, which helped him to escape the scrutiny that the American sprinter Helen Stephens and other gold medalists battled. He continued to play sports, and in September 1938, Ratjen set a new world record, scoring 1.7 meters in the high jump at the European Championships in Vienna.[14]

It all began to collapse on the train ride home from Vienna. When a ticket inspector saw Ratjen, dressed in a gray two-piece suit, during a train stop in Magdeburg, Germany, the inspector asked a pair of Nazi soldiers to pull him aside.[15] They believed him to be a cis man who was dressing up as a woman in order to cross the border—potentially a British or French spy. Ratjen offered up his identity card from the European Championships, but the police didn't believe him. They noticed he had hair on his hands and seized on that fact as proof that he was in disguise. They arrested him and brought him to the police station, where they took his mug shot and put him through an invasive medical exam. A police doctor wrote after examining Ratjen that "this person is indisputably to be regarded as a man."[16] Ratjen, who had a mix of biological traits traditionally associated with both male and female sex, did seem to want to embrace his masculine side, telling police that he was "happy" now that "everything is out in the open." But the pressure the Nazis put on him must have been immense. There wasn't room to say no to the brownshirts even if he had wanted to.

In September 1938, directly because of his arrest, the German Amateur Athletic Union quietly banned Ratjen from women's sports. The Germans also contacted the IAAF and applied to have Ratjen's name erased from their records.[17] Fearing embarrassment from the revelation, they allowed only one article about Ratjen's status to appear, in the sports magazine *Der Leichtathlet*. "As a

result of a medical examination," *Der Leichtathlet* wrote cryptically, "it has been established that [Heinz] Ratjen cannot be admitted to female competitions."[18] Though the paper never explicitly
said that Ratjen was intersex, or that he had chosen to live as a man,
anyone who had been following sporting news over the past three
years would have been able to read between the lines. On October 12, the Reich Propaganda Ministry demanded that "nothing further" be published about Ratjen. The press obeyed. A high-ranking
Nazi SS officer, Reinhard Heydrich, expressed his gratitude that
"the Ratjen case has not led to undesirable discussions in the public
sphere or even to conflicts in international sport."[19]

Ratjen's nightmare didn't end there. At the end of 1938, prose-
cutors began investigating him for fraud, accusing him of intentionally misleading the public. But on March 10, 1939, the charges were
dropped. "Fraud cannot be deemed to have taken place because
there was no intention to reap financial reward," a senior prosecu-
tor explained in internal memos.[20] Ratjen took the name Heinz—
short for his father's name, Heinrich—and received new government
documents identifying him as a man. In exchange, officials offered
him membership in the German Labor Front, the Nazi state's amal-
gamated trade union, allowing him to work and live freely. That the
Nazis had validated Ratjen's own desire to live as a man probably
did not occur to these officials; certifying him as a man perhaps
seemed like the easiest way to sweep the entire controversy under
the rug. In this one case, it seemed, it was politically expedient to
acknowledge that sex and gender *were* in fact quite porous, and
someone assigned female at birth might be able to live a full life as
a man. Whatever the case, Ratjen knew not to discuss it: for the
next two decades, he lived under the radar.

Ratjen's ordeal didn't become a major news story, but it quietly
shaped IAAF policy. The Nazis didn't want a repeat, and they used
their influence over international sports to continue to crack down
on athletes who didn't fit normative gender standards. On Novem-

ber 21, 1938, just a month after Ratjen's arrest, Karl Ritter von Halt—the close friend of Avery Brundage and Sigfrid Edström who was rising in the ranks of the Nazi Party—suggested that the IAAF amend its sex testing rules once again. Rather than physically examine only the athletes against whom a competitor lodged a protest, as the IAAF had decided at the Berlin Olympics, he thought that all "ladies taking part in the Games 1940 shall produce doctors' certificates stating that they are <u>women</u>."[21]

Von Halt's sudden concern for women's sports was certainly hypocritical; he once said that "competing disfigures the female face" and "is not female in nature."[22] But the risk of embarrassment to the Nazis from the Ratjen news forced his hand. In a letter to the IAAF on February 16, 1939, Avery Brundage voiced his support, saying, "I am in favor of Karl von Halt's suggestion that all female competitors be required to obtain doctor's certificates."[23]

A blanket sex testing requirement, in which all female competitors had to sit for an invasive medical exam, was on the slate for the 1940 Olympics. Only war, it turned out, could get in its way. At the end of 1939, Hitler invaded Poland. War in Europe eliminated the possibility that the Olympic Games could be held in 1940, no matter how hard true believers like Brundage tried to fight it. In October 1939, Hitler called off the Winter Olympics, which his country had been planning to host.[24] Brundage was crushed. A staunch detractor of American president Franklin Delano Roosevelt, he at first seemed to feel sympathy for the Nazis. He complained that FDR was too close to France and England,[25] and he joined the America First cause, the isolationist and often antisemitic movement that attempted to keep the United States out of World War II. Entering the war, Brundage said in a speech in August 1940, was "stupid, dishonest and criminal politics."[26] In a letter to IOC president Henri de Baillet-Latour, he lamented the "propaganda" and "misinformation" that was turning the "gullible" American public toward battle.[27]

While pushing back against the war, Brundage began organizing an alternative Olympic Games, which he hoped could be held in the Americas instead of war-torn Europe. Only on December 3, 1941, four days before the attack on Pearl Harbor, did Brundage finally give up on trying to rescue the Olympics. The world war, he concluded, was not going to end soon. "The Olympic flame is temporarily extinguished," he told an NBC radio reporter.[28]

World War II swallowed up the discussions of sex testing that von Halt had helped to bring to the forefront of the IAAF. But his proposal had long-lasting impacts. After World War II, when international sports resumed, the policy requiring all women to obtain medical exams from doctors was firmly in place at the IAAF. It didn't matter that some of the regulations' most vocal supporters, like von Halt and the sports doctor Wilhelm Knoll, were Nazis. Sex testing had already become part of the fabric of track-and-field sports. And even though officials and the media quickly forgot the context in which they were introduced, these policies would continue to haunt athletes, and civil rights, for decades.

O N JULY 1, 1941, a white, twenty-nine-year-old interior decorator petitioned a Los Angeles court to change her name to Barbara Ann Richards.[1] Richards, who had been assigned male at birth, was still registered with a traditionally masculine name she no longer claimed as her own. Richards was trans, but she had a clever way of explaining her gender to the court. She had "always lived and worked as a man until about two years ago," she told the court, at which point, she said, "I realized that some vital physiological change was taking place." She had, she said, undergone a physical metamorphosis. Without warning, her beard—which she used to shave twice a day—stopped growing. Her voice changed pitch. "I began to observe that my skin had become smoother, that the shape of my face was different, my waist was smaller, my hips heavier, my throat smaller," she said.

Her petition became a blockbuster news story, especially when, in October 1941, a Los Angeles judge agreed to recognize Richards as a woman. Headlines like "Court Rules 'Man' Who Changed Sex

Is Now a Woman" blanketed American newspapers, interspersed between dispatches from the European war. By then, the press mostly seemed to have forgotten about Koubek and Weston, but a few made the connection. On July 19, the newsmagazine *Pathfinder* published an article on Richards, pointing out that her story sounded a lot like what happened with Koubek and Weston a few years prior. While those two athletes had transitioned as men, "a case of the reverse has been occupying the attention of a Los Angeles court," the magazine said, referring to Richards.[2]

By the 1950s, gender transitions were once again front-page news across the United States. In 1952, tabloids throughout the country covered the story of Christine Jorgensen, an American ex-soldier who had opted to undergo a gender-affirmation surgery months earlier. Jorgensen helped to bring a rudimentary understanding of trans identity into the public consciousness. While Jorgensen, who was white and blond, was undoubtedly the biggest trans celebrity of the 1950s, other trans women received a blitz of press coverage in the postwar years, too. As the historian C. Riley Snorton has documented, stories of Black trans women abounded in the years directly following World War II. In 1945, *Time* published an extensive story on Lucy Hicks Anderson,[3] a Black woman who worked as a brothel owner and who hosted elaborate parties for many of California's elite families. In 1951, *Ebony* wrote about another woman, Georgia Black, under the headline "The Man Who Lived 30 Years as a Woman." *Jet* began episodically covering the life of a third Black trans woman, Carlett Brown, starting in June 1953.[4]

The stories of Jorgensen and Hicks Anderson popularized the notion of gender transition for a new generation, just as Koubek had done fifteen years prior. Yet it wasn't an increased awareness of trans identity that led the IAAF and the IOC each to ramp up its sex testing procedures at the end the 1950s. Instead, a seemingly unrelated geopolitical reality was turning sex testing—once a perfunctory rule

that Avery Brundage had pushed to add to the IAAF handbook—
into a top concern of world sports officials.

○○○

By time the dust settled on World War II, the IOC emerged with a
new leader. Henri de Baillet-Latour had died unexpectedly in January 1942, putting the IAAF leader Sigfrid Edström in line to suc-
ceed him as president. When the IOC met for the first time after
the war, on September 4, 1946, Edström officially assumed the
presidency. Avery Brundage received the title of vice president of
the IOC.[5]

At that meeting, Edström highlighted his postwar agenda. "The
great problem will be the question of Russia," Edström told the
members.[6] The United States and Russia exited World War II as
the indisputable global superpowers, yet Russia was not a member
of the IOC or the IAAF. Edström felt the omission of Russia had
become glaring, and in his position as president of the IOC, he began making overtures to the USSR.

He had his work cut out for him. The USSR had long considered
the Olympics a "bourgeois" event, and members of the IOC, who
did quite literally belong to the bourgeoisie, if not the actual aristocracy, weren't itching to welcome a Communist state into their
fold, either. As a form of protest against the Bolsheviks, the IOC
had allowed a longtime member, Lev Urusov, a Russian prince who
had joined the IOC during the tsarist years, to continue to serve on
the committee until his death in the 1930s.[7] The IOC, in other
words, preferred to recognize a felled Russian monarchy rather
than a Communist-run Russian state.

Brundage and Edström were also not fans of the USSR. Though
Brundage, who had traveled to Russia in 1912 and 1934, admitted
that the country had made significant strides in sports since the Bol-
shevik Revolution,[8] he hated their ideology. "I seriously doubt that

it is possible to have friendly sport contacts with any country that adheres to the Communist system," he admitted to a friend.[9] But contempt alone couldn't stop him. Edström and Brundage were institutionalists first and foremost, and they worried that the absence of one of the two world superpowers made the competition look lopsided.

Bringing on Russia was going to be a long, complicated task. To become an IOC member, each country needed to appoint delegates to all the international federations, including the IAAF. To kick-start the process, Edström invited Russia to join the IAAF twice in the fall of 1945; he received no reply and assumed they were not interested. Both he and Brundage were shocked, then, when they flew in for the European Championships in Oslo in 1946, only to find a team of thirty-five Russian athletes waiting to compete.[10] When Brundage landed at the Oslo airport, the chairman of the Oslo organizing committee rushed over to him and blurted out: "The Russians are here. What shall we do?" Ultimately, despite the breach of policy, the IAAF decided to let them play.

Another problem was that Russia did not follow the rules of amateurism that Edström and Brundage each treasured. The men were repeatedly chagrined by reports from abroad that top Russian athletes were receiving stipends and salaries. Russian athletic officials, knowing their use of cash rewards could pose a problem for international competition, requested—and received—a pardon for any athletes who had been paid for their sport prior to July 1, 1947, when Russia did eventually join the IAAF.[11]

Four years later, in May 1951, the IOC voted to accept the USSR as a member. Brundage was disappointed but probably not surprised when the first two IOC members that Russia selected were Communist Party loyalists who had worked as state bureaucrats.[12] The IOC that the Russians were joining looked notably different from the group of men that had met in Berlin in 1936. At the 1946 IOC meeting, half of the members were new to the organization.[13]

The IOC stubbornly retained other members who seemed like obvious candidates for removal. Brundage was particularly concerned with keeping his close German friends, despite their ties to the Nazi regime, on the IOC.

At most risk was Karl Ritter von Halt, the registered Nazi who had become Hitler's sports czar after the death of Hans von Tschammer.[14] Von Halt, who had funneled money from Deutsche Bank into the coffers of Heinrich Himmler, the architect of the Holocaust, was complicit in genocide. Yet in 1950, Brundage wrote letters on behalf of him and Carl Diem, insisting that neither man was a true believer in the Nazi cause.[15] "Dr. von Halt is not a politician and was never a Nazi," Brundage told a US State Department official. Though other IOC members, including P. W. Scharroo of the Netherlands, raised the topic of von Halt's very recent past, Brundage and Edström were more than willing to overlook it. Brundage called him "un parfait gentleman," and Edström, as president, wouldn't allow the committee to vote on his removal.[16] Von Halt stayed on the IOC. On January 6, 1951, he became president of the newly formed West German Olympic Committee, unscathed following his Nazi past.[17]

Diem's situation was only slightly less complicated. Though Diem never registered as a member of the Nazi Party, he was, at the very least, uncritical of Hitler. During World War II, Diem led a group of German officials who attempted to stage a takeover of the IOC. Diem told then president Baillet-Latour that all future Olympic Games were to be held in Berlin.[18] At one point, he broke into the IOC headquarters in Switzerland. "When Professor Diem attempted to remove the Olympic headquarters [from Switzerland] to Germany, I hid the most important documents in the cellar, and convinced the community that Diem was a spy," an IOC secretary remembered later. Diem also seemed deeply supportive of his country's war. In 1945, as Russian forces closed in on Berlin, Diem urged a group of Hitler Youth to defend the capital with their lives.[19]

Other controversial IOC members included two delegates from Italy who were former members of Mussolini's Fascist party,[20] as well as a French delegate who collaborated with the Nazis and about whom a British diplomat once said, "No decent French person will meet either him or his wife."[21] The IOC refused to expel any of them.

o o o

With the war over and 1948 Olympics looming, Sigfrid Edström realized he needed an actual plan for women's sports. It was going to be the first Olympics since Berlin, and owing to the dissolution of Alice Milliat's FSFI, it was the first time the IAAF would have complete control over the governance of women's athletics. Edström had fought for decades for this outcome. Yet now that he'd won, he seemed to lose interest in actually governing. He instead tasked Britain's Lord Burghley, who had succeeded him as president of the IAAF, to appoint a commission of IAAF members to deal with women's sports.

A French council member named Paul Mericamp took charge of the new committee, and in the spring of 1947, he issued his first report. In it, he included a section titled "The Question of Sex," which built on the suggestion that Karl Ritter von Halt had made just before the outbreak of World War II. Mericamp proposed that the IAAF adopt a new rule that made sex testing a blanket requirement for all female athletes: "Each woman athlete taking part in the Olympic Games and the European Championships must produce at the time of entry a recent medical certificate of sex." In "cases which appear doubtful," Mericamp added, officials on the ground could demand a "special examination" of the athlete.[22] Mericamp was never particularly specific about whom he was trying to screen out. Like his predecessors, he never endeavored to define what he meant by "doubtful" cases. Presumably, Mericamp was referring to women with physically masculine features. As with previous iterations of sex testing policy, the motivation seemed beside the point. Was Mericamp concerned broadly about intersex participants? About any woman with a muscular body? Or was his fear that a cis man might pose as a woman and compete specifically for the purpose of cheating?

His suggestion received swift approval, and a year later, at the 1948 Olympics in London, it went into effect.[23] For the first time in history, all athletes who took part in women's track-and-field sports needed to present a medical certificate, signed by their doctors, attesting to their sex, just as Karl Ritter von Halt and Avery Brundage had imagined it. Athletes in other sports notably didn't have this same requirement; in the years immediately following World War II, no other federation seemed to consider sex testing necessary. The IAAF, because its leadership felt that women's track and field was most likely to attract "doubtful" athletes, remained on its own.

What was peculiar about the IAAF's postwar discussion of sex testing was the amnesia around its origins. IAAF members did not mention Koubek, Weston, or any of the actual athletes who had inspired the policy in the first place. It was as if, during the course of World War II, the IAAF had simply forgotten. A newcomer to the council could be forgiven for assuming that the rules had always been there, a natural part of the business of sports governance.

And these rules—their provenance lost, their institutional support cemented—were now reorienting the careers of up-and-coming track-and-field athletes. On July 8, 1950, a group of Dutch track-and-field athletes reported to the Westeinde Hospital in The Hague, Netherlands, where, one by one, they walked into an examination room, sat down in a gynecology chair, and spread their legs.[24] The group was preparing to enter the European Championships in Brussels, Belgium, and they needed to present a certificate verifying their sex. Getting that certificate meant sitting through an invasive medical exam, in which a doctor inspected the most intimate parts

of their bodies. Nearly every Dutch woman sprinter showed up—
except for the team's rising star, Foekje Dillema, who had decided
that she wanted no part in the process. She wrote a letter to the
Dutch Athletic Union that morning, informing them, without further explanation, that she was not going to sit for the exam.

Born in 1926 in a village near Friesland, the Netherlands, Dillema grew up poor, in a tiny, two-room house barely able to fit her
seven siblings. For years, three of her sisters shared a single bed.
She'd worked as a domestic servant since she was twelve.[25] In her
free time, Dillema discovered that she had a talent for running, and
in 1947, she joined a sports club that was headquartered twenty
miles from her house. A year later, she ran the one-hundred-meter
sprint in 12.7 seconds, an incredibly fast time for a newcomer. In a
subsequent tournament in England, she "provided two shocks for
England's sprinters," according to reports in the British press,[26]
when she won back-to-back races. Dutch officials began to position
her for the 1952 Olympics in Helsinki.

The 1950 European Championships were supposed to be her
first big showcase. Then she refused to show up for her medical
exam. Five days later, on July 13, the Dutch Athletic Union sent a
telegram to her house, informing her that she was disqualified from
competition.[27] The telegram didn't arrive in time. Dillema was already biking to the nearest train station, where she planned to join
her team for a competition on their way to the European Championships. At the station, Dutch officials told her she had to leave. She
couldn't come with the team unless she presented a certificate verifying that she'd had her body inspected. Dillema biked back home,
humiliated. A representative for the Dutch Athletic Union told the
press that "due to a medical condition Foejke would never be able to
compete again,"[28] without elaborating on what that "medical condition" might involve. Dillema never took part in a sex test and never
played with the team again. She was embarrassed and ashamed and
barely spoke to anyone for years after the incident.[29]

What was Dillema so afraid of? Later coverage identified her as having a chromosome mosaic,[30] meaning more than the standard XX and XY chromosomes—a rare genetic feature that suggested, depending on her exact situation and her self-identity, that she may have fallen under the contemporary umbrella of intersex. There's no connection between a chromosome mosaic and athletic performance, but perhaps Dillema backed out of the test because she didn't want to have her body and her identity scrutinized so crudely.

Dillema was one of the first victims of the IAAF's sex testing regime, which from the start gave little thought to natural biological variations—whether that be in terms of chromosomes, reproductive organs, hormones, or something else—contained within the category of "woman." Dillema wasn't alone in discovering that the new IAAF policies had cut short her career. Another prominent French athlete, Léon Caurla, refused to undergo a medical examination in 1948;[31] he was immediately disqualified from international competition. (Two years later, Caurla transitioned gender and began living as a man.)

Dillema and Caurla were only the best known of a much wider array of athletes who dropped out of competition, or opted against pursuing sports, because they refused examinations. What made—and still makes—sex testing especially cruel was that its victims were forced to live in silence and shame. The public saw failing a sex test as proof that someone wasn't "truly" a woman. It was a ludicrous conclusion, considering that many subcategories of women—cis, trans, intersex, and any intersections thereof—would soon fail tests. But many of the people who were pushed out of sports did not speak up because doing so risked further marginalization and unwanted attention.

The IAAF, which had regulatory control only over track-and-field sports, was the earliest and most prominent proponent of sex testing among the many international sports federations, but other sports leagues would soon join in. In the next three decades, the federations governing basketball, volleyball, handball, and more would all adopt their own sex testing policies.[32] Because of the specific anxieties around working-class and masculine-appearing women sprinters, track and field was out in front—but the idea eventually spread.

○○○

Not long after Avery Brundage became vice president of the IOC, he set his sights on the top job. Sigfrid Edström, who turned eighty in 1950, was looking ahead to his retirement. Brundage was the obvious choice for his replacement as president, but Brundage began to worry that his enemies might use his past against him. He had not apologized for his cozy relationship to Nazi officials, and even after the horrors of the Holocaust, he never felt he had to. He professed not to understand why IOC members from the rest of Europe felt "so much bitterness and hatred" toward Germany.[33] When Carl Diem met with Brundage in the late 1940s, Diem reported the official was "in a depressed mood" owing to the criticism of his politics.[34] "He has many enemies and these miserable creatures are at work everywhere," Diem wrote.

The opposition to Brundage was not trivial. Edström worried that many of the European members wouldn't allow Brundage to become president of the IOC, in part because of Brundage's historic stances and in part because the IOC was still seen as a necessarily European institution. As an IOC delegate from Denmark bluntly summarized it to Brundage, "no American should be president of the IOC."[35]

Brundage had other problems, too. He was not a people pleaser. He almost never ate meals with his colleagues. He refused to go out to bars with anyone but Edström and von Halt. He "never visited anybody, never went to anybody's house," one colleague remembered.[36] Worse, Brundage was nervous that a personal secret might spill out into the open, potentially spoiling his election odds.

Though he'd been married since 1927, for years he'd had an affair with a Finnish athlete named Lilian Dresden. On August 27, 1951, Dresden secretly gave birth to Brundage's first son.[37] Knowing that Edström would be retiring in 1952, Brundage kept his child under wraps. He had his name removed from the child's birth certificate, and he refused to acknowledge his son publicly; the world wouldn't find out about the affair until November 1, 1954, when a *San Francisco Examiner* columnist wrote a blind item about it.

In the end, the opposition to Brundage, while strong, wasn't enough to stave off destiny. When the IOC delegates filed into a meeting room in Helsinki in August 1952, after a brutal twenty-five rounds of voting, Brundage finally cleared a two-thirds majority, winning 30–17 in the last round.[38] Two delegates refused to fill out their ballots, perhaps as a protest.

On August 14, at a dinner in honor of his election, Brundage described himself as a hard-nosed steward of IOC rules. Sports, he told the gathered IOC officials, were "perhaps the most saving grace in the world at the moment, with its spirit of rules kept, and regard for the adversary, whether the fight is going for or against."[39] The speech's focus on integrity and rule-following was especially ironic in light of Brundage's own personal misadventures. At the dinner, Brundage's longtime wife was by his side to congratulate him on the fulfillment of his lifelong dream. Neither she nor anyone else in the room had any idea when, five days later, Brundage's Finnish mistress secretly gave birth to another child, the new IOC president's second son.

ooo

As Avery Brundage assumed the most powerful office in sports, many of his contemporaries were disappearing from the spotlight. In the years since Berlin, Alice Milliat fell into obscurity. Though she was largely responsible for bringing women's track-and-field sports to the Olympics—not to mention advocating for the legitimacy of women's sports in general—few members of the public knew her name. In 1937, shortly after the dissolution of the Women's World Games, the IAAF published a report on the history of women's sports, which noted the existence of a "special women's sports federation"—the FSFI, though it was not named—that held women's sports competitions in the 1920s. This federation, according to the IAAF, existed "owing to the fact that the IAAF had hesitated in accepting the control of women's sports."[40] In a cruel erasure of her legacy, Alice Milliat was never mentioned by name. She died alone, forgotten, in 1957, and was buried in a cemetery in Nantes. Her grave wasn't identified until a historian located it over a half century later.[41]

For the athletes who transitioned gender in the 1930s, fading from public life was more of a calculated choice. In the summer of 1936, Mark Weston seemed uncomfortable with the amount of attention that he and his new wife, Alberta Bray, were receiving. He hated the spotlight. After the Berlin Olympics, he disappeared into the life of a private citizen. With Bray at his side, he continued his massage business in Plymouth. The following February, Weston moved his practice to a new address along the waterfront.[42] Sometime in early 1942, Weston's younger sibling—who had been assigned female at birth—decided to undergo a gender transition of his own at the age of twenty-six.[43] The Westons started calling him Harry, and like his older brother, he saw a surgeon for two operations. Before his transition, Harry had been depressed, and that continued even after he began living as a man. In July 1942, police in Plymouth reported that Harry had ended his own life. Weston never talked about his brother's suicide publicly, but it appeared to expedite his disillusionment with England. On June 1, 1951, Weston and Bray boarded a ship from Southampton, England, to New York City.[44]

By 1954,[45] the couple had settled in Clifton, New Jersey, where they rented a house from a landlord named Vincent Laterza at 367 Harding Avenue.[46] The couple seemed to be close to Laterza, with Weston driving his landlord to church every morning at 10:00 a.m.[47] Weston worked as a mixer at a bakery, according to the Clifton city directory. After his move to New Jersey, Weston only shows up in records in a pair of car accident reports. In 1970, he was listed as retired and still residing in Clifton.[48] Then, at some point in the 1970s, he and Bray moved back to Plymouth, where they lived out their final days together. Weston died at Freedom Fields Hospital in Plymouth in 1978. Bray continued to live in town as a widow for the next seventeen years, before dying in 1995.

The American sprinter Helen Stephens never returned to the Olympics, either. No matter what she did, the whispers about her gender continued to haunt her. By the end of 1936, when Stephens enrolled at William Woods University in her hometown of Fulton, Missouri, rumors spread among the faculty about her supposedly masculine traits. When a first-year student befriended Stephens, the dean of students called the young student into her office to warn her about Stephens.[49] "I'm sure you're aware that there are two sexes," the dean, fidgeting with her pencil, told the student. "Well, you know there are some that are not truly male or female." Helen Stephens, the dean warned, belonged to this third category, and the first-year needed to stay away: "Don't let them touch you or get near you."[50]

In February 1937, in its inaugural issue, the magazine Look— billed as a competitor to Life—ran a spread of photos under the headline "When Is a Woman Actually a Woman?" The question, according to Look, was a "chief worry among athletic officials."[51] The spread included photos of Koubek, Weston, and other people who had actually transitioned gender, but on the second page, Look added a particularly unflattering photo of Helen Stephens. "Is this a man or a woman?" the magazine asked. "Study the above picture closely and see whether you can tell if it's a man or a woman." Stephens was so furious that she decided to sue. That August, she collected a $4,500 libel settlement.[52]

As the decades passed, however, Stephens began to earn her due. To make extra money after her Olympic career ended, she had turned professional, alternating between basketball and baseball. In 1938, she began managing a semiprofessional basketball team, becoming one of the first women in the United States to do so. Decades later, even though she'd moved on from track-and-field sports, tales of her successes as a sprinter in Berlin continued to circulate. In 1993, Stephens was inducted into the National Women's Hall of Fame. She died a year later, at the age of seventy-five. Though she'd known for decades that she was a lesbian, she had never discussed it.[53] She feared that coming out publicly would hurt her reputation in the sports world. "Homosexuality won't be accepted in my lifetime," Stephens told her biographer, Sharon Kinney Hanson, shortly before her death. "*Lesbian* is a scare word. It can be very hurtful if applied incorrectly to young girls who are athletic."[54]

World War II radicalized Witold Smętek, the Polish javelin thrower. In 1946, shortly after Poland had fully expelled the Nazis, he joined the Polish Workers' Party and began a job in a trade union council.[55] In 1950, he decided to go back to school: he started studying history at the University of Warsaw, where he wrote a master's thesis on revolutionary movements in Warsaw between November 1918 and August 1919. On the side, he earned money as a tour guide for the Polish government, and he volunteered as an instructor in a men's sports association. Few records remains of Smętek discussing his gender transition. In a résumé he submitted to prospective employers, he wrote that "a significant part of my life was marked by" a "congenital defect," but "the natural changes that took place when my body matured made it possible to carry out the aforementioned operation, to arrange the formalities for a sex change, and then to take on the name Witold."[56]

CHAPTER 21

SOON AFTER THE NAZIS ARRESTED the German high jumper Heinz Ratjen in 1938, Karl Ritter von Halt applied to have the IAAF strike the athlete's records. But the group took nearly two decades to do it. In 1957, the IAAF finally reached out to the new recordholder, a British woman named Dorothy Odam, to tell her that she was now the top-place high jumper.[1]

It didn't take long for the story to leak to the press. With headlines like "High Jump Mark Set by 'Woman' in '38 Was Male," news outlets in the 1950s characterized Ratjen not as a likely intersex person assigned female at birth but as a cis man who had donned female clothing for the purpose of cheating. *Time* reported—inaccurately—that Ratjen "had been forced by the Nazis to pose as a woman 'for the sake of the honor and glory of Germany.'" The magazine quoted Ratjen as saying, "For three years I lived the life of a girl. It was most dull."[2] *Time* implied that, prior to the Olympics, Ratjen had publicly identified as a man and had only entered women's competitions so he could win. The reality was more complicated: Ratjen had spent his whole life being perceived as a woman, and he didn't come to terms with his identity until after the Olympics. Many historians have since questioned whether *Time* spoke to Ratjen at all. It seems unlikely, especially considering that Ratjen never did any other press.[3]

The mischaracterization of Ratjen's story wasn't the only damaging lie in the *Time* article. The magazine also reported on Shin Keum-dan (or Sin Kim Dan, as American journalists called her), a North Korean sprinter who dropped out of the Olympics because the IOC had barred her country from participating. Yet somehow, *Time* bungled the story. The magazine claimed, utterly without evidence, that she dropped out because her father had revealed her to be a man in disguise. The lie stuck. Ratjen and Keum-dan were continually cited as examples of men who had posed as women at the Olympics, giving off the impression that "men in masquerade" were a legitimate threat to the integrity of women's sports.[4]

The historical myth that at one point in Olympic history cis men had successfully disguised themselves as women in order to notch world records became an animating justification for sex testing. By way of explaining the history of sex testing, a nationally syndicated news story characterized the 1930s like this: "Even with the emergence of women athletes in the modern games, it was getting harder to tell the girls from the boys. In fact some of the girls were boys."[5] Time, and prejudice, had flattened the nuances in the lives of Zdeněk Koubek, Mark Weston, and Heinz Ratjen.

In America, the transmogrification of Ratjen's story proved to be politically expedient. In the early 1950s, around the time that Ratjen resurfaced in the tabloids, the USSR was setting itself apart in women's track-and-field sports. Americans, already prone to suspicion and rumor about the USSR, began to speculate that the Russians were cheating. No duo set off more alarm bells than Irina and Tamara Press, a pair of Ukrainian track-and-field athletes who first entered the Olympics in 1960 and quickly racked up gold medals for the USSR. Tamara Press, a five-foot-eleven track-and-field athlete, won a combined three gold medals and one silver at the Olympics in 1960 and in 1964, while her sister, Irina, won a gold in both the hurdles and in the pentathlon.[6] Starting in the early 1960s, American newspapers implied that the Press sisters could not possibly be women. An Associated Press report noted that while the US women's track-and-field team had "some mighty attractive practitioners," the USSR's women's contingent was "more of a beef trust." One American track athlete bragged to the wire service, "Right now we live more femininely than the USSRs."[7]

It wasn't uncommon for American sports fans to speculate that the Press sisters were, in fact, cis men in disguise. "The Press brothers" became a common insult.[8] "We never thought about it in our sport," one American slalom racer said of sex tests, "then we read about some husky Russian woman beating our women."[9] As track-and-field athletes, the Press sisters did have to present sex certificates "verifying" their womanhood, but critics became convinced that the Russian doctors who signed them were lying.

Ratjen's reappearance in the press in 1957 lent an air of credibility to these tales of nefarious cross-dressing. "We shall never know the exact number of men who have competed in the Olympics posing as women," the *Chicago Tribune* announced in an article about sex testing, failing to mention that the number was almost certainly zero, "but athletes of questionable gender have been common enough to warrant changing rules this year."[10] *The New York Times* noted the rise of "complaints that some competitors, principally from Communist countries, were of questionable femininity."[11] Exacerbating the distrust, perhaps, was the USSR's tendency to distance itself from the rest of the national teams. At the 1952 Olympics in Helsinki, the USSR didn't allow its athletes to live with the rest of the teams in the Olympic Village, instead housing them at a nearby

USSR navy base.[12] When the IOC asked to carry the Olympic torch across Soviet territory, the Russians politely refused.

By the end of the 1960s, the IAAF decided to respond with an escalation of its policies. At a series of competitions in 1966, it began requiring female athletes to submit to *on-site* sex testing for the first time.[13] Rather than present certificates signed by doctors from their home countries, which Americans had charged could be manipulated, track-and-field athletes would now sit for an exam by a doctor associated with the IAAF. These were crude physical exams during which doctors would strip down women and inspect their genitalia. This, the IAAF claimed, could eliminate accusations of fraud. The organization either ignored, or did not care to understand, the reality that genitalia was not uniform across people and could not be cleaved into binary sex categories of "male" and "female."

To the delight of some reporters, as soon as the IAAF toughened up its sex testing rules, some prominent athletes began dropping out. The year that the IAAF made on-site sex testing mandatory, three high-profile Russian women, including the Press sisters, chose not to attend. Though the Press sisters claimed the reason for their nonattendance was their mother's illness, close watchers of the Olympics, including many athletes who'd competed against the Press sisters, were suspicious.[14] "Did Sex Tests Scare 'Em?" asked one headline.[15] Speculating that she had dropped out of competition in order to avoid the sex tests, the *Vancouver Sun* called Irina Press a "husky, out-going queen (or king, as the case might be)."[16]

If the idea that such a prominent competitor in women's athletics could actually be a cis man in disguise sounded a bit far-fetched, a London newspaper had an explanation for how Russia could get away with dressing up male athletes as women. "What happens? A big boy in his teens may show all the signs of being a good hammer-thrower or shot-putter. So in some countries they don't hesitate to feed him on female hormones."[17] Other reporters began linking the need for sex testing explicitly to the dishonesty of the USSR. "If the Commies hadn't been guilty of substituting men for women in the first place, the new rule by the IAAF wouldn't have been necessary," a columnist reported in a Florida newspaper in 1966.[18]

The Boston Globe, meanwhile, interviewed a Soviet whistleblower who alleged that Tamara Press was in fact raised as a boy named Tim until she was fifteen.[19] (This wasn't true; records from when Press was five years old list her as female.)[20] The doctor, Nahum Sternberg, said the USSR had a system in place for recruiting male athletes into women's sports. The article opened with a factual inaccuracy—the *Globe* stated that "instances in which a 'woman' athlete turned out to be a man have been recorded in the past"—and then dug its heels in further. Sternberg alleged that the Soviet state had a system for enrolling boys in female sports and intentionally deceiving the Olympics.[21] When Soviet doctors encountered "female-looking boys," they reported them to physical education authorities, who brought them to special training camps, injected them with female hormones "until the last vestiges of manhood disappear and the boys become neuters," changed their name, and then enrolled them in women's sports. Tamara Press was one of these "neuters," though she "still is a man from a legal point of view," according to Sternberg. For as far-fetched as these reports might sound, they lodged into the American psyche. From then on, an athlete taking female hormones became indelibly linked to fraud.

The bombastic reporting was enough to convince the American public that physical examinations for women athletes were necessary to preserve the sanctity of women's sports. Up until 1966, sex testing was a solution in search of a real problem. But the rise of Cold War hostilities intensified the sense, on both sides of the world, that the other global power was cheating. Subjecting every woman—but notably no athletes in men's competitions—to invasive and humiliating sex tests seemed like a small price to pay for supposedly weeding out frauds and preserving "fairness."

The argument unsurprisingly found a receptive audience in the new IOC president, Avery Brundage. Though Brundage had become more sympathetic to women's sports since the war, pushing the IAAF to add more events for women,[22] he remained skeptical of masculine-appearing female athletes. "His suspicion is that some of them—perhaps even a considerable number—are really men," the magazine *Life* told readers.[23] Brundage himself admitted to preferring "lithe, supple, physically disciplined, strong, slender and efficient" women athletes,[24] not their bigger, more muscular counterparts.

That skepticism fueled his continued interest in sex testing. Sometime in either the late 1940s or early 1950s, Brundage solicited comments on women's sports from an all-male group of his correspondents.[25] The group was largely split on the issue, with Franz Joseph II, the prince of Lichtenstein and an IOC member, complaining of the "unaesthetic spectacle of women trying to look and act like men." Brundage's friend Norman Cox, a former swimming coach he had known in Chicago, offered a more bombastic response. "One thing the fathers of the Olympics overlooked was making provision for competition among hermaphrodites," Cox said. "Certainly the 'child-bearing' type of woman [. . .] is under a handicap when up against the hermaphrodite, even in swimming. And how normal women are to be protected against such handicap except through the institution of anatomical examination is beyond me."

Whether or not Brundage actually believed that the USSR was dressing up cis men to compete as women, he didn't consider it outside the realm of possibility. Brundage declared in 1960 that, owing to the requirements that they did "hard manual labor," women athletes from the USSR were "a different type of women anyway." He wouldn't elaborate further, but the implication was clear. What did they look like? a reporter asked. "Get a picture for yourself," Brundage replied.[26]

As the head of the IOC, Brundage couldn't risk his home country losing faith in the validity of the women's competitions. By the end of the sixties, however, sports authorities decided to adopt a different approach to testing. Why not use the new science of chromosomes to measure sex? It was supposed to be a simple solution. In place of the bodily inspections of years past, first the IAAF, followed quickly by the IOC, would now test whether women athletes possessed XX chromosomes. Athletes would show up at an office at the site of the Olympics, where a nurse, using a small spatula, would scrape off a sample from the inside of their cheeks,[27] smear it on a slide, and then repeat the process to get a second sample. Under a microscope, nurses then examined the nuclei of the cells to see each athlete's chromosomes. They did this through a slightly simpler process called a Barr body test, but the result was the same: XX women were given a card supposedly certifying their womanhood. All other women would sit for more tests.

The IAAF first used the chromosome test in 1967, then debuted it at the Olympics the following year.[28] It backfired almost immediately. Since the 1940s, sex testing had cut short the careers of athletes largely in silence. When the Dutch runner Foekje Dillema dropped out of athletic competition, it wasn't widely reported in the press. That would change in 1967, when, for the first time, a woman failed her sex test outright. Poland's Ewa Kłobukowska, according to reports from the IAAF, was removed from competition when a test found she "had one chromosome too many."[29] Like Dillema, the sprinter had a chromosome mosaic, that rare condition with no bearing on a person's biological sex or athletic performance. At the time, however, IAAF officials saw the presence of the extra chromosome as proof that she was "not truly female" and boasted that it had "managed to keep out six who were hermaphrodites" that year.[30]

Medical experts could see just how illogical the IAAF and IOC policies had become. Were the two sports bodies saying that a

chromosome mosaic made someone inherently not a woman? That
the presence of XX chromosomes was now the defining trait of femaleness? Brundage began fielding complaints from sports officials. The president of the Polish Olympic Committee, the group
that represented Kłobukowska, wrote to the IOC in October 1967,
arguing that the sex tests not only created an "unpleasant atmosphere" for women athletes, but that they also amounted to "a form
of discrimination." When it came to how the group was defining
"woman," the Polish president called the IOC president's bluff. He
wanted to know: With all these new medical examinations, what,
exactly, were they trying to test for? "There are no generally accepted criteria of sex for woman athletes," he said, and the "arbi-
trariness" with which the group was deciding who would be eligible
for competition was damaging.[31]

In his reply two weeks later, Brundage ignored these bigger questions and instead fixated on a lesser complaint in the Polish Olympic
Committee letter: that Kłobukowska's dismissal from international
sport should not have happened so publicly. Brundage agreed that
"this is a very delicate subject," and that the IOC would work to
"avoid unwarranted invasion of personal privacy."[32] Brundage made
no effort to roll back his sex testing regime. If anything, he doubled
down. Two months later, Monique Berlioux, his close confidante
who oversaw IOC publications, penned an article titled "Femininity" for the IOC's official magazine, *Olympic Review*, defending
the sex testing policy. In it, Berlioux emphasized that the new sex
tests "will make it possible to put an end to the cheating, which
takes place, whether intentionally or not." Sure, she wrote, "one
feels sorry for the 'unfortunate' girl who has been disqualified, but
is there a voice raised against the person responsible for such cheating? Does anyone think of all those young girls who have been
ousted from first place simply because they are women and they
have taken part honestly?" Berlioux used the platform of the IOC to
air her unfounded belief that intersex women held an unfair ad-

vantage over their peers. Allowing these women to compete, she thought, would destroy women's sports itself. "Nothing is more prejudicial to female sport than this charlatanry; nothing can kill it more surely."[33]

○○○

Even as Brundage continued to profess support for sex testing, he decided to delegate authority over it.[34] At the 1967 session of the IOC, Brundage pushed for the formation of a medical commission within the IOC that could draft rules for administering sex and drugs tests. The commission decided that, starting in 1968, officials would begin testing all women a month ahead of the Olympics, when they first arrived, to avoid a scandal if an athlete needed to be sent home.[35]

Like the IAAF before it, the IOC's Medical Commission made chromosome-based tests its metric of choice. A doctor named Jacques Thiébault, who oversaw the implementation of these tests at the 1968 Olympics, had full confidence in their usefulness. These chromosome tests were "among the surest examinations for determining the sex," he told colleagues. While he expressed some sympathy for people who failed sex tests, noting that "in feminine checks, it is only a natural irregularity which comes to light, and these people are to be pitied," he saw sex tests as a necessary evil. These tests, he said, were really about protecting women. Without them, "the lay press" would spread rumors about "so-called females who are as strong as oxen and who break so many records." By introducing sex tests, the IOC was ensuring that "the real representatives of the weaker sex" would not "feel persecuted" by more masculine-appearing women entering the competition.[36]

Whatever fractured vision the IOC might have had for its sex testing regime in 1968 quickly eroded. In the following years, medical experts began expressing concern that chromosome-focused tests didn't consider that many people had more than two chromosomes, or that people with XY chromosomes didn't always get assigned male at birth. The IOC therefore risked excluding certain women who lacked the XX chromosome from the Olympics for no discernable reason. On February 3, 1972, a group of Danish researchers issued a report declaring the IOC testing policy inadequate. "The definition of sex," they wrote, "is so difficult that it cannot be given ambiguously."[37]

These criticisms worked their way back up to Brundage, who, in April 1972, in one of his last letters as IOC president, wrote to tell the Medical Commission he found reports of discrimination against people with chromosomal variations to be "disquieting."[38] Thirty-six years after he first proposed that the IOC get into the business of sex testing, Brundage had finally realized that "apparently technical tests are not the answer" to determining an athlete's sex. In typical fashion, he couldn't help but make a joke out of it. If the Medical Commission was unable to draft a policy to screen out masculine women, he said, "maybe the eye of a 25 year old would be better."

That didn't mean Brundage wanted the IOC to abandon the idea. Sex testing was his legacy, and publicly, he continued to praise it, insisting that women athletes "are more feminine now" that the procedures were in place.[39] On September 11, 1972, just before his eighty-fifth birthday, Brundage retired from the IOC. He died three years later in Garmisch-Partenkirchen, Germany, the site of the Berlin Winter Games in 1936, while on an international trip.

o o o

As the years elapsed, and as virtually all the original 1936 IOC and IAAF members died, the origin story of sex testing faded from memory. Zdeněk Koubek and Mark Weston were no longer recognizable names, and neither were Witold Smętek, Willy de Bruyn, and the other athletes who publicly transitioned in the 1930s. The oft-referenced story of Heinz Ratjen continued to be misremembered and misunderstood as an example of a cis man who had "posed" as a woman with the intention of cheating.

By the close of the twentieth century, in fact, few sports executives seemed to understand why sex testing existed at all. In 1987, Mary Glen-Haig, one of the first women to receive a seat on the IOC, consulted with three doctors about how to revise the IOC's sex testing policies. After the conversation, Glen-Haig realized the IOC had a problem. It wasn't clear to the public which athletes the organization was trying to weed out with its sex tests. "We should define who we wish to exclude from female competitions," she wrote to Alexandre de Merode, the head of the Medical Commission. "As an example should women with androgen producing tumors or with congenital adrenal hyperplasia be excluded?"[40]

As it turned out, no one had a great answer. When pressed, various members of the Medical Commission referred to "abnormal cases." The IOC Medical Commission member Jacques Thiébault said that sex tests were designed "above all to dissuade the 'hybrids' from competing in the Olympics,"[41] but the problem was that "hybrids" as a label didn't really mean anything. Was a so-called hybrid someone who had a chromosome mosaic, someone who had been assigned male at birth but who now lived as a woman, or someone with adrenal congenital hyperplasia, a natural condition that sometimes resulted in a person producing elevated testosterone levels? And why was the IOC focused on these slight variations in chromosomes or sex assignment at birth, given that all athletes had different body types that could give them advantages in some sports and disadvantages in others? No one was limiting how tall a basketball player could be.

The more the IOC tried to defend its sex testing policy, the clearer its historical amnesia became. In 1988, Arne Ljungqvist, the chair of the IAAF Medical Committee, wrote a memo offering a historical perspective on sex testing at the Olympics, in which he claimed that "femininity testing was introduced in the late 1960s after reports that men had been masquerading as women in female sport."[42] Alexandre de Merode remembered the origin of sex testing as a desire "to put a stop to the development of a particularly immoral form of cheating which had been spreading insidiously within high-level competition sport." In the 1960s, de Merode recounted, "we were informed that in certain regions, a systematic search was taking place for young people presenting sexual anomalies"[43] to enroll in sports—seemingly a reference to the accusations against the USSR. Echoing this, another IOC Medical Commission member wrote in December 1987 that sex testing "had to be introduced in 1968 when it became obvious that males tried to participate in female events." The commission member added, "This type of cheating could reappear if testing would be dropped."[44]

When Albert de la Chapelle, a Finnish doctor who repeatedly voiced his opposition to the IOC's sex testing policy, heard the claim that men had once tried to participate in women's sports, he found it "surprising." He asked for more information. What man had ever masqueraded as a woman at the Olympics? If there was truth to this claim, and "if the main target is males posing as females, then a method will certainly be easy to devise" to weed them out, he claimed.[45]

De la Chapelle never received a reply to his question. It's not clear which athletes, exactly, the IOC members were referring to when they claimed that "males" had previously been caught "posing as females" at the Olympics. Were they discussing Ewa Kłobukowska, who had a chromosome mosaic? Irina and Tamara Press, who had never actually sat for a sex test? Heinz Ratjen, whose story had been misreported in the press and who never actually "posed" as anyone? Or perhaps they were thinking of Zdeněk Koubek and Mark Weston, the two athletes who introduced gender transition to the mainstream in 1935 and 1936? In a way, it probably didn't matter.

None of these athletes was an example of a "male posing as female." Decades of geopolitical turmoil and personnel changes had simply erased the origins of sex testing—the specific conflagration of Nazi ideology, 1930s understandings of sex, and the ambitious personalities of men like Avery Brundage that ushered these policies into existence one summer day in 1936.

In fact, the false claims of men masquerading as women offered a distraction from the realities of the IOC's contemporary sex testing project. What the IOC and the IAAF largely failed to acknowledge was that, by instituting sex tests, they were constructing their own definitions of femaleness. The IOC and the IAAF revised their policies to lend the categories of "woman" and "man" an air of coherence. First, they relied on physical inspections of each athlete's outward body; then they shifted to chromosomes, which they claimed would be more precise and scientific; later, and continuing into the present, they tried defining sex based on testosterone. Even as these shifts were underway, it was clear to astute observers what the IOC was doing. Daniel F. Hanley, the top physician on the US Olympic Committee, complained in 1967 that chromosome-based sex tests "will establish a new definition of femaleness."[46] Even de Merode once admitted that "it was practically impossible, scientifically, to define the sex of an athlete."[47]

Yet the IOC had backed itself into a corner. By implementing sex tests, they were keeping alive the illusion that sports could be inherently segregated by sex, as they had been since the earliest days of the Olympics. Sex testing became part of the fiction that "men's sports" and "women's sports" were logical concepts. Abolishing sex testing would mean acknowledging that people cannot be sorted inherently into male and female categories. And if human sex is not built on a binary, fans might start to ask: Why, then, should sports be?

The ultimate irony was that, until 1986, Zdeněk Koubek was alive and able to answer their questions, if the IOC had just thought to ask. Koubek fell off the radar after the war, but neither he nor his legacy disappeared. His world record of two minutes and twelve seconds was broken in 1960, the first year that the eight-hundred-meter dash was put back on the Olympic program. That year, a Russian woman named Lyudmila Shevtsova turned in a time of two minutes and four seconds in the eight hundred meters.[48]

In 1944, after ten years away, Koubek had quietly returned to sports. He enrolled in a newly formed men's rugby league, RC Říčany, which practiced in the suburbs of Prague.[49] He took the train out twice a week to play.[50] Koubek was fast, the quickest-footed athlete on the team. "We knew who he was," one teammate said in an interview in 2001, though "his past was not discussed" unless he himself brought it up.

In a way, Koubek was living his dream. He had always planned to sign up for men's sports, even though, because of his advancing age, he suspected he could never reach world-record status in the men's category. He didn't care. "Breaking records doesn't have to be a condition for participating in sport," he wrote in his essay in the *Prague Illustrated Reporter* in 1936, because "a true athlete loves their sport even when they end up in last place."[51] By the time he died in Prague on June 12, 1986, he had spent several decades in club sports, far from the glory of the games and his faded international celebrity. But he remained, in his definition, a true athlete. By the time his world record was broken in 1960, Koubek was too tired of his track-and-field trophies to care. He dumped all the medals he'd won into the trash can.[52]

AUTHOR'S NOTE

In 2021, when I first stumbled on the rich, interconnected lives of the athletes in this book in a digital newspaper archive, I couldn't believe they had been forgotten—and that they had been largely embraced by the public in their time. They seemed to defy my understanding of the 1930s as being a period when the queer community was forced to exist underground. I needed to know more. And so, ultimately, this book is less a history of sex testing in sports than it is a story of queer possibilities.

When I say my focus is on "queer possibilities," then, I mean bringing to light these narratives that challenge our assumption that history is linear. Today, even in an era of intense governmental backlash to queer and particularly trans people, it is easy to imagine that the distant past was a worse time to be queer—that, for all our faults, we've achieved social progress. Maybe that's true. But queer history is not, and has never been, so simple. Compare the raft of transphobic coverage written in publications like *The New York Times* today to the magazine articles about the athletes Zdeněk Koubek and Mark Weston published in 1936, and you start to see the complexities. My intent here is not to romanticize the 1930s. I simply want to un-flatten those years, to start with the premise that maybe this decade has something to tell us, that buried in its temporal crevices are radical queer stories that can add contours to our understanding of gender, sexuality, the body, and queer community today.

This book operates from the premise that sex is not a stable category. That statement might sound self-evident to some and outrageous to others, but the point is historically true: we do not, and have never had, a definitive indicator that separates "male" from "female." Throughout recent centuries, sexologists who studied chromosomes, hormone levels, external genitalia, physical phenotype, internal organs like ovaries, and more have found again and again that all these traits exist on a broad spectrum. Chromosomes don't always fit a neat XY and XX pattern; there is no cutoff hormone level that separates male from female; and so on. Many individuals are born with some qualities that we typically associate with maleness and some that we typically associate with femaleness. How a government or regulatory body defines "sex" is actually a subjective choice, one that, over the last century, governments and regulatory bodies have taken it upon themselves to make.

Understanding this is important, because it allows us to see that when the Department of Motor Vehicles adds sex markers to driver's licenses or, more to the point, when the International Olympic Committee decides whether someone should be allowed to participate in men's or women's sports, they are not reflecting some objective reality. Instead, they are making arbitrary decisions about what "male" or "female" means to them at each historical juncture. We tend to think these processes are rooted in science, but they are not and have never been.

The Other Olympians traces the origins of one of the most publicized and controversial versions of sex regulation: sex testing. Beginning in the 1930s, sports executives began cleaving people into poorly defined categories of "man" and "woman" and expelling the largely trans and intersex athletes who didn't fit their definitions. You can trace a direct line between the International Olympic Committee's policies of 1936 and more recent institutionalized discrimination, such as World Athletics' 2023 ban on nearly all trans women athletes. (World Athletics is the new name for the IAAF.) In each moment, athletic officials decided to codify a sex binary, then purged anyone who challenged it.

Today, in a time when we understand gender and sex as distinct categories, it often makes more sense to speak of gender than sex. But throughout the book, I focused on the meaning of "sex" in an attempt to show its holes. "Sex" still masquerades as an objective indicator, one that can be easily cleaved into two categories: male or female. Advocates for sex testing tend to—falsely— assume that "female" and "male" are coherent biological categories with their own unique set of markers. By zeroing in on how sex has been constructed, I hoped to dispel the idea that "sex" was ever a stable category. This line between "male" and "female" was something that top sports officials needed to invent.

In his book *Sex Is as Sex Does: Governing Transgender Identity*, Paisley Currah analyzes how states regulate sex markers on birth certificates and driver's licenses—and how and why those regulations shift over time. Currah argues that bureaucracies make decisions on when to allow people to amend their identity documents based not on what sex *is* to them but on what sex *does* for them. Currah writes, "The only thing we can say for sure about what sex means is what a particular state actor says it means." For many years, in the United States, bureaucrats worried that allowing trans people to amend their driver's licenses would lead to a collapse of heterosexual marriage. A New York–based committee in 1966, for instance, predicted that giving trans people legal recognition would allow anyone to enter into marriages "fraudulently." Policies loosened up only when same-sex marriage became a more tolerable prospect, starting in the early 2000s. Using Currah's framework, we can see what defining sex *does* for sports leaders: namely, that it offers "male" and "female" sports categories an illusion of coherence.

Today, sex testing most often takes the form of measuring testosterone, even though the evidence that testosterone confers any kind of athletic advantage is slim. Scientists like Severine Lamon, for instance, have found that naturally high testosterone levels have no real impact on athletic performance in women. The journalist Katie Barnes also discusses how little we still know about the role of testosterone in athletic performance in their book *Fair Play: How Sports Shape the Gender Debates*. Testosterone also does not have a 1:1 relationship to sex. Some people who are assigned female naturally produce more testosterone than some people assigned male. Further, testosterone testing relies on a blatant double standard. Many athletic federations put caps on women's hormone levels, but they do not do the same for men. Let's say sports officials are right, and testosterone neatly maps onto athletic performance. Why, then, do we measure hormone levels only in women's sports, when men could also benefit from higher-than-average testosterone levels? It doesn't make sense to cap women at certain testosterone levels, just as it doesn't make sense to cap men, either.

The more we probe, the more we can see that sex testing does not exist to ensure "fairness" in sports, as many supporters claim, but rather to lend credibility to the rigid separation between men's and women's sports. Sex testing allows athletic organizations to sort people into neat categories of male and female, and, more important, to push out the athletes—most often trans and intersex people—who complicate binary assumptions of sex. It is not a coincidence that modern sex testing originates at the Berlin Olympics of 1936, when the Nazis had deep influence within the sporting world. As we have seen, a small cadre of officials, including a Nazi sports doctor and a number of Nazi sympathizers, first came up with the idea of medical exams to determine sex.

Lastly, a note on sourcing: There is, as ever, not enough of it. Much of the chapters on Koubek and Weston are reconstructed from a series of public interviews that both athletes gave, and, in Koubek's case, a lengthy narrative essay he wrote for a Czech magazine in 1936. I try to hew as closely as I can to these accounts, even at points that feel slightly exaggerated. Certainly, there are some holes in the narratives that Koubek and Weston presented to the public, some pieces that don't add up. It is worth keeping in mind that everything we know about Koubek and Weston was filtered. These men were speaking to an audience not versed in the nuances of trans or intersex identities; with every interview they gave, they were, in some sense, put in the position of trying to justify their existence. Perhaps they intentionally obscured some details, like their love lives, that they assumed the public wasn't ready to hear.

It would certainly be thrilling to uncover an unvarnished account of their lives, an autobiography that Weston or Koubek wrote just for their friends, that fills in the gaps in the narratives we do have. I like to believe that such a memoir is out there somewhere. But a part of me is glad Koubek and Weston saved the full, unfiltered story for themselves.

NOTES

CHAPTER 1

1. See *Olympia-Vorspiele 1914* booklet, June 27–28, 1914, Central Library for Sport Sciences, German Sport University Cologne, Cologne, Germany; Carl Diem, *Ein Leben für den Sport: Erinnerungen aus dem Nachlaß* (Düsseldorf, Germany: A. Henn Verlag, 1974), 93.
2. Arnd Krüger, "The Ministry of Popular Enlightenment and Propaganda and the Nazi Olympics of 1936," Fourth International Symposium for Olympic Research (October 1998): 33.
3. Mehmet Tunckol and Yasar Sahin, "Carl Diem and the Olympics," *Ovidius University Annals* 10, no. 2 (June 2010): 914.
4. Ansgar Molzberger, "The Intended 1916 Olympic Games through the Eyes of the German Sport University Cologne's Historical Collections," *Diagoras: International Academic Journal on Olympic Studies* 4 (2020): 223.
5. Dikaia Chatziefstathiou and Ian P. Henry, *Discourses of Olympism: From the Sorbonne 1894 to London 2012* (London: Palgrave Macmillan, 2012), 149.
6. Molzberger, "The Intended 1916 Olympic Games," 224.
7. Diem, *Leben*, 85.
8. Diem, *Leben*, 90.
9. "Prince Karl Real Olympic Athlete," *San Antonio Express*, June 27, 1914.
10. Barry A. Jackisch, "The Nature of Berlin: Green Space and Visions of a

New German Capital, 1900–45," *Central European History* 47 (June 2014): 311.

11. Jackisch, "The Nature of Berlin," 324.

12. Evi Zemanek, "An Entangled History of Environmental and Cultural Sustainability," in *Cultural Sustainability: Perspectives from the Humanities and Social Sciences*, ed. Torsten Meireis and Gabriele Rippl (Milton Park, UK: Routledge, 2019), 162.

13. Volker Kluge, "Cancelled but Still Counted, and Never Annulled: The Games of 1916," *Journal of Olympic History* 2 (2014): 10.

14. "Kaiser Opens Berlin's New Stadium Today," *The Boston Globe*, June 8, 1913.

15. Diem, *Leben*, 86.

16. David Clay Large, *Nazi Games: The Olympics of 1936* (New York: W. W. Norton, 2007), 36.

17. Kluge, "Cancelled but Still Counted," 13.

18. Diem, *Leben*, 93.

19. Kluge, "Cancelled but Still Counted," 13.

20. Molzberger, "The Intended 1916 Olympic Games," 230.

CHAPTER 2

1. Unless otherwise specified, the accounts relating directly to Koubek's personal life come from Zdeněk Koubek, "Zdeněk Koubek: The Story of a World-Record Woman" ("Zdeněk Koubek, Příběh světové rekordwoman"), *Prague Illustrated Reporter* (*Pražský ilustrovaný zpravodaj*), 1936. Published serially, February 13, 1936, to July 2, 1936, issues 7–27. English translation by Meghan Forbes. The text is relied upon heavily in this chapter, as well as in all future chapters centered around Koubek.

2. Nancy M. Wingfield, *Flag Wars and Stone Saints: How the Bohemian Lands Became Czech* (Cambridge, MA: Harvard University Press, 2007), 30.

3. Milan Neužil, "The Press as a Factor of Political Mobilization: Brno's Periodical Deutsches Blatt" (PhD diss., Masaryk University, 2019), 126, https://is.muni.cz/th/ckg15/Disertacni_prace_Milan_Neuzil.pdf.

4. Wingfield, *Flag Wars & Stone Saints*, 84.

5. Mark Cornwall, "News, Rumour and the Control of Information in Austria-Hungary, 1914–1918," *History* 77, no. 249 (February 1992): 57.

6. Cornwall, "News, Rumour and the Control of Information," 56.

7. Cornwall, "News, Rumour and the Control of Information," 51.

8. See the population tables in Alice Teichova, *The Czechoslovak Economy 1918–1980* (Milton Park, UK: Routledge, 1988), 2–5.

9. Nancy M. Wingfield, "Democracy's Violent Birth: The Czech Legion-

naires and Statue Wars in the First Czechoslovak Republic," *Austrian History Yearbook* 53 (April 2022), 7.

10. Václav Šmidrkal, "The First World War in the Czech and Slovak Cinema," in *Habsburg's Last War: The Filmic Memory (1918 to the Present)*, ed. Hannes Leidinger (New Orleans: University of New Orleans Press, 2018), 72.

11. Antonín Bartonek, "History and Bibliography of Classical Scholarship in Czecho-Slovakia, 1900–1987," *The Classical Bulletin* 68 (January 1992): 21.

12. Wingfield, *Flag Wars and Stone Saints*, 277.

13. Wingfield, "Democracy's Violent Birth," 10.

14. Wingfield, "Democracy's Violent Birth," 7.

15. Šmidrkal, "The First World War in the Czech and Slovak Cinema," 74.

16. Wingfield, "Democracy's Violent Birth," 8.

17. Rudolf Kučera, "Exploiting Victory, Sinking into Defeat: Uniformed Violence in the Creation of the New Order in Czechoslovakia and Austria, 1918–1922," *The Journal of Modern History* 88, no. 4 (December 2016): 844.

18. Kučera, "Exploiting Victory, Sinking into Defeat," 827.

19. Kučera, "Exploiting Victory, Sinking into Defeat," 828.

CHAPTER 3

1. Florence Carpentier, "Alice Milliat: A Feminist Pioneer for Women's Sport," in *Global Sport Leaders: A Biographical Analysis of International Sport Management*, ed. Emmanuel Bayle and Patrick Clastres (London: Palgrave Macmillan, 2018), 63.

2. Carpentier, "Alice Milliat," 63.

3. Carpentier, "Alice Milliat," 64.

4. Carpentier, "Alice Milliat," 65.

5. "French Women Heed Call of the World of Sports," *The Kansas City Star*, October 9, 1919.

6. "French Women Heed Call of the World of Sports."

7. Carpentier, "Alice Milliat," 66.

8. Carpentier, "Alice Milliat," 67.

9. Carpentier, "Alice Milliat," 67.

10. Keith Rathbone, "'Save the Long Skirt': Women, Sports, and Fashion in Third Republic and Vichy France," *The International Journal of the History of Sport* 36, nos. 1–2 (January–February 2019): 306.

11. "Lady Footballers: French Team's Rousing Welcome in Preston," *Lancashire Evening Post*, April 29, 1920.

12. "Mother as Footballer," *Evening Standard*, May 1, 1920.

13. Florys Castan-Vicente and Anaïs Bohuon, "Emancipation Through Sport?:

Feminism and Medical Control of the Body in Interwar France," *Sport in History* 40, no. 2 (2019): 245.

14. "Lady Footballers."

15. "World Games Dramatize Women's Athletics," *Independent Woman* 13 (October 1934): 336.

16. Carpentier, "Alice Milliat," 69.

17. Florence Carpentier, "Alice Milliat et le premier 'sport féminin' dans l'Entre-deux-guerres," *Revue D'Histoire* 142, no. 2 (2019): 98.

18. Carpentier, "Alice Milliat," 76. According to Carpentier, Milliat wrote to Coubertin twice, first in 1919 and again in 1922. Milliat mentioned these letters in the minutes of the 1922 FSFI Congress, but neither letter appears to have survived, and we don't have their exact text.

19. Jules Boykoff, *Power Games: A Political History of the Olympics* (New York: Verso, 2016), 49.

20. Boykoff, *Power Games*, 11.

21. Diem, *Leben*, 87.

22. M. Patrick Cottrell and Travis Nelson, "Not Just the Games?: Power, Protest and Politics at the Olympics," *European Journal of International Relations* 17, no. 4 (December 2011): 736.

23. Dikaia Chatziefstathiou, "Reading Baron Pierre de Coubertin: Issues of Gender and Race," *Aethlon: The Journal of Sport Literature* 25, no. 2 (Spring–Summer 2008): 95.

24. Chatziefstathiou, "Reading Baron Pierre de Coubertin," 105.

25. Chatziefstathiou, "Reading Baron Pierre de Coubertin," 107.

26. Chatziefstathiou, "Reading Baron Pierre de Coubertin," 108.

27. "Chart Showing the Growth of the International Olympic Committee," Series 15, Box 116, Folder 5, Avery Brundage Collection, University of Illinois Archives, Champaign, Illinois.

28. Sheila Mitchell, "Women's Participation in the Olympic Games, 1900–1926," *Journal of Sport History* 4, no. 2 (Summer 1977): 210.

29. Joanna Davenport, "Breaking into the Rings: Women on the IOC," *Journal of Physical Education, Recreation & Dance* 67, no. 5 (1996): 26.

30. Chatziefstathiou, "Reading Baron Pierre de Coubertin," 99.

31. Fae Brauer, "Vitalist Cubisms: The Biocultures of Virility, Militarism and *La Vie Sportive*," in *Sport and the European Avant-Garde (1900–1945)*, ed. Andreas Kramer and Przemysław Strożek (Leiden, Netherlands: Brill, 2022), 20.

32. Chatziefstathiou, "Reading Baron Pierre de Coubertin," 103.

33. Chatziefstathiou, "Reading Baron Pierre de Coubertin," 100.

34. Sandra Heck, "A Sport for Everyone?: Inclusion and Exclusion in the Or-

ganisation of the First Olympic Modern Pentathlon," *The International Journal of the History of Sport* 31, no. 5 (2014): 532.

35. Patricia Campbell Warner, *When the Girls Came Out to Play: The Birth of American Sportswear* (Amherst: University of Massachusetts Press, 2006), 97.

36. Chris Turner, "From Pigeons to Olympic Participation—Centenary of the First Women's Olympiad," Museum of World Athletics, March 24, 2021, https://worldathletics.org/heritage/news/centenary-first-womens-olympiad.

37. "Women Athletes," *The Daily Telegraph*, April 7, 1921.

38. The restaurant was called Taverne Pousset, located at 14 Boulevard des Italiens. George R. Goethals, Georgia J. Sorenson, and James MacGregor Burns, eds., *Encyclopedia of Leadership* (Thousand Oaks, CA: Sage Publishing, 2004), 1681.

39. See the photograph *Menu Card for the Taverne Pousset*, taken by Jean Louis Forain in 1924. Held by the School of the Art Institute of Chicago.

40. "First Women's Olympiad," *Daily News* (London), August 21, 1922.

41. "Women Athletes," *Westminster Gazette*, August 21, 1922.

42. "Women's Olympiad Today," *Los Angeles Times*, August 20, 1922.

43. "American Girl Athletes Sail for Women's Olympiad at Paris," *The Boston Globe*, August 1, 1922.

44. Mary Henson Leigh, "The Evolution of Women's Participation in the Summer Olympic Games, 1900–1948" (PhD diss., Ohio State University, 1974), 164.

45. Carpentier, "Alice Milliat et le premier 'sport féminin,'" 104.

46. Milliat taught herself German in 1926, when she expected that Germany would host the Women's World Games. Lilian Campbell, "With the Women of Today," *Scranton Times*, December 16, 1926.

47. "Women's Athletic Contest," *The Vote* (London), February 1, 1929.

48. China and India are mentioned in "Women of Every Clime and Color Going In for Athletics, It Seems," *The Boston Globe*, March 14, 1925; Milliat's correspondence with Palestine is discussed in San Charles Haddad, *The File: Origins of the Munich Massacre* (New York: Post Hill Press, 2020), at the start of Chapter 3.

49. Carpentier, "Alice Milliat," 71.

50. Castan-Vicente and Bohuon, "Emancipation Through Sport?," 241.

51. Daniel M. Rosen, *Dope: A History of Performance Enhancement in Sports from the Nineteenth Century to Today* (Westport, CT: Praeger, 2008), 2.

52. See, for example, Dorando Pietri, an Italian marathon runner who, dehydrated and exhausted, fell four times throughout his race at the 1908 London Olympics. Matthew P. Llewellyn, "'Viva l'Italia! Viva l'Italia!': Dorando

Pietri and the North American Professional Marathon Craze, 1908–10," *The International Journal of the History of Sport* 25, no. 6 (2008): 713.

53. "L'Accident de la Passerelle des Invalides," *L'Aurore* (Paris), August 19, 1900. According to the Olympic archival website OlympStats, one of the victims was an Olympic fencer named Eugène Edmond Brassart, https://olympstats.com/2021/04/07/edmond-brassart/.

54. The athlete chased off course was Len Taunyane, one of the first Black Africans to participate in the Olympics, representing British-colonial South Africa. See George Matthews and Sandra Marshall, *St. Louis Olympics 1904* (Chicago: Arcadia Publishing, 2003), 68.

55. "Stops to Eat Peaches: Loses Marathon Race," *The Indianapolis Star*, September 4, 1904.

56. Allen Guttmann, *The Olympics: A History of the Modern Games* (Champaign: University of Illinois Press, 1992), 23.

57. "American Wins the Great Marathon Race," *The Courier-Journal* (Louisville, KY), August 31, 1904.

58. Many sources claim Lorz posed for photos with Alice Roosevelt Longworth, although that story is perhaps apocryphal; the anecdote first appears in print in the *New York Daily News* on August 11, 1935, two decades after the event.

59. Matthew P. Llewellyn, "The Battle of Shepherd's Bush," *The International Journal of the History of Sport* 28, no. 5 (2011): 692.

60. "Ugly Work in Games," *Sioux City Journal*, July 24, 1908.

61. Luke Harris and Iain Adams, "Wyndham Halswelle and the 1908 Olympic 400 Metres Final, the Most Controversial Race in Olympic History?," *Sport in History* 38, no. 2 (2018): 228.

62. Llewellyn, "The Battle of Shepherd's Bush," 692.

63. Harris and Adams, "Wyndham Halswelle and the 1908 Olympic 400 Metres Final," 235.

64. Jörg Krieger, *Power and Politics in World Athletics: A Critical History* (Milton Park, UK: Routledge, 2021), 15.

65. Krieger, *Power and Politics*, 18.

66. "J. Sigfrid Edström: Administrative / Biographical History," International Olympic Committee Historical Archives, Olympic Studies Centre, April 14, 2011.

67. Krieger, *Power and Politics*, 18.

68. "Development of Zurich Tramways," *Lane County Journal* (Dighton, KS), December 27, 1900.

69. Krieger, *Power and Politics*, 19.

70. Heck, "A Sport for Everyone?," 529.

71. See Krieger, *Power and Politics*, 19: "Coubertin regarded Edström as an ally . . ."

72. Large, *Nazi Games*, 30.

73. Krieger, *Power and Politics*, 19.

74. "International Athletics Regulations," *The San Francisco Call*, July 12, 1913.

75. Hans Bolling, "The Beginning of the IAAF: A Study of Its Background and Foundation," Stockholm, 2007, 15–16.

76. Krieger, *Power and Politics*, 24.

77. Krieger, *Power and Politics*, 24.

78. Krieger, *Power and Politics*, 26.

79. "International Jury to Decide Protests in Olympic Games," *Democrat and Chronicle* (Rochester, NY), June 11, 1914.

80. Krieger, *Power and Politics*, 18.

81. See, for example, the discussion of wind velocity in the Minutes of the Thirteenth Congress of the International Amateur Athletic Federation, held in Berlin on August 10–11, 1936. My gratitude to Doudou Sall Gaye and Chris Turner of World Athletics for providing copies of the meeting minutes.

82. For a detailed chronicle of the thinking of the IAAF and the IOC, see generally Jörg Krieger, Michele Krech, and Lindsay Parks Pieper, "'Our Sport': The Fight for Control of Women's International Athletics," *The International Journal of the History of Sport* 37, nos. 5–6 (2020): 451–72.

83. Krieger, Krech, and Pieper, "'Our Sport,'" 455.

84. Krieger, Krech, and Pieper, "'Our Sport,'" 455.

85. Krieger, Krech, and Pieper, "'Our Sport,'" 455. The members were Frantz Reichel, Harry Barclay, Fr. Wydemans, Allan Muhr, Sophie Eliott-Lynn, and Alice Milliat.

86. Krieger, Krech, and Pieper, "'Our Sport,'" 459.

CHAPTER 4

1. The first part of this chapter is sourced entirely from Koubek's recounting of his life in Koubek, "Zdeněk Koubek: The Story of a World-Record Woman."

2. It's possible that Koubek had the name "Karla Sychrová" slightly wrong. I was not immediately able to find sources documenting an athlete by this name.

3. The school was UMPRŮM, known in English as the Academy of Arts, Architecture & Design in Prague. See Karla Huebner, *Magnetic Woman: Toyen and the Surrealist Erotic* (Pittsburgh: University of Pittsburgh Press, 2021), 5.

4. The Huebner text refers to Toyen using she/her pronouns, but in light of

Toyen's intentionally androgynous presentation, I am choosing to use they/them pronouns for Toyen.

5. Huebner, *Magnetic Woman*, 33.

6. Huebner, *Magnetic Woman*, 12.

7. Karla Huebner, "The Czech 1930s through Toyen," in *Czech Feminisms: Perspectives on Gender in East Central Europe*, ed. Iveta Jusová and Jiřina Šiklová (Bloomington: Indiana University Press, 2016), 65.

8. Huebner, "The Czech 1930s through Toyen," 71.

9. Huebner, *Magnetic Woman*, xiv.

10. Huebner, "The Czech 1930s through Toyen," 70.

11. When it was founded in 1931, the publication that became *New Voice* was known as *The Voice of the Sexual Minority* (*Hlas sexuální menšiny*). See Huebner, "The Czech 1930s through Toyen," 70.

12. Huebner, "The Czech 1930s through Toyen," 62.

13. Huebner, "The Czech 1930s through Toyen," 63.

14. Karla Huebner, "The Whole World Revolves Around It: Sex Education and Sex Reform in First Republic Czech Print Media," *Apasia* 4 (Spring 2010): 31.

15. Mark Cornwall, "Heinrich Rutha and the Unraveling of a Homosexual Scandal in 1930s Czechoslovakia," *GLQ: A Journal of Lesbian and Gay Studies* 8, no. 3 (2002): 325.

16. Zavier Nunn, "Trans Liminality and the Nazi State," *Past & Present* (September 2022): 8.

17. Nunn, "Trans Liminality," 4.

18. Leah Tigers, "On the Clinics and Bars of Weimar Berlin," Tricky Mother Nature, 2022, http://www.trickymothernature.com/insideout1.html.

19. The surgeon is Ludwig Levy-Lenz. See Tigers, "On the Clinics and Bars of Weimar Berlin," citing page 204 of the 1953 book *Diskretes und Indiskretes* by Ludwig Levy-Lenz.

20. Tigers, "On the Clinics and Bars of Weimar Berlin."

21. Tigers, "On the Clinics and Bars of Weimar Berlin."

22. For further reading on Tong, see generally Laurie Marhoefer, *Racism and the Making of Gay Rights: A Sexologist, His Student, and the Empire of Queer Love* (Toronto: University of Toronto Press, 2022).

23. Marhoefer, *Racism and the Making of Gay Rights*, ix. See the caption on figure 3.

24. See, for example, "Want to Change Your Sex? It's Simple They Say," *Colton (CA) Daily Courier*, May 12, 1921.

25. See "Science Can Alter Sex at Will, Prof. Guyer Says," *The Capital Times* (Madison, WI), January 31, 1925. The article notes that even "among human beings," there are "persons who are of both sexes."

26. "Oyster Changes from Sex to Sex," *The News-Democrat* (Carrollton, KY), August 18, 1912.

27. F. A. E. Crew, "Studies in Intersexuality: Sex-Reversal in the Fowl," *Proceedings of the Royal Society B* 95, no. 667 (September 1, 1923): 273.

28. Oscar Riddle, "A Case of Complete Sex-Reversal in the Adult Pigeon," *The American Naturalist* 58, no. 655 (March–April 1924): 169.

29. Riddle, "A Case of Complete Sex-Reversal in the Adult Pigeon," 175.

30. United Press, "Girls Who Would Be Boys May Gain Wish," *The Columbus Telegram*, December 28, 1923.

31. Associated Press, "Changes Sex of a Dove," *The Kansas City Star*, December 28, 1923.

32. "Want Your Girl to Be a Boy? Call on Dr. Riddle," *Fort Wayne Sentinel*, December 28, 1923.

33. Riddle, "A Case of Complete Sex-Reversal in the Adult Pigeon," 175.

34. "Want Your Girl to Be a Boy?"

35. Oscar Riddle, "Can We Control Sex?," *Science and Invention* (December 1928): 683.

36. "Court Decrees Change of Sex," *The Buffalo Enquirer*, December 16, 1911.

37. Huebner, "The Czech 1930s through Toyen," 67.

38. Lennox Broster, *The Adrenal Cortex and Intersexuality* (London: Chapman and Hall, 1938), 47.

39. See the Mark Edward Weston entry in England & Wales Deaths 1837–2007, a database of government records available on findmypast.com.

40. "Devon Woman Athlete Who Has Become a Man," *Western Morning News* (Plymouth, UK), May 28, 1936.

41. See 1911 Census for England and Wales, a digitized file available on findmypast.com. Mark is listed as "Mary Edith Louise Weston," living in Oreston, a village within Plymouth.

42. Jean Williams, *Britain's Olympic Women: A History* (Milton Park, UK: Routledge, 2020), 132.

43. Milton Bronner, "The Girl Who Became a Bridegroom," *Brownsville (TX) Herald*, September 29, 1936.

44. "Lady Athletes," *Western Morning News* (Plymouth, UK), August 8, 1922. The club, which was known variously as the Plymouth & District Ladies' Athletic and Football Club and the Plymouth Ladies Amateur Athletic Club, was formed around 1921, but it initially appeared to focus on soccer matches. Track and field came only in 1922.

45. "Pretty Bobbed Hair Girl's Athletic Prowess," *Weekly Dispatch* (London), August 9, 1925.

46. "Women's Championships," *Western Morning News* (Plymouth, UK), July 3, 1924. The article refers to Weston as "Miss M. C. L. Weston."

47. "Lady Athletes Prominent Competitors in Torquay Sports," *Western Morning News* (Plymouth, UK), August 18, 1924.

48. F. A. M. Webster, *Athletics of Today for Women* (London: Frederick Warne and Company, 1930), 337.

49. Bronner, "The Girl Who Became a Bridegroom."

50. Bronner, "The Girl Who Became a Bridegroom."

51. "Oreston Girl Athlete," *Western Morning News* (Plymouth, UK), July 23, 1930; "Strong Girl. Javelin-Discus Champion," *Daily News* (London), August 19, 1930.

52. "Devon Athlete Miss Mary Weston Leaves for Hanover," *Western Morning News* (Plymouth, UK), August 22, 1931. The article notes that Weston practiced on the Cattewater. Per the census, Weston was living in Bayley's Cottages in Oreston, Plymouth, at the time. The following establishes that the cottages were off Marine Road, near the Cattewater: "Collapse on Raft," *Western Morning News* (Plymouth, UK), January 1, 1936.

53. "Team of 'Babes' Who Will Make Germans Move," *Reynolds's Newspaper* (London), August 16, 1931.

54. "New Record for Discus Throwing," *Western Morning News* (Plymouth, UK), July 20, 1931.

55. "Broke Two Records," *Western Morning News* (Plymouth, UK), July 17, 1928.

56. "Kicking Sex into 'Limbo,'" *Daily Herald* (London), April 21, 1922.

57. "Women's Olympiad (1922)," British Pathé, April 24, 1922, https://www.britishpathe.com/asset/49332.

58. Lindsay Parks Pieper, *Sex Testing* (Champaign: University of Illinois Press, 2016), 17.

59. United Press, "2 Operations Make Man of Girl Athlete," *Shamokin (PA) News-Dispatch*, May 28, 1936.

60. "English Champion Back at Oreston," *Western Morning News* (Plymouth, UK), August 25, 1928.

61. "Middlesex Ladies' Athletic Club," *West London Observer*, July 23, 1926.

62. "To Represent Britain," *Daily Mirror*, August 9, 1926.

63. See "J. Sigfrid Edström: Administrative / Biographical History."

64. Natalie Barker-Ruchti, Karin Grahn, and Claes Annerstedt, "Moving Towards Inclusion: An Analysis of Photographs from the 1926 Women's Games in Gothenburg," *The International Journal of the History of Sport* 30, no. 8 (2013): 876.

65. Email correspondence with Claes Annerstedt, who is cowriting a paper

on the 1926 Women's World Games, tentatively titled "The Second Women's Olympic Games, Gothenburg 1926."

66. Email correspondence with Claes Annerstedt.

67. Email correspondence with Claes Annerstedt. It's difficult to prove an absence with absolute certainty, but Annerstedt wrote, "As far as I know, Sigrid Edström did not visit the games."

68. Weston placed sixth in the shot put. See FSFI Meeting Minutes, August 27–29, 1926, Musée National du Sport, Nice, France, 4. With gratitude to Léna Schillinger for scanning the meeting minutes.

69. The following section draws entirely on the full-length interview that Willy de Bruyn gave of his life immediately after his gender transition. See "A New Life: How I Changed from a Woman into a Man," *De Dag* (Belgium), April 24–25, 1937. (The article was published over the course of two days.) Translated into English by Charlotte Emma Vanhecke. Much gratitude as well to Hilde Laenen and Steven Van Impe of the Hendrik Conscience Heritage Library, both of whom assisted in scanning the original copy.

CHAPTER 5

1. Erik N. Jensen, *Body by Weimar* (Oxford: Oxford University Press, 2010), 100.

2. Karl Lennartz and Jürgen Buschmann, "Carl Diem—Still Controversial 50 Years On," *Journal of Olympic History* 3 (2012): 28.

3. "Chronicle, 1920," German Sport University Cologne, accessed May 2023, https://www.dshs-koeln.de/english/university-facilities/profile/chronicle/1920.

4. Jensen, *Body by Weimar*, 106.

5. Jensen, *Body by Weimar*, 106.

6. Jensen, *Body by Weimar*, 107.

7. "Chronicle, 1920."

8. Henning Eichberg, "Race-Track and Labyrinth: The Space of Physical Culture in Berlin," *Journal of Sport History* 17, no. 2 (Summer 1990): 257.

9. Jensen, *Body by Weimar*, 107.

10. Jensen, *Body by Weimar*, 124.

11. Jensen, *Body by Weimar*, 132.

12. This letter is mentioned in Walter Borgers, Karl Lennartz, Dietrich R. Quanz, and Walter Teutenberg, "Foundation Dates of the German Olympic Committee," Carl Diem Archive digitized by LA84 Foundation, 1995, 8. See also Carl Diem, *Leben*, 110.

13. Diem, *Leben*, 110.

14. Large, *Nazi Games*, 36.

15. Lewald's role in the effort is chronicled in "Sore on Olympic Fund," *Washington Evening Star*, February 15, 1914. The 200,000 marks figure comes from Kluge, "Cancelled but Still Counted," 12.

16. Thomas Zawadzki, "Fundamental Thoughts into a Research on German IOC Member and Politician: Theodor Lewald," *Journal of Olympic History* 14, no. 1 (March 2006): 60.

17. Zawadzki, "Fundamental Thoughts," 61.

18. Darren M. O'Byrne, "'Self-Coordination' and Its Origins: Civil Servants and Regime Change in 1933 and 1918/19," *Contemporary European History* (2022): 10.

19. O'Byrne, "'Self-Coordination' and Its Origins," 11.

20. Zawadzki, "Fundamental Thoughts," 59. "Germany's largest sports organization" refers to DRA für Leibesübungen, often translated as the German Reich's Committee for Physical Exercise.

21. Borgers, Lennartz, Quanz, and Teutenberg, "Foundation Dates of the German Olympic Committee," 10.

22. Diem, *Leben*, 110–12.

23. Large, *Nazi Games*, 49.

24. Diem, *Leben*, 113.

25. Diem, *Leben*, 113.

26. Jonathan Shaw, "The Unexpected Olympians," *Harvard Magazine*, July 1996.

27. Barbara Keys, "Spreading Peace, Democracy, and Coca-Cola: Sport and American Cultural Expansion in the 1930s," *Diplomatic History* 28, no. 2 (April 2004): 169.

28. Keys, "Spreading Peace, Democracy, and Coca-Cola," 174.

29. Keys, "Spreading Peace, Democracy, and Coca-Cola," 169.

30. See Keys, "Spreading Peace, Democracy, and Coca-Cola," 170, fn16.

31. Peter-Jan Mol, "Sport in Amsterdam, Olympism and Other Influences: The Inter-War Years," *The International Journal of the History of Sport* 17, no. 4 (2000): 147.

32. Mol, "Sport in Amsterdam," 147.

33. Mol, "Sport in Amsterdam," 147.

34. See Keys, "Spreading Peace, Democracy, and Coca-Cola," 170, fn16.

35. Diem, *Leben*, 114.

36. Ahead of the games, Diem had publicly predicted that Germany would place third in the medal count. See "Germany Hopes to Be Third in Olympic Games," *Blackwell (OK) Journal-Tribune*, February 29, 1928.

37. Diem, *Leben*, 115.

38. Large, *Nazi Games*, 49.

39. Diem, *Leben*, 115.
40. Darren M. O'Byrne and Christopher Young, "The Will of the Führer?: Financing Construction for the 1936 Olympics," *Journal of Contemporary History* 57, no. 1 (January 2022): 28.
41. O'Byrne and Young, "The Will of the Führer," 28.
42. Barbara J. Keys, *Globalizing Sport* (Cambridge, MA: Harvard University Press, 2006), 124.
43. Large, *Nazi Games*, 50.
44. William Gerard Durick, "To the Berlin Games: The Olympic Movement in Germany from 1896–1936" (master's thesis, North Texas State University, 1984), 59.
45. Durick, "To the Berlin Games," 60.
46. Durick, "To the Berlin Games," 61.
47. "Olympia Learns Lessons," *Athletic News* (Manchester, UK), May 18, 1931.
48. Large, *Nazi Games*, 51.
49. Durick, "To the Berlin Games," 63.
50. Large, *Nazi Games*, 52.
51. Crombie Allen, "Germany Plans Sports Revival," *Los Angeles Times*, August 2, 1931.

CHAPTER 6

1. Associated Press, "Miss Hitomi Is Japan's Foremost Woman Athlete," *Kenosha (WI) News*, September 11, 1926.
2. Dennis J. Frost, *Seeing Stars: Sports Celebrity, Identity, and Body Culture in Modern Japan* (Cambridge, MA: Harvard University Press, 2010), 125. According to a contemporaneous writer quoted by Frost, Hitomi, with no coach to speak of, practiced "all alone, day after day."
3. Frost, *Seeing Stars*, 110.
4. Frost, *Seeing Stars*, 121.
5. Frost, *Seeing Stars*, 121.
6. Frost, *Seeing Stars*, 122.
7. Frost, *Seeing Stars*, 122.
8. Frost, *Seeing Stars*, 126.
9. "Miss Hitomi Again," *Daily Mirror*, August 9, 1928.
10. Frost, *Seeing Stars*, 122.
11. Frost, *Seeing Stars*, 144.
12. Negley Farson, "Kimmie Hitomi Not Only Sport Star but She Is 'Some Girl,'" *Washington Evening Star*, July 30, 1928. "Kimmie" was one of many misspellings American journalists made of Hitomi's name.
13. Krieger, Krech, and Pieper, "'Our Sport,'" 460.

14. Krieger, Krech, and Pieper, "'Our Sport,'" 461.

15. Krieger, *Power and Politics*, 41.

16. Leigh, "The Evolution of Women's Participation," 181.

17. Frost, *Seeing Stars*, 127–28. "Her face felt hot" is a slight departure from Hitomi's own words. Hitomi actually said, "My eyes suddenly became hot," according to Frost's translation.

18. Colleen English, "'Beyond Women's Powers of Endurance': The 1928 800-Meter and Women's Olympic Track and Field in the Context of the United States," *Sport History Review* 50, no. 2 (2019): 187.

19. Frost, *Seeing Stars*, 110.

20. Exactly what happened still remains murky, but according to Colleen English, "the veracity of this narrative is questionable at best." Recently unearthed footage suggests that few women did actually fall after the race. See English, "'Beyond Women's Powers of Endurance,'" 188.

21. All quoted newspapers first appeared in English, "'Beyond Women's Powers of Endurance,'" 188. Much gratitude to English for unearthing these reports.

22. English, "'Beyond Women's Powers of Endurance,'" 188.

23. Krieger, Krech, and Pieper, "'Our Sport,'" 461, quotes the IAAF meeting minutes as stating that the eight-hundred-meter dash was "too hard for women, this race not being an endurance competition but a long sprint."

24. "New Leader Named for the Olympics," *The Vancouver Sun*, May 29, 1925.

25. Florence Carpentier, "Henri de Baillet-Latour: Globalising the Olympic Movement," in *Global Sport Leaders*, ed. Bayle and Clastres, 107.

26. Carpentier, "Henri de Baillet-Latour," 114.

27. Letter from Henri de Baillet-Latour to Alice Milliat, November 21, 1926, "Women and Sport: Correspondence About the Women's Federations— Alice Milliat," International Olympic Committee Historical Archive, Olympic Studies Centre, reference code F-A02-PS-FEMSP/011. Thanks in particular to Diego Girod for the invaluable help in using these archives.

28. Florence Carpentier and Jean-Pierre Lefèvre, "The Modern Olympic Movement, Women's Sport and the Social Order During the Inter-War Period," *The International Journal of the History of Sport* 23, no. 7 (2006): 1126, fn36.

29. Krieger, Krech, and Pieper, "'Our Sport,'" 460.

30. Carpentier and Lefèvre, "The Modern Olympic Movement," 1119.

31. Carpentier and Lefèvre, "The Modern Olympic Movement," 1122.

32. Krieger, Krech, and Pieper, "'Our Sport,'" 462, notes that Edström was "apathetic about women's athletics" and largely saw them "as a means to maintain and increase the power of the IAAF."

33. The meeting minutes of the FSFI are riddled with frank discussions of its financial straits. Krieger, Krech, and Pieper, "'Our Sport,'" quote the 1926 meeting minutes, which note that "only prodigious efforts of economy have allowed the Federation to survive to date with such meagre resources."

34. Krieger, Krech, and Pieper, "'Our Sport,'" 462.

35. Krieger, Krech, and Pieper, "'Our Sport,'" 462.

36. Krieger, Krech, and Pieper, "'Our Sport,'" 463.

37. Krieger, Krech, and Pieper, "'Our Sport,'" 463.

38. See, for instance, FSFI Meeting Minutes, September 11–12, 1932.

39. "Oreston Girl Honoured," *Western Morning News* (Plymouth, UK), August 1, 1929.

40. "Oreston Carnival," *Western Morning News* (Plymouth, UK), August 6, 1928.

41. "For the Hospital: How Plymstock Has Helped Fundraise," *Western Morning News* (Plymouth, UK), September 9, 1929.

42. "Oreston Athletic Heroine," *Western Morning News* (Plymouth, UK), August 17, 1929.

43. "To Represent England," *Western Morning News* (Plymouth, UK), August 8, 1930.

44. "Oreston Girl Athlete Leaves Plymouth for Women's Games at Prague," *Western Morning News* (Plymouth, UK), September 2, 1930.

45. Frost, *Seeing Stars*, 128.

46. "Japan's Woman Champion," *The Guardian*, September 26, 1930.

47. Frost, *Seeing Stars*, 129.

48. Weston placed in fourteenth in the javelin-throwing competition, twelfth in the shot put, and sixth in the discus. See the FSFI Meeting Minutes, September 6–8, 1930, 7.

49. Frost, *Seeing Stars*, 129.

50. "Oreston Girl Athlete on German Methods," *Western Morning News* (Plymouth, UK), September 16, 1930.

51. Sigfrid Schultz, "Germans Vote Today; 1 Slain, 8 Dying in Riot," *Chicago Tribune*, September 14, 1930.

52. "Oreston Girl Athlete on German Methods."

53. See James K. Pollock Jr., "The German Reichstag Elections of 1930," *American Political Science Review* 24, no. 4 (November 1930).

54. In a later interview, Weston noted that in 1930, "My continued studies in anatomy as part of my massage work led me to begin wondering whether I was really a woman." See Bronner, "The Girl Who Became a Bridegroom."

55. Program for the 1930 Women's World Games, Marguerite Radideau Collection, Musée National du Sport, Nice, France.

56. Frost, *Seeing Stars*, 129.

57. "Miss Kinuye Hitomi, Athlete, Dies at 24," *The New York Times*, August 3, 1931.

58. Frost, *Seeing Stars*, 131.

59. Frost, *Seeing Stars*, 143. This article was published in the *Fujin gahō* in May 1931, as Hitomi was in the hospital, but shortly before her death.

60. Koubek, "Zdeněk Koubek: The Story of a World-Record Woman."

61. Koubek does not mention this detail in his narrative essay, but see FSFI Meeting Minutes, September 9, 1930; Bléha is listed among the Czech representatives.

62. O'Byrne and Young, "The Will of the Führer," 30.

63. O'Byrne and Young, "The Will of the Führer," 30.

64. Diem, *Leben*, 119.

65. Guy Walters, *Berlin Games: How the Nazis Stole the Olympic Dream* (New York: Harper Perennial, 2006), 12.

66. Boykoff, *Power Games*, 67.

67. Mark Dyreson and Matthew Llewellyn, "Los Angeles Is *the* Olympic City: Legacies of the 1932 and 1984 Olympic Games," *The International Journal of the History of Sport* 25, no. 14 (2008): 1995.

68. Keys, "Spreading Peace, Democracy, and Coca-Cola," 169.

69. Keys, "Spreading Peace, Democracy, and Coca-Cola," 172.

70. Keys, "Spreading Peace, Democracy, and Coca-Cola," 175–76, notes that a group of Japanese visitors were reportedly visiting "three or four parties a day."

71. Keys, "Spreading Peace, Democracy, and Coca-Cola," 173.

72. Keys, "Spreading Peace, Democracy, and Coca-Cola," 170.

73. Dyreson and Llewellyn, "Los Angeles Is *the* Olympic City," 1992.

74. Walters, *Berlin Games*, 12.

75. Boykoff, *Power Games*, 68.

76. Diem, *Leben*, 123.

77. Peter Fritzsche, *Hitler's First Hundred Days: When Germans Embraced the Third Reich* (New York: Basic Books, 2020), 67.

CHAPTER 7

1. Maynard Brichford, "Avery Brundage: Chicago Businessman," *Journal of the Illinois State Historical Society* 91, no. 4 (Winter 1998): 218.

2. Allen Guttmann, *The Games Must Go On* (New York: Columbia University Press, 1983), 2.

3. Guttmann, *The Games Must Go On*, 3.

4. Guttmann, *The Games Must Go On*, 3.

5. Guttmann, *The Games Must Go On*, 4.

6. "Is Best All-Around Athlete," *The Lahoma Sun* (Oklahoma), December 29, 1916.

7. Guttmann, *The Games Must Go On*, 6.

8. Guttmann, *The Games Must Go On*, 11.

9. Avery Brundage, *The Olympic Story*, unpublished memoir, 1, dated February 24, 1972, Series 34, Box 354, Folder 3, Avery Brundage Collection.

10. Brundage, *The Olympic Story*, 3.

11. "Is Best All-Around Athlete."

12. "Title Games Billed Today," *The Chicago Tribune*, August 29, 1914.

13. "Avery Brundage Nation's Champion Athlete," *The Birmingham News*, September 20, 1914.

14. Guttmann, *The Games Must Go On*, 24.

15. Brundage, *The Olympic Story*, 3.

16. Guttmann, *The Games Must Go On*, 22.

17. Guttmann, *The Games Must Go On*, 26.

18. Guttmann, *The Games Must Go On*, 10.

19. Guttmann, *The Games Must Go On*, 40.

20. Guttmann, *The Games Must Go On*, 39.

21. Guttmann, *The Games Must Go On*, 4.

22. Guttmann, *The Games Must Go On*, 29. Guttmann speculates, but does not know for sure, that there is a connection.

23. Guttmann, *The Games Must Go On*, 28.

24. Guttmann, *The Games Must Go On*, 67.

25. Guttmann, *The Games Must Go On*, 2.

26. Guttmann, *The Games Must Go On*, 29.

27. Brichford, "Avery Brundage," 222.

28. Brichford, "Avery Brundage," 220.

29. Guttmann, *The Games Must Go On*, 32.

30. "Murray Hulbert Is Head of A.A.U.," *The Miami Herald*, November 18, 1925.

31. "Brundage Should Iron Out A.A.U. Troubles," *The Brooklyn Daily Eagle*, November 22, 1928.

32. Nearly a year into office, Brundage got into a public spat with—and threatened to suspend—the famous American sprinter Charles Paddock. See "Story Enraged Athletic Head," *Los Angeles Times*, August 16, 1929.

33. "Avery Brundage Elected Head of American Olympic Body," *The Salt Lake Tribune*, November 20, 1930.

34. Letter from Avery Brundage to Sigfrid Edström, September 3, 1929, Series 5, Box 44, Folder 12, Avery Brundage Collection.

35. Krieger, *Power and Politics*, 47.
36. Carly Adams, "Fighting for Acceptance: Sigfrid Edström and Avery Brundage: Their Efforts to Shape and Control Women's Participation in the Olympic Games," *The Global Nexus Engaged: Past, Present, Future Interdisciplinary Olympic Studies: Sixth International Symposium for Olympic Research*, ed. Kevin B. Wamsley, Robert Knight Barney, and Scott G. Martyn (London, Ontario: International Centre for Olympic Studies, University of Western Ontario, 2002), 145.
37. Krieger, *Power and Politics*, 47.
38. Leigh, "The Evolution of Women's Participation," 161. Leigh interviewed Brundage shortly before his death.
39. Letter from Sigfrid Edström to Avery Brundage, January 3, 1935, Series 5, Box 44, Folder 12, Avery Brundage Collection.
40. Letter from Avery Brundage to Knute Rockne, July 17, 1930, Series 1, Box 8, Folder 19, Avery Brundage Collection.
41. "Brundage Defends A.A.U. in Case Concerning Babe Didrikson," *The Mansfield (OH) Journal*, December 24, 1932.
42. Mary Henson Leigh, "The Enigma of Avery Brundage and Women Athletes," *Arena Review* 4 (1980): 14, quotes Brundage as lobbying a colleague, William May Garland, to support women's sports for political benefit.
43. Jörg Krieger and Austin Duckworth, "Annexation or Fertile Inclusion?: The Origins of Handball's International Organisational Structures," *Sport in History* 42, no. 2 (2022): 241.
44. Krieger, *Power and Politics*, 47.
45. Leif Yttergren, "J. Sigfrid Edström and the Nurmi Affair of 1932," *Journal of Olympic History* 15, no. 3 (November 2007): 22.
46. Yttergren, "J. Sigfrid Edström and the Nurmi Affair of 1932," 25.
47. Yttergren, "J. Sigfrid Edström and the Nurmi Affair of 1932," 21.
48. Letter from Sigfrid Edström to Avery Brundage, November 5, 1932, Series 5, Box 44, Folder 12, Avery Brundage Collection.
49. See, for example, letter from Sigfrid Edström to Justice Bartow S. Weeks, March 7, 1919, IAAF Correspondence (1914–1972) folder, International Olympic Committee Historical Archive, Olympic Studies Centre.
50. Durick, "To the Berlin Games," 75.
51. Dieter Petzina, "Germany and the Great Depression," *Journal of Contemporary History* 4, no. 4 (October 1969): 60. According to Petzina, "We shall not go far if we assume that in 1932 one in every three of the working population had no job."
52. Peter D. Stachura, *Unemployment and the Great Depression in Weimar Germany* (London: Palgrave Macmillan, 1986), 136.

53. Fritzsche, *Hitler's First Hundred Days*, 31.
54. Fritzsche, *Hitler's First Hundred Days*, 28.
55. Fritzsche, *Hitler's First Hundred Days*, 52.
56. "Cabinet Changes Foreseen in Reich," *The New York Times*, January 15, 1933.
57. O'Byrne and Young, "The Will of the Führer," 30.
58. Larry Eugene Jones, "Hindenburg and the Conservative Dilemma in the 1932 Presidential Elections," *German Studies Review* 20, no. 2 (May 1997): 237.
59. Durick, "To the Berlin Games," 75.
60. O'Byrne and Young, "The Will of the Führer," 31.
61. Anton Rippon, *Hitler's Olympics: The Story of the 1936 Nazi Games* (Barnsley, UK: Pen and Sword, 2012), 32.
62. Rippon, *Hitler's Olympics*, 33.
63. Rippon, *Hitler's Olympics*, 33.
64. "German Government to Give Full Co-Operation," *Western Morning News* (Plymouth, UK), January 27, 1933.
65. "Group Formed by Papen," *The New York Times*, January 31, 1933.
66. Fritzsche, *Hitler's First Hundred Days*, 122.
67. Monika Meyer, "Berlin 1936," in *Olympic Cities: City Agendas, Planning, and the World's Games*, ed. John R. Gold and Margaret M. Gold (Milton Park, UK: Routledge, 2007), 271.
68. Associated Press, "Nazi Leaders Appear Well Satisfied with the Boycott on Jews," *Deadwood (SD) Pioneer-Times*, April 4, 1933.
69. Large, *Nazi Games*, 36.
70. O'Byrne and Young, "The Will of the Führer," 31; Large, *Nazi Games*, 63.
71. O'Byrne and Young, "The Will of the Führer," 31.
72. Large, *Nazi Games*, 63.
73. O'Byrne and Young, "The Will of the Führer," 34.
74. Borgers, Lennartz, Quanz, and Teutenberg, "Foundation Dates of the German Olympic Committee," 10.
75. Arnd Krüger, "'Once the Olympics Are Through, We'll Beat Up the Jew': German Jewish Sport 1898–1938 and the Anti-Semitic Discourse," *Journal of Sport History* 26, no. 2 (Summer 1999): 356. The two clubs were Schild and Maccabi.
76. Letter from Karl Jarres to Theodor Lewald, April 15, 1933, in *German Reich, 1933–1937*, ed. Wolf Gruner and Caroline Pearce (Berlin: De Gruyter Oldenbourg, 2019), 157.
77. Large, *Nazi Games*, 65.
78. Large, *Nazi Games*, 66.

79. Leif Yttergren, "Questions of Propriety: J. Sigfrid Edström, Anti-Semitism, and the 1936 Berlin Olympics," *Olympika: The International Journal of Olympic Studies* 16 (2007): 84.

80. Yttergren, "Questions of Propriety," 84.

81. Peter Longerich, *Heinrich Himmler: A Life* (Oxford: Oxford University Press, 2007), 259.

82. Associated Press, "Brundage Predicts Games Will Not Be Held in Germany," *Palladium-Item* (Richmond, IN), April 17, 1933.

83. Associated Press, "Brundage Predicts."

84. "U.S. May Boycott Berlin Olympics," *The Daily Worker*, April 20, 1933.

85. International News Service, "Hitlerites Disturbed by Threatened Loss of Olympic Games," *The Lincoln (NE) Star*, April 18, 1933.

86. Large, *Nazi Games*, 71.

87. International News Service, "Hitlerites Disturbed."

88. Large, *Nazi Games*, 73.

89. Large, *Nazi Games*, 73.

90. Arnd Krüger, *The Nazi Olympics: Sport, Politics, and Appeasement in the 1930s* (Champaign: University of Illinois Press, 2003), 48.

91. Associated Press, "German Sports Head Says Games for Aryans," *The Boston Globe*, May 9, 1933.

92. George Eisen, "The Voices of Sanity: American Diplomatic Reports from the 1936 Berlin Olympiad," *Journal of Sport History* 11, no. 3 (Winter 1984): 59.

93. Letter from Henri de Baillet-Latour to Avery Brundage, December 1, 1933, Series 5, Box 44, Folder 10, Avery Brundage Collection.

94. Letter from Henri de Baillet-Latour to Avery Brundage, November 3, 1933, Series 5, Box 44, Folder 10, Avery Brundage Collection.

95. Krüger, *The Nazi Olympics*, 49.

96. Arthur J. Daley, "A.A.U. Boycotts 1936 Olympics Because of the Nazi Ban on Jews," *The New York Times*, November 21, 1933.

97. Baillet-Latour to Brundage, November 3, 1933.

98. Letter from Sigfrid Edström to Avery Brundage, February 8, 1934, Series 5, Box 44, Folder 13, Avery Brundage Collection.

99. Letter from Sigfrid Edström to Avery Brundage, December 4, 1933, Series 5, Box 44, Folder 12, Avery Brundage Collection.

100. Letter from Avery Brundage to Sigfrid Edström, December 28, 1933, Series 5, Box 44, Folder 12, Avery Brundage Collection.

CHAPTER 8

1. Robert Beachy, "The German Invention of Homosexuality," *The Journal of Modern History* 82, no. 4 (December 2010): 836–37.

2. Matthew H. Birkhold, "A Lost Piece of Trans History," *The Paris Review*, January 15, 2019.

3. Laurie Marhoefer, "Lesbianism, Transvestitism, and the Nazi State: A Microhistory of a Gestapo Investigation, 1939–1943," *American Historical Review* 121, no. 4 (October 2016): 1176. The use of "asocial" appears on page 1178 of the same text.

4. Tigers, "On the Clinics and Bars of Weimar Berlin."

5. Ben Miller, "Friedrich Radszuweit and the False Security of Collaboration," OutHistory, https://outhistory.org/blog/in-the-archives-friedrich -radszuweit-and-the-false-security-of-collaboration/ (page discontinued).

6. Andrew Stewart, "A Journal for Manly Culture: An Exploration of the World's First Gay Periodical," *Papers of the Bibliographical Society of Canada* 57 (2019): 86.

7. Stewart, "A Journal for Manly Culture," 86.

8. Heike Bauer, *The Hirschfeld Archives* (Philadelphia: Temple University Press, 2017), 92–93. In German, the chant was "Brenne Hirschfeld."

9. "German Libraries 'Purged,'" *Civil & Military Gazette* (British-colonial India), May 8, 1933.

10. Associated Press, "Dr. Hirschfeld Dead at Age 67," *South Bend (IN) Tribune*, May 17, 1935.

11. W. Jake Newsome, *Pink Triangle Legacies: Coming Out in the Shadow of the Holocaust* (Ithaca, NY: Cornell University Press, 2022), 25. The actual number is 7,957.

12. Keira Roberson, "Underground Circles and Clandestine Romance: Queer Resistance Under the Third Reich" (master's thesis, University of North Carolina at Charlotte, 2021), 32.

13. Dagmar Herzog, *Sexuality in Europe: A Twentieth-Century History* (Cambridge: Cambridge University Press, 2011), 73.

14. Newsome, *Pink Triangle Legacies*, 27.

15. Roberson, "Underground Circles and Clandestine Romance," 37.

16. Roberson, "Underground Circles and Clandestine Romance," 40.

17. Roberson, "Underground Circles and Clandestine Romance," 46.

18. Roberson, "Underground Circles and Clandestine Romance," 45.

19. Roberson, "Underground Circles and Clandestine Romance," 45.

20. Joseph B. Treaster, "Overlooked No More: Claude Cahun, Whose Photographs Explored Gender and Sexuality," *The New York Times*, June 19, 2019.

21. Konrad Henlein, "The German Minority in Czechoslovakia," *Bulletin of International News* 15, no. 4 (March 6, 1937): 747.

22. Cornwall, "News, Rumour and the Control of Information," 320.

23. Cornwall, "News, Rumour and the Control of Information," 323.

24. Ronald M. Smelser, "At the Limits of a Mass Movement: The Case of the Sudeten German Party, 1933–1938," *Bohemia* 17 (1976): 240.

25. Smelser, "At the Limits of a Mass Movement," 242.

26. Cornwall, "News, Rumour and the Control of Information," 323.

27. Cornwall, "News, Rumour and the Control of Information," 323–24.

28. "Fights U.S. Okay of Olympic Bid," *Washington Evening Star*, January 26, 1934.

29. William Fuchs, "Boycott the Olympics!," *The Daily Worker*, May 11, 1934.

30. Large, *Nazi Games*, 77.

31. Krüger, *The Nazi Olympics*, 50.

32. Krüger, *The Nazi Olympics*, 51.

33. Eisen, "The Voices of Sanity," 64.

34. "The American Olympic Team," *The Jewish Press* (Omaha, NE), August 24, 1934.

35. Large, *Nazi Games*, 78.

36. Letter from Avery Brundage to Henri de Baillet-Latour, July 9, 1934, Series 5, Box 44, Folder 10, Avery Brundage Collection.

37. Guttmann, *The Games Must Go On*, 47.

38. Fritzsche, *Hitler's First Hundred Days*, 232.

39. Fritzsche, *Hitler's First Hundred Days*, 265.

40. Fritzsche, *Hitler's First Hundred Days*, 111.

41. Large, *Nazi Games*, 79.

42. Krüger, "'Once the Olympics Are Through,'" 357–58.

43. Krüger, "'Once the Olympics Are Through,'" 358.

44. Robert Atlasz, *Barkochba: Makkabi-Deutschland, 1898–1938* (Tel Aviv: publisher unknown, 1977), 141–42. With gratitude to the United States Holocaust Memorial Museum for providing this scan.

45. Krüger, "'Once the Olympics Are Through,'" 358.

46. Atlasz, *Barkochba*, 141.

47. Large, *Nazi Games*, 79.

48. Guttmann, *The Games Must Go On*, 70.

CHAPTER 9

1. Koubek, "Zdeněk Koubek: The Story of a World-Record Woman."

2. Sheldon Anderson, *The Forgotten Legacy of Stella Walsh: The Greatest Female Athlete of Her Time* (Lanham, MD: Rowman & Littlefield, 2017), 55. The breaking point for Walsh, however, was the delay of not just her US citizenship but also the school scholarship and stable job that the Polish government had promised her.

3. Anderson, *The Forgotten Legacy*, 68.

4. Anderson, *The Forgotten Legacy*, 84.

5. Koubek, "Zdeněk Koubek: The Story of a World-Record Woman."

6. Williams, *Britain's Olympic Women*, 121.

7. Pavlína Vostatková, "Czechoslovak Female Athletes at the International Scene During the Interwar Period Between WWI and WWII," *Sport and Tourism: Central European Journal* 3, no. 4 (2020): 24–25.

8. Koubek, "Zdeněk Koubek: The Story of a World-Record Woman."

9. David Littlefield, "White City: The Art of Erasure and Forgetting the Olympic Games," *Architectural Design* 82, no. 1 (January/February 2012): 73.

10. Littlefield, "White City," 72.

11. Williams, *Britain's Olympic Women*, 121.

12. Vostatková, "Czechoslovak Female Athletes," 24–25.

13. "Women's World Games," *The Western Daily Press* (Bristol, UK), August 10, 1934.

14. Koubek, "Zdeněk Koubek: The Story of a World-Record Woman."

15. Vostatková, "Czechoslovak Female Athletes," 25, quotes (and translates) Koubek's own entry on his win in *Star*.

16. "Athletic Wonders in Women's Games," *Daily Herald* (London), August 13, 1934.

17. Vostatková, "Czechoslovak Female Athletes," 25.

18. "Germany's Girl Athletes Win 9 Events at World Games," *Daily News* (London), August 13, 1934.

19. "Athletic Wonders in Women's Games."

20. Koubek, "Zdeněk Koubek: The Story of a World-Record Woman."

21. For confirmation of Sims's job title, see "Colour Bar in Empire Games," *Daily Mirror*, July 10, 1934.

22. This account borrows Koubek's own claims in his narrative essay; however, because Koubek appears to have gotten the details of who Sims was wrong, it should be taken with a dose of skepticism. Koubek was not in attendance at the banquet, so it's unclear what his source of his information was. The banquet also does not appear to have been reported in the press. Because Sims did stir a panic about women athletes a month later, my best guess is that Koubek combined these two events in his memory.

23. Minutes of the Meeting of the Council of the South African Olympic and British Empire Games Association, August 24, 1934. With gratitude to Francois Johannes Cleophas for sending photos of these minutes.

24. The full meeting minutes, which presumably include these quotes, are unavailable. I am pulling these quotes from the contemporaneous newspaper coverage of the issue. See, for instance, "Were They Women? Doubts Cast

on World Games Competitors," *Sheffield Independent*, September 20, 1934.

25. "World Games 'Women' Really Men, Says Track Coach," *The Vancouver Sun*, September 20, 1934.

26. "Claims Men Posed as Girls in Sport Events at London," *The Coshocton (OH) Tribune*, September 20, 1934.

27. Alexandrine Gibb, "No Man's Land of Sport," *Toronto Daily Star*, December 3, 1935.

28. Alexandrine Gibb, "No Man's Land of Sport," *Toronto Daily Star*, May 30, 1936.

29. M. Ann Hall, "Alexandrine Gibb: In 'No Man's Land of Sport,'" *The International Journal of the History of Sport* 18, no. 1 (2001): 154.

30. Minutes of the IAAF Congress, 1932; the section on Elections of the Committee for Women's Sports was excerpted for me via email by Doudou Sall Gaye of the World Athletics Library, Monaco.

31. Alexandrine Gibb, "No Man's Land of Sport," *Toronto Daily Star*, August 17, 1934.

32. Alexandrine Gibb, "No Man's Land of Sport," *Toronto Daily Star*, September 25, 1934.

33. "Women Athletes Who Looked Like Men," *Liverpool Post and Mercury*, September 21, 1934.

34. "Those Empire Games 'Men-Women' Athletes," *Hartlepool Northern Daily Mail*, October 6, 1934.

35. United Press, "A Woman's Prerogative?," *The Oklahoma News*, December 4, 1935, quotes the Czech newspaper *Prager Tagblatt* from sometime in 1934. Unfortunately, I was unable to locate the original copy of the *Prager Tagblatt* article.

36. Koubek, "Zdeněk Koubek: The Story of a World-Record Woman."

37. Koubek, "Zdeněk Koubek: The Story of a World-Record Woman." It's unclear how Koubek knew the inner workings of the FSFI, and I could neither verify nor challenge this in the publicly available reporting.

38. Krieger, Krech, and Pieper, "'Our Sport,'" 465.

39. Krieger, Krech, and Pieper, "'Our Sport,'" 464.

40. "Milliat, Alice," in *Bibliothèque Marie-Louise Bouglé: Dossiers de coupures de presse biographiques*, 1933, reference number 4-MS-FS-21-0517.

41. Avery Brundage to Sigfrid Edström, September 20, 1934, Series 5, Box 44, Folder 14, Avery Brundage Collection.

42. Sigfrid Edström to Avery Brundage, January 3, 1935, Series 5, Box 44, Folder 15, Avery Brundage Collection.

43. Koubek, "Zdeněk Koubek: The Story of a World-Record Woman." Kou-

bek himself is the main source for this account, even though he presumably was not present throughout.

44. Smelser, "At the Limits of a Mass Movement," 240.

45. Koubek, "Zdeněk Koubek: The Story of a World-Record Woman."

CHAPTER 10

1. O'Byrne and Young, "The Will of the Führer," 25.

2. Meyer, "Berlin 1936," 273.

3. O'Byrne and Young, "The Will of the Führer," 33.

4. Meyer, "Berlin 1936," 273.

5. Meyer, "Berlin 1936," 274.

6. Meyer, "Berlin 1936," 273.

7. O'Byrne and Young, "The Will of the Führer," 41.

8. Krüger, "The Ministry of Popular Enlightenment and Propaganda and the Nazi Olympics of 1936," 33.

9. Large, *Nazi Games*, 83.

10. Moshe Gottlieb, "The Berlin Riots of 1935 and Their Repercussions in America," *American Jewish Historical Quarterly* 59, no. 3 (March 1970): 302.

11. Gottlieb, "The Berlin Riots of 1935," 303.

12. Gottlieb, "The Berlin Riots of 1935," 304.

13. Large, *Nazi Games*, 80.

14. Letter from Avery Brundage to Sigfrid Edström, August 29, 1935, Series 5, Box 44, Folder 15, Avery Brundage Collection.

15. Letter from Avery Brundage to Sigfrid Edström, August 29, 1935.

16. Letter from Avery Brundage to Henri de Baillet-Latour, September 24, 1935, Series 5, Box 44, Folder 11, Avery Brundage Collection.

17. Krüger, "'Once the Olympics Are Through,'" 359.

18. Krüger, "'Once the Olympics Are Through,'" 359. "Purely German Olympics" is quoting Krüger's paraphrase.

19. Rippon, *Hitler's Olympics*, 53.

20. "New Anti-Jew Laws," *Birmingham Gazette*, September 16, 1935.

21. "L.A. Olympic Chief Refuses to Attend Games in Berlin!," *Los Angeles Evening Post-Record*, November 27, 1935.

22. Letter from Sigfrid Edström to Avery Brundage, September 12, 1935, Series 5, Box 44, Folder 15, Avery Brundage Collection.

23. Henri de Baillet-Latour to Avery Brundage, October 10, 1935, Series 5, Box 44, Folder 10, Avery Brundage Collection.

24. H. Bernett, "Sport History: Sport and National Socialism—A Focus of Contemporary History," in *Sport Science in Germany: An Interdisciplin-*

ary Anthology, ed. Herbert Haag, Ommo Grupe, and August Kirsch (Berlin: Springer-Verlag, 1992), 454.

25. Avery Brundage to Henri de Baillet-Latour, October 28, 1935, Series 5, Box 44, Folder 10, Avery Brundage Collection.

26. Telegram from Daniel J. Ferris to Avery Brundage, October 29, 1935, Series 5, Box 44, Folder 10, Avery Brundage Collection.

27. Walters, *Berlin Games*, 57.

28. Avery Brundage to Sigfrid Edström, October 28, 1935, Series 5, Box 44, Folder 15, Avery Brundage Collection.

29. Letter from Hans von Tschammer to Charles Sherrill, September 21, 1935 (containing copy of undated letter from von Tschammer to Helene Mayer), Box 18, Volume 35, Scrapbook 35, Charles H. Sherrill Collection, New-York Historical Society, New York, NY.

30. "Helene Mayer, at Mills College, Accepts Bid," *Oakland Tribune*, October 26, 1935.

31. "Nazi Sports Authorities Give Written Promise Not to Discriminate Against Jews," *The Modern View* (St. Louis, MO), October 3, 1935. In these reports, Mayer in fact denied that she had received an invitation to join the German Olympic team.

32. John Lucas, "Ernest Lee Jahncke: The Expelling of an IOC Member," *Stadion* 17 (1991): 54.

33. Lucas, "Ernest Lee Jahncke," 57.

34. Lucas, "Ernest Lee Jahncke," 57.

35. Charles Sherrill to Ernest Lee Jahncke, June 22, 1932, Box 1, Correspondence Folder (Olympics, 1919–1933), Ernest Lee Jahncke, Sr., Papers, Louisiana State University, Baton Rouge, LA.

36. Lucas, "Ernest Lee Jahncke," 63.

37. Letter from Ernest Lee Jahncke to Henri de Baillet-Latour, November 25, 1935. A copy appears in Series 5, Box 44, Folder 10, Avery Brundage Collection.

38. Letter from Henri de Baillet-Latour to Avery Brundage, December 10, 1935, Series 5, Box 44, Folder 11, Avery Brundage Collection.

39. "Fight on Olympics Gets New Support," *The New York Times*, November 28, 1935.

40. Letter from Henri de Baillet-Latour to Avery Brundage, December 5, 1935, Series 5, Box 44, Folder 11, Avery Brundage Collection.

41. Letter from Brundage to Baillet-Latour, December 2, 1935, Series 5, Box 44, Folder 11, Avery Brundage Collection.

42. Koubek, "Zdeněk Koubek: The Story of a World-Record Woman."

43. "Koubková Is Undergoing Surgery," *The Czech Word* (*České slovo*),

November 30, 1935, accessed via the digital library Kramerius. In his personal essay, Koubek identifies the headline as "The Case of a World Record Woman," but he appears to have been mistaken.

44. Koubek, "Zdeněk Koubek: The Story of a World-Record Woman."

45. Koubek, "Zdeněk Koubek: The Story of a World-Record Woman."

46. See, for instance, the mention of Koubek's victory at the Women's World Games in "Germany Is First in Women's Meet," *The New York Times*, August 12, 1934.

47. I was not able to locate the name of the Reuters reporter who broke the story, but the first international article about Koubek cited Reuters, with a dateline in Prague. See, for example, "Woman Athlete Changing Sex," *Lancashire Evening Post*, December 3, 1935.

48. "Girl Athlete's Sex to Be Changed," *New York Daily News*, December 3, 1935; "Champion Girl Athlete Will Become 'Man,'" *San Francisco Examiner*, December 4, 1935; "Girl Athlete Changes Sex and Legal Status," *Los Angeles Times*, December 29, 1935.

49. "Woman Track Star Decides to Change Sex," *Pittsburgh Post-Gazette*, December 4, 1935.

50. "Girl Athlete May Become a Man," *Brooklyn Times Union*, December 3, 1935.

51. "Woman Track Star Decides to Change Sex."

52. "Champion Girl Athlete Will Become 'Man.'"

53. "Man to Keep Two Women's Race Records," *Wilkes-Barre Times Leader*, December 3, 1935.

54. "Athlete's Astounding Change of Sex," *London Life*, January 18, 1936. Many thanks to Clare Tebbutt, who wrote about Weston and Koubek in "The Spectre of the 'Man-Woman Athlete': Mark Weston, Zdenek Koubek, the 1936 Olympics and the Uncertainty of Sex," *Women's History Review* 24, no. 5 (2015): 721–38, for scanning their copies of *London Life* for me.

55. "Mysteries of Sex Metamorphosis," *London Life*, August 29, 1936.

56. International News Service, "Sorry Sex Is Changing," *Akron Beacon Journal*, December 16, 1935.

57. "Girl-into-Man Star Tells How It Feels," *New York Daily News*, February 23, 1936.

58. "Sorry Sex Is Changing."

59. Koubek, "Zdeněk Koubek: The Story of a World-Record Woman."

60. Zdeněk Koubek, letter to Prague Police Headquarters, May 23, 1936, from Policejní ředitelství Praha II—všeobecná spisovna (Police Headquarters Prague II—General Register), 1921–1950, Národní archiv

(National Archives of the Czech Republic). Thank you to Lukáš Pátý for providing the scan and to Barbora Bartunkova for translating these files into English.

61. "The Woman Who Became a Man," *Paris-soir*, January 3, 1936. Translated into English by Marion Renault.

62. Koubek, "Zdeněk Koubek: The Story of a World-Record Woman."

63. Koubek, "Zdeněk Koubek: The Story of a World-Record Woman."

64. "The Woman Who Became a Man."

65. "Czech Athlete Now a Man," *The New York Times*, December 29, 1935.

66. "Girl Who 'Turned to Man' Starts New Job," *Los Angeles Evening Post-Record*, December 28, 1935.

67. "Ex-Woman Makes Debut as Man," *The Western Daily Press* (Bristol, UK), December 21, 1935.

68. "Sex-Change Profitable," *Nottingham Evening Post*, January 4, 1936.

69. "Woman into Man. New Terror Added to Life," *Ireland's Saturday Night*, January 11, 1936.

70. "Sorry Sex Is Changing."

71. "Sex-Change Profitable."

72. United Press, "Operation Changes Girl Athlete to Man," *The Courier-Journal* (Louisville, KY), December 29, 1935.

73. "Sex-Change Profitable." *Paris-soir* is possibly the culprit, as the newspaper interviewed Koubek around the time.

74. "Woman Athlete Who May Become a Man," *Dundee Courier*, December 13, 1935.

75. "Girl Athlete Now a Man, and Sports World's Agog," *New York Daily News*, January 5, 1936.

76. "Women Who Shave Daily," *Dundee Courier*, January 2, 1936.

77. "Girl Athlete Now a Man, and Sports World's Agog."

78. Alexandrine Gibb, "No Man's Land of Sport," *Toronto Daily Star*, December 3, 1935.

79. Fabio Pigozzi et al., ed., *Ninety Years Contribution to Health in Sport* (Italy: International Federation of Sport Medicine, 2018), 10.

80. Paolo Colombani and Boris Gojanovic, "Über die frühen Jahre der organisierten Sportmedizin in der Schweiz," *Schweizerische Zeitschrift für Sportmedizin und Sporttraumatologie* 61 (2013): 6.

81. Jensen, *Body by Weimar*, 106.

82. Urban Fraefel, "Der gut getarnte Nazi," *Tagblatt*, September 12, 2015.

83. Hans-Peter de Lorent, "Wilhelm Knoll," Behörde für Schule und Berufsbildung (excerpting Lorent's book, *Täterprofile: Die Verantwortlichen im Hamburger Bildungswesen unterm Hakenkreuz*, 2016). Accessible

online at https://www.hamburg.de/clp/dabeigewesene-dokumente/clp1 /ns-dabeigewesene/onepage.php?BIOID=575.

84. Fraefel, "Der gut getarnte Nazi."

85. Lorent, "Wilhelm Knoll."

86. Fraefel, "Der gut getarnte Nazi."

87. Walter Aeschimann, "Die dunkle Vergangenheit des Elitesports," *Neue Zürcher Zeitung*, September 14, 2013.

88. For the bulk of the following quotes, see "Seek Ban on Czech 'Man-Woman' Star," *The Omaha Morning Bee-News*, January 11, 1936. For confirmation that Knoll wrote this as an op-ed in *Sport*, see "Zdenka Koubkowa wurde Zdenek Koubek," *Der Führer*, January 11, 1936 (accessed via Deutsches Zeitungsportal).

89. "Seek Ban on Czech 'Man-Woman' Star."

90. "Zdenka Koubkowa wurde Zdenek Koubek."

91. Letter from Czechoslovak Amateur Athletic Union to Dr. Borkovec, March 5, 1936, Policejní ředitelství Praha II—všeobecná spisovna (Police Headquarters Prague II—General Register), 1921–1950, Národní archiv (National Archives of the Czech Republic). English translation by Barbora Bartunkova.

92. Letter from Czechoslovak Amateur Athletic Union to Dr. Borkovec, March 5, 1936.

93. Letter from Dr. Borkovec to Czechoslovak Amateur Athletic Union, March 6, 1936, Policejní ředitelství Praha II—všeobecná spisovna. According to the police, "It is unclear from the files whether a name change was approved." Translation by Barbora Bartunkova.

94. Letter from Czechoslovak Amateur Athletic Union to Dr. Borkovec, March 5, 1936.

95. Ceskoslovenské Atletické Amatérské Unie (Czechoslovak Amateur Athletic Union) Annual Report, 1936, 9. Accessible online at https://www .atletika.cz/_sys_/FileStorage/download/16/15842/1936vod.pdf.

CHAPTER 11

1. Stephen R. Wenn, "Death-knell for the Amateur Athletic Union: Avery Brundage, Jeremiah Mahoney, and the 1935 AAU Convention," *The International Journal of the History of Sport* 13, no. 3 (1996): 262.

2. Henry Super, "A.A.U. Vote Will Not Change U.S. Olympic Stand," *The Minneapolis Star*, December 5, 1935.

3. Krüger, *Nazi Olympics*, 57.

4. Wenn, "Death-knell," 267.

5. Wenn, "Death-knell," 268.

6. Minutes of the annual meeting come from *Amateur Athletic Union of the United States, 1932–1937*, 129 (hereafter 1935 AAU Minutes). Courtesy of Utah State University, Logan, UT.

7. 1935 AAU Minutes, 142.

8. 1935 AAU Minutes, 146.

9. 1935 AAU Minutes, 149.

10. 1935 AAU Minutes, 153.

11. 1935 AAU Minutes, 153.

12. 1935 AAU Minutes, 155.

13. 1935 AAU Minutes, 161.

14. 1935 AAU Minutes, 162.

15. 1935 AAU Minutes, 186.

16. 1935 AAU Minutes, 192.

17. 1935 AAU Minutes, 238.

18. 1935 AAU Minutes, 240.

19. Large, *Nazi Games*, 100.

20. Krüger, *Nazi Olympics*, 92.

21. Large, *Nazi Games*, 105.

22. Krüger, *Nazi Olympics*, 92.

23. Large, *Nazi Games*, 106.

24. Krüger, *Nazi Olympics*, 72.

25. Walters, *Berlin Games*, 39.

26. Walters, *Berlin Games*, 40.

27. Eisen, "The Voices of Sanity," 68.

28. Letter from Henri de Baillet-Latour to Avery Brundage, December 12, 1935, Series 5, Box 44, Folder 10, Avery Brundage Collection.

29. Letter from Sigfrid Edström to Avery Brundage, April 3, 1934, Series 5, Box 44, Folder 13, Avery Brundage Collection.

30. Mateusz Rozmiarek, "The Legacy of the 1936 Winter Olympics in Garmisch-Partenkirchen in the Context of Sports Tourism," *Studies in Sport Humanities* 29 (2021): 53.

31. Krüger, *Nazi Olympics*, 74.

32. Arkadiusz Włodarczyk, "Olympic Games in Garmisch-Partenkirchen 1936—Sport, Logistics, Media," *Studies in Sport Humanities* 23 (2018): 19.

33. Large, *Nazi Games*, 110.

34. Large, *Nazi Games*, 136.

35. Walters, *Berlin Games*, 81.

36. Large, *Nazi Games*, 117.

37. Large, *Nazi Games*, 120.

38. Large, *Nazi Games*, 120.

39. "Hockey Opens Olympics Today; Two English Players Barred," *The New York Times*, February 5, 1936.

40. Large, *Nazi Games*, 144.

41. Stephen A. Schuker, "France and the Remilitarization of the Rhineland, 1936," *French Historical Studies* 14, no. 3 (Spring 1986): 299.

42. United Press, "French Plan to Bolt Berlin Olympics in Reprisal for Scrapping of Pact," *Democrat and Chronicle* (Rochester, NY), March 9, 1936.

43. United Press, "Fate of Berlin Olympics May Turn on Outcome of Rhineland Reoccupation," *The Hanford (CA) Sentinel*, March 10, 1936.

44. "Fate of Berlin Olympics May Turn on Outcome of Rhineland Reoccupation."

45. Krüger, *Nazi Olympics*, 96.

46. Mario Kessler, "Only Nazi Games? Berlin 1936: The Olympic Games Between Sports and Politics," *Socialism and Democracy* 25, no. 2 (July 2011): 129.

47. Large, *Nazi Games*, 151.

48. Large, *Nazi Games*, 150.

49. Kessler, "Only Nazi Games?," 130.

50. Large, *Nazi Games*, 151.

51. Krüger, *Nazi Olympics*, 98.

52. Guttmann, *The Games Must Go On*, 73.

53. Guttmann, *The Games Must Go On*, 73.

54. Walters, *Berlin Games*, 112.

CHAPTER 12

1. "Girl-into-Man Star Tells How It Feels," *New York Daily News*, February 23, 1936.

2. "Athlete Who Changed Sex Plans to Beat Men," *Daily Mirror*, November 2, 1936.

3. Grantland Rice, "Separate Olympics for Sexes in 1940 Planned," *Los Angeles Times*, August 12, 1936.

4. "Sport: Olympic Games," *Time*, August 24, 1936.

5. See Dirk Schultheiss, Alexander I. Gabouev, and Udo Jonas, "Nikolaj A. Bogoraz (1874–1952): Pioneer of Phalloplasty and Penile Implant Surgery," *The Journal of Sexual Medicine* 2, no. 1 (January 2005).

6. Analysis of Koubek, Ministry of Public Health and Physical Education, September 30, 1936, from the fonds of the Ministerstvo veřejného zdravotnictví a tělesné výchovy (Ministry of Public Health and Physical Education), Box 892, Inventory number 3352, Národní archiv (National Archives of the Czech Republic).

7. Koubek, "Zdeněk Koubek: The Story of a World-Record Woman."

8. Reuters, "Sex Changed: Woman Athlete's Operation," *Sheffield Independent*, April 4, 1936.

9. "The Astounding Case of the Man Who Was Changed into a Woman," *Evansville Press*, October 22, 1933.

10. C. Riley Snorton, *Black on Both Sides: A Racial History of Trans Identity* (Minneapolis: University of Minnesota Press, 2017), 60.

11. See Jen Manion, *Female Husbands: A Trans History* (Cambridge: Cambridge University Press, 2020).

12. Zoë Playdon, *The Hidden Case of Ewan Forbes: And the Unwritten History of the Trans Experience* (New York: Scribner, 2021), 22.

13. "Girl Who Fell Ill Recovers, but Becomes a Boy," *Pittsburgh Sun-Telegraph*, August 11, 1935.

14. "Woman with Changed Sex Discovered," *Los Angeles Times*, October 27, 1933.

15. "Changing Sex," *Daily Mirror*, February 21, 1921.

16. Elizabeth Reis, *Bodies in Doubt: An American History of Intersex* (Baltimore: Johns Hopkins University Press, 2012), 89.

17. Reis, *Bodies in Doubt*, 87.

18. Reis, *Bodies in Doubt*, 107.

19. Reis, *Bodies in Doubt*, 94.

20. International News Service, "Girl Becomes Man," *The Birmingham News*, March 26, 1936. Burian's name is shortened as "Franz Burian" here.

21. Václav Smrčka, Vlasta Mádlová, and Ahmed Edriss, "František Burian (September 17, 1881–October 15, 1965) and the Beginning of Plastic Surgery in Czechoslovakia," *European Journal of Plastic Surgery* 35 (2012): 449.

22. Smrčka, Mádlová, and Edriss, "František Burian," 454.

23. Koubek later said he earned more in New York than in half a year in Europe. See Pavel Kovář, *Příběh české rekordwoman* (Prague: Nakladatelství Pejdlova Rosička, 2017), 207.

24. "Girl Olympic Champ Who Became Man Looks Forward to Marriage and Family," *Brooklyn Times Union*, August 25, 1936.

25. Letter from Zdeněk Koubek to Prague police headquarters, May 23, 1936, Policejní ředitelství Praha II—všeobecná spisovna (Police Headquarters Prague II—General Register) 1921–1950, Národní archiv (National Archives of the Czech Republic).

26. Letter from Prague police headquarters to Zdeněk Koubek, May 25, 1936, Národní archiv.

27. See Radka Šmídová, "Reklama v časopisech Pestrý týden a Pražský ilustrovaný zpravodaj" (PhD diss., Charles University, 2019).

28. Koubek, "Zdeněk Koubek: The Story of a World-Record Woman."

29. Publication timeline courtesy of Kateřina Trnavská of the National Museum of Prague.

CHAPTER 13

1. "2 Operations Make Man of Girl Athlete."

2. Broster, *The Adrenal Cortex*, 47.

3. Broster, *The Adrenal Cortex*, 48.

4. Bronner, "The Girl Who Became a Bridegroom."

5. Bronner, "The Girl Who Became a Bridegroom."

6. "Items of Interest from All Parts," *Coventry Evening Telegraph*, February 29, 1932.

7. Broster, *The Adrenal Cortex*, 48.

8. "New Record for Discus Throwing," *Western Morning News* (Plymouth, UK), July 20, 1931, notes that Weston "was accompanied by [his] friend Miss Bertha [*sic*] Bray" to a match.

9. The timeline of when this began is fuzzy, probably because social acceptance would have been difficult pre-transition, but Weston is pictured locking arms with Bray on May 30, 1936. See *Daily News* (London), May 30, 1936.

10. Stephen Carder Weston, death certificate, accessed via Archives.com.

11. Broster, *The Adrenal Cortex*, 47.

12. "L. R. Broster," Obituary Notices, *British Medical Journal*, April 24, 1965, 1130.

13. L. R. Broster, "Eight Years' Experience with the Adrenal Gland," *Archives of Surgery* 34, no. 5 (1937): 768.

14. "Sex Changes: Important Scientific Discoveries Expected," *Nottingham Evening Post*, May 5, 1932.

15. "Doctor Changes Sex of 24: Patients Have Married," *Daily Mirror*, May 5, 1938.

16. Broster, "Eight Years' Experience," 772.

17. "Drifting Towards a Neuter Sex," *Halifax Evening Courier*, April 20, 1934.

18. Broster, "Eight Years' Experience," 780.

19. "Drifting Towards a Neuter Sex."

20. "Drifting Towards a Neuter Sex."

21. Broster, *The Adrenal Cortex*, 48.

22. Broster, *The Adrenal Cortex*, 48.

23. "Devon Woman Athlete."

24. "Devon Woman Athlete." The following page is almost entirely sourced from here.

25. "Devon Woman Athlete."

26. "Mark Weston at Home," *Western Morning News* (Plymouth, UK), May 29, 1936.

27. "Change to Etiquette of Living as Man," *Western Morning News* (Plymouth, UK), May 29, 1936.

28. Bronner, "The Girl Who Became a Bridegroom."

29. Bronner, "The Girl Who Became a Bridegroom."

30. "Change to Etiquette."

31. "Marriage: By Man Who Was a Woman," *Weekly Dispatch* (London), May 31, 1936.

32. Bronner, "The Girl Who Became a Bridegroom."

33. "Sports Official Offer to Mr. Mark Weston, of Oreston," *Western Morning News* (Plymouth, UK), May 30, 1936.

34. Bronner, "The Girl Who Became a Bridegroom."

35. James Thomas Sears, *Behind the Mask of the Mattachine: The Hal Call Chronicles and the Early Movement for Homosexual Emancipation* (Milton Park, UK: Routledge, 2006), 340. Barker said, "When I was a teenager, another gay boy and I [. . .] would go to the newsstand and read *Sexology* magazine."

36. "Happiness for Homosexuals," *Sexology*, December 1935, 225; "Do Women Marry Each Other?," *Sexology*, June 1936, 627. Microfiche held by New York Public Library.

37. Jim Elledge, *An Angel in Sodom: Henry Gerber and the Birth of the Gay Rights Movement* (Chicago: Chicago Review Press, 2022), 42.

38. "(611) Man into Woman," from the "Questions and Answers" section, *Sexology*, June 1936. The letter writer is identified only as "J. S., Georgia."

39. "Bisexuality—Desire for Both Sexes," *Sexology*, January 1935, 309.

40. "Women into Men by Surgery?," *Sexology*, August 1936, 774.

41. "They Want to Change Sexes," *Sexology*, September 1937, 32.

42. Jules Gill-Peterson, *Histories of the Transgender Child* (Minneapolis: University of Minnesota Press, 2018), 84.

43. "They Want to Change Sexes," 32.

44. Thomas Baty, *Alone in Japan* (Tokyo: Maruzen, 1959), Appendix I, 185. Baty/Clyde was only ever identified with he/him pronouns at the time, but I am using they/them to account for a wide range of gender possibilities.

45. Baty, *Alone*, 188.

46. Alison Oram, "Feminism, Androgyny and Love Between Women in *Urania*, 1916–1940," *Media History* 7, no. 1 (2001): 58.

47. "Authentic Change of Sex," *Urania*, January 1936. Thanks to Sage Milo for sending me their scans of *Urania*.

48. "Another Extraordinary Triumph," *Urania*, June 1936. Courtesy of Sage Milo.

49. "A New Life: How I Changed from a Woman into a Man." Except where otherwise stated, the de Bruyn section is sourced entirely from this article.

50. The technical details of the race are verified by the following: "English Girl's Fall in International Cycle Race," *Leeds Mercury*, September 18, 1934; "Girl Rider's Bad Luck," *Daily Mirror*, September 19, 1934.

CHAPTER 14

1. "Medicine: Change of Sex," *Time*, August 24, 1936.

2. Reis, *Bodies in Doubt*, 84.

3. Donald Furthman Wickets, "Can Sex in Humans Be Changed?," *Physical Culture*, January 1937.

4. Morris Fishbein, "Explaining the Strange Mystery of Women Becoming Men," *Dayton Daily News*, October 11, 1936.

5. Knoll mentions that he wrote letters to multiple federations in Wilhelm Knoll, "Sportkanonen und Cracks," *Sportmedizin und Olympische Spiele 1936*, August 1–16, 1936. Copy courtesy of Dennis Krämer. Only the letter to the IAAF survives, however.

6. Wilhelm Knoll to Carl Diem, June 19, 1936, World Athletics Library, Monaco. My gratitude to Jörg Krieger for sharing these letters and to Eliza Levinson for translating them into English.

7. Knoll to Diem, June 19, 1936.

8. Sigfrid Edström to Wilhelm Knoll, June 25, 1936, World Athletics Library. Copy provided by Krieger, translation by Levinson.

9. Knoll discusses the reaction in Knoll, "Sportkanonen und Cracks."

10. "Der Stolz der Leichtathletinnen," *Alpenzeitung*, November 17, 1936. Translation by Alexander Luckmann. Accessed via the Dr. Friedrich Tessmann Provincial Library.

11. Alexandrine Gibb, "No Man's Land of Sport," *Toronto Daily Star*, May 30, 1936.

12. Avery Brundage quoted the letter he'd received, without naming the source, in a message to Henri de Baillet-Latour. See Brundage to Baillet-Latour, June 23, 1936, Series, Box 44, Folder 10, Avery Brundage Collection. The anonymous letter, as we will discuss later, was almost certainly referring to Helen Stephens.

13. Roger Butterfield, "Avery Brundage," *Life*, June 14, 1948, 115. In the profile, Butterfield writes that Brundage "has always been suspicious of athletic

women," and "his suspicion is that some of them—perhaps even a considerable number—are really men."

14. Brundage to Baillet-Latour, June 23, 1936.

15. Reis, *Bodies in Doubt*, 99.

16. Reis, *Bodies in Doubt*, 99–100.

17. "Mary Baker," Hugh Ryan on Patreon, December 29, 2019, https://www .patreon.com/posts/mary-baker-32696069. Thank you to Hugh Ryan for sharing with me this outtake from his book, *The Women's House of Detention: A Queer History of a Forgotten Prison* (New York: Bold Type Books, 2022).

18. I extensively researched pre-1950 judging decisions surrounding trans name change cases for an article. See Michael Waters, "Barbara Ann Richards Designed—and Then Demanded—the Life She Deserved," Slate .com, March 20, 2022, https://slate.com/human-interest/2022/03/barbara -ann-richards-trans-history-california.html.

19. John P. Holloway, "Transsexuals—Their Legal Sex," *University of Colorado Law Review* (1967–1968): 283.

20. Margot Canaday, "'Who Is a Homosexual?': The Consolidation of Sexual Identities in Mid-Twentieth-Century American Immigration Law," *Law & Social Inquiry* 28, no. 2 (Spring 2003): 359, fn18.

21. United States Public Health Service, *Manual of the Mental Examination of Aliens* (Washington, DC: Government Printing Office, 1918), 21.

22. United States Public Health Service, *Report of the Federal Security Agency: Public Health Service* (Washington, DC: Government Printing Office, 1906), 273.

23. Margot Canaday, *The Straight State: Sexuality and Citizenship in Twentieth-Century America* (Princeton, NJ: Princeton University Press, 2009), 31–32.

24. Canaday, *The Straight State*, 34.

25. Heinrich Voss, "Frauen und Mädchen bei den Olympischen Spielen? Ja!," *Reichssportblatt*, June 10, 1936, International Olympic Committee Historical Archives, Olympic Studies Centre.

CHAPTER 15

1. The 1934 minutes of the FSFI meeting, tellingly, note that "today the FSFI has increased considerably and the IAAF is coming back to appropriate the results of work that is not its own." Translation courtesy of Marion Renault.

2. Krieger, Krech, and Pieper, "'Our Sport,'" 465.

3. Krieger, Krech, and Pieper, "'Our Sport,'" 465.

4. Letter from Alice Milliat to Henri de Baillet-Latour, February 24, 1926,

"Women and Sport: Correspondence About the Women's Federations—Alice Milliat," International Olympic Committee Historical Archive, Olympic Studies Centre, reference code: F-A02-PS-FEMSP/011.

5. "Pauvre Sport Féminin!," *L'Écho de Paris*, March 7, 1935.

6. FSFI Meeting Minutes, August 6, 1936, 5–6. The minutes note that "Milliat found herself there alone with M. Genet, who had received credentials and a number of telegrams of instructions."

7. 1936 FSFI Meeting Minutes, 6.

8. Letter from Joseph Genet to Sigfrid Edström, June 30, 1936, J. Sigfrid Edström Archive, Riksarkivet, Stockholm, Sweden. Photos provided by Jörg Krieger.

9. 1936 FSFI Meeting Minutes, 6. Translation by Marion Renault.

10. Letter from Genet to Edström, June 30, 1936.

11. Krieger, Krech, and Pieper, "'Our Sport,'" 466.

12. Details are sparse, but traveling seemed to be difficult for Milliat at this time; the 1934 FSFI meeting minutes note that "Milliat, despite her health, went to Stockholm" that year.

13. According to the FSFI meeting minutes from 1936, in fact, several members of the FSFI—Australia, Belgium, the Netherlands, Japan, and Palestine—were not paying their dues.

14. Guttmann, *The Games Must Go On*, 76.

15. Walters, *Berlin Games*, 118.

16. Minutes of the Meeting of the American Olympic Committee, July 5, 1936, 186. Thanks to Amanda McGrory of the US Olympic and Paralympic Committee Archives for providing a copy.

17. Letter from Avery Brundage to Sigfrid Edström, June 22, 1936, Series 5, Box 44, Folder 14, Avery Brundage Collection.

18. Walters, *Berlin Games*, 118.

19. Large, *Nazi Games*, 100.

20. Michael J. Socolow, *Six Minutes in Berlin: Broadcast Spectacle and Rowing Gold at the Nazi Olympics* (Champaign: University of Illinois Press, 2016), 77.

21. Socolow, *Six Minutes*, 10.

22. Socolow, *Six Minutes*, 80.

23. Walters, *Berlin Games*, 136.

24. Helen Stephens, Olympic diary, entry from July 16, 1936, Athletic Series, Folder 63, Helen Stephens Collection, the State Historical Society of Missouri, Columbia, MO.

25. Robert Morrison, "Helen Stephens, Sprinter, and Flachmann, Swimmer, District's Olympic 'Hopes,'" *St. Louis Post-Dispatch*, May 22, 1936.

26. Socolow, *Six Minutes*, 80.

27. "Strongest Team Ever to Represent Country, Says Avery Brundage," *Hartford Courant*, July 16, 1936.

28. Bob Cavagnaro, "U.S. Olympic Team Sails Today for Games in Berlin," *Asheville Citizen-Times*, July 15, 1936.

29. "Strongest Team Ever."

30. Sharon Kinney Hanson, *The Life of Helen Stephens: The Fulton Flash* (Carbondale: Southern Illinois University Press, 2004), 59.

31. Krüger, *Nazi Olympics*, 60.

32. "Record Squad Heading for Berlin Games," *The Tampa Tribune*, July 16, 1936.

33. Socolow, *Six Minutes*, 81.

34. "Strongest Team Ever."

35. Socolow, *Six Minutes*, 81.

36. Alan Gould, "Crewmen Are Sea Sick on Olympic Boat," *Elmira (NY) Star-Gazette*, July 17, 1936.

37. Helen Stephens, Olympic diary, entry for July 16, 1936.

38. Socolow, *Six Minutes*, 81.

39. Walters, *Berlin Games*, 154.

40. Cavagnaro, "U.S. Olympic Team Sails."

41. Hanson, *The Life of Helen Stephens*, 68.

42. Brundage to Baillet-Latour, June 23, 1936.

43. Hanson, *The Life of Helen Stephens*, 12.

44. Hanson, *The Life of Helen Stephens*, 14.

45. Hanson, *The Life of Helen Stephens*, 23.

46. Hanson, *The Life of Helen Stephens*, 24.

47. Hitomi and Walsh had a mutual respect. At a dinner for the winners following the Women's World Games in 1930, Hitomi declared that Walsh was going to break a world record at the coming Olympics Games in 1932. She gave Walsh a pair of spikes for her track shoes. Walsh said later, "I'll never forget her." See Anderson, *The Forgotten Legacy*, 43.

48. Anderson, *The Forgotten Legacy*, 85.

49. Anderson, *The Forgotten Legacy*, 87.

50. Alexandrine Gibb, "No Man's Land of Sport," *Toronto Daily Star*, January 6, 1936.

51. For the timing of the letter, see letter from Hans von Tschammer und Osten to Gretel Bergmann, July 16, 1936, United States Holocaust Memorial Museum #14932. For the translation of its contents, see Krüger, *Nazi Olympics*, 30.

52. Walters, *Berlin Games*, 141.

53. "Jewish Athletes—Gretel Bergmann," United States Holocaust Memorial Museum, https://www.ushmm.org/exhibition/olympics/?content=jewish _athletes&lang=en, accessed May 2023. The record Bergmann tied was a jump of five feet and three inches.

54. This was obvious to some at the time. See "Two Jewesses Invited, But—," *Reynolds's Newspaper* (London), January 5, 1936, which notes that "no Aryan team would risk Hitlerite wrath by competing against Jews" and speculates, of Bergmann and Helene Mayer, "they are only invited to the Olympiad as a gesture to America."

55. "Reich Jewish Papers Barred from Reporting on Jews in Olympics," *Jewish Telegraphic Agency*, July 20, 1936.

56. Socolow, *Six Minutes*, 84.

57. Walters, *Berlin Games*, 160.

58. Socolow, *Six Minutes*, 85.

59. Socolow, *Six Minutes*, 87.

60. Walters, *Berlin Games*, 166.

61. Socolow, *Six Minutes*, 89.

62. Avery Brundage, "Talk for Germany Day," October 4, 1936, Series 25, Box 278, Folder 19, Avery Brundage Collection.

63. Socolow, *Six Minutes*, 90.

64. Hanson, *The Life of Helen Stephens*, 71.

65. Large, *Nazi Games*, 159.

66. Large, *Nazi Games*, 182.

67. Walters, *Berlin Games*, 173.

68. Socolow, *Six Minutes*, 148.

69. Edward J. Beattie, "Nazis Cheer U.S. Athletes," United Press wire service, July 24, 1936.

70. Brundage himself noted as much. See Brundage, "Talk for Germany Day."

71. Walters, *Berlin Games*, 168.

72. Socolow, *Six Minutes*, 109.

73. Socolow, *Six Minutes*, 90.

74. Socolow, *Six Minutes*, 93.

75. Socolow, *Six Minutes*, 90.

76. Socolow, *Six Minutes*, 69.

77. Krüger, *Nazi Olympics*, 25.

78. Walters, *Berlin Games*, 238.

79. "American Flag Will Not Salute Hitler at Olympic Games," *Wisconsin Jewish Chronicle*, July 24, 1936.

80. Large, *Nazi Games*, 183.

81. Krüger, *Nazi Olympics*, 25.

82. Large, *Nazi Games*, 223.

83. Krüger, *Nazi Olympics*, 27.

84. Large, *Nazi Games*, 222.

85. Walters, *Berlin Games*, 204.

CHAPTER 16

1. Associated Press, "Damp, Cold Berlin Weather Puts More Than 100 Yankee Olympic Hopes on Sick List," *The Buffalo News*, July 30, 1936.

2. Walters, *Berlin Games*, 169.

3. Walters, *Berlin Games*, 171.

4. The lamps detail comes from Prussian Palaces and Gardens Foundation Berlin-Brandenburg, "Audio Station and Plan of Isle / Peacock Island," April 2011, https://www.spsg.de/fileadmin/user_upload/Pfaueninsel_Flyer -Hoerstationen_04-2011_download.pdf, accessed May 2023.

5. Guttmann, *The Games Must Go On*, 79.

6. Brundage, *The Olympic Story*, chapters 4, 16.

7. Theodor Lewald to Henri de Baillet-Latour, July 9, 1936, correspondence of the Organizing Committee of the 1936 Olympic Summer Games in Berlin, 1936 Berlin Olympic Games, International Olympic Committee Historical Archives, Olympic Studies Centre, reference code: CIO JO-1936S-COJO.

8. Details of the party from Brundage, *The Olympic Story*, chapters 4, 17. Proof that Göring lived there is from "Interior view of room in Hermann Göring's Berlin home at Leipziger Platz 11a, after the renovation," Library of Congress online catalog, https://www.loc.gov/item/2009632861.

9. Brundage, *The Olympic Story*, chapters 4, 18.

10. Brundage, "Talk for Germany Day."

11. "Mysteries of Sex Metamorphosis," *London Life*, August 29, 1936.

12. Walters, *Berlin Games*, 210.

13. Volker Kluge, "Scandal About 'Dora' and the 'Bergmann Case,'" *Journal of Olympic History* 17, no. 3 (December 2009): 23.

14. "Women Athletes Tackle That 'Man-Woman' Problem," *Daily Mirror*, August 10, 1936.

15. Quoted in Kluge, "Scandal About 'Dora,'" 23.

16. Knoll, "Sportkanonen und Cracks." With gratitude to Nita Tyndall for translating this article into English.

17. Hanson, *The Life of Helen Stephens*, 78. Hanson does not immediately identify this crush, but it becomes clear in later references.

18. See discussion of Stephens's sexuality in Hanson, *The Life of Helen Stephens*, 238.

19. Minutes of the Meeting of the Council of the IAAF, July 28, 1936, World

Athletics Archive. Courtesy of Doudou Sall Gaye. This entire section is taken from the minutes.

20. For a discussion of the weather, see Damon Runyon, "Cool, Damp Berlin Weather Hampers U.S. Athletes," *The Buffalo News*, July 29, 1936.

21. Minutes of the Meeting of the 1936 IOC Congress, July 29–31, 1936, *Official Bulletin of the International Olympic Committee*, 2.

22. It wasn't really a secret: a few weeks prior, the Associated Press wrote that Brundage was "slated for election to the International Olympic Committee." See Associated Press, "Brundage Named," *The Caledonian-Record* (St. Johnsbury, VT), July 17, 1936.

23. Minutes of the Meeting of the 1936 IOC Congress, July 29–31, 1936, 6.

24. Minutes of the Meeting of the 1936 IOC Congress, July 29–31, 1936, 7.

25. Associated Press, "Japan, Finns Vie for '40 Olympics," *Okmulgee Daily Times* (Oklahoma), July 31, 1936.

26. Associated Press, "Bitter Battle on 1940 Games Award," *The Gazette and Daily* (York, PA), July 31, 1936.

27. Associated Press, "Japan Wins Award for 1940 Games," *The Fresno Bee*, July 31, 1936.

28. Alan Gould, "Olympiad Opens with Elaborate Ceremony Today," *The San Bernardino County Sun*, August 1, 1936.

29. The meeting minutes themselves are extremely sparse. They note only the existence of "a letter from the American Olympic Committee," without further elaboration. Because Brundage's letter to Baillet-Latour is the only surviving correspondence on this subject in the IOC archives, it is very likely this is the same letter. See Minutes of the Meeting of the 1936 IOC Congress, July 29–31, 1936, 10.

30. Minutes of the Meeting of the 1936 IOC Congress, July 29–31, 1936, 10.

31. Associated Press, "Brundage Advises Sex Examination," *The San Bernardino County Sun*, August 1, 1936.

32. United Press, "Discuss Exams for Women Track Stars," *El Paso Times*, August 2, 1936.

33. "Brundage Asks Sex Exams for Olympic Girls," *New York Daily News*, August 1, 1936.

34. United Press, "A Woman's Only a Woman Except When She's a Man!," *The Richmond News Leader*, August 1, 1936.

35. A strange twist in this saga is that Brundage, at one point, denied taking the initiative on sex testing; he told one newspaper, "I did not bring the matter up and did not take the lead favoring it more than anyone else" (see "Sex Tests Hinted for Girl Athletes," *Capitol Hill Beacon* [Oklahoma City, OK], August 1, 1936). Because of the correspondence trail in which

Brundage did raise the issue in June, and because of the reporting confirming this, I don't take much stock in his denial.

36. Jimmy Powers, "The Powerhouse," *New York Daily News*, August 2, 1936.

37. United Press, "Delicate Question of Physical Exam Given Women Stars Heard," *Sapulpa (OK) Herald*, August 1, 1936.

38. Large, *Nazi Games*, 191.

39. Socolow, *Six Minutes*, 122.

40. "Americans Recovering from Illness as Games Start," *The Binghamton Press*, August 1, 1936.

41. Hanson, *The Life of Helen Stephens*, 80.

42. Socolow, *Six Minutes*, 123.

43. Socolow, *Six Minutes*, 124.

44. Guttmann, *The Games Must Go On*, 79. Though 384 athletes had originally traveled to Berlin, one athlete, Eleanor Holm, was disqualified during the voyage and didn't join the opening ceremony.

45. Walters, *Berlin Games*, 189.

46. Walters, *Berlin Games*, 186.

47. Walters, *Berlin Games*, 190.

48. Guttmann, *The Games Must Go On*, 80.

49. Large, *Nazi Games*, 223.

50. Helen Stephens, Olympic diary, entry for August 1, 1936.

51. Matthew J. Bruccoli and Park Bucker, ed., *To Loot My Life Clean: The Thomas Wolfe–Maxwell Perkins Correspondence* (Columbia: University of South Carolina Press, 2000), 197.

52. Gerhard L. Weinberg, "Hitler's Memorandum on the Four-Year Plan: A Note," *German Studies Review* 11, no. 1 (February 1988): 133.

53. Hanson, *The Life of Helen Stephens*, 86.

54. Helen Stephens, Olympic diary, entry for August 4, 1936.

55. Hanson, *The Life of Helen Stephens*, 86.

56. Hanson, *The Life of Helen Stephens*, 87.

57. Hanson, *The Life of Helen Stephens*, 88.

58. "Helen Stephens Beats Stella Walsh for Olympics," *St. Louis Star and Times*, August 4, 1936.

59. Helen Stephens, Olympic diary, entry for August 4, 1936.

60. Socolow, *Six Minutes*, 151.

61. "Owens Wins Broad Jump and Cracks Record," *Los Angeles Times*, August 5, 1936.

62. "Helen Stephens Beats Stella Walsh for Olympics."

63. "Woodruff Was Certain He'd Win 800-Meter," *Brooklyn Times Union*, August 5, 1936.

64. "Polish Writer Calls Helen Stephens 'Man,'" *Los Angeles Times*, August 6, 1936.

65. Anderson, *The Forgotten Legacy*, 107.

66. This translation appears in William Murray, "France: Liberty, Equality, and the Pursuit of Fraternity," in Krüger, *The Nazi Olympics*, 102.

67. Hanson, *The Life of Helen Stephens*, 95–96.

68. Though Stephens implied in this quote that all athletes were sex tested ahead of competition, this was not true in 1936; it is worth keeping in mind that Stephens relayed this quote to her biographer over half a century later and likely forgot the specifics. The quote does not appear in contemporaneous press reports in the 1930s. See Hanson, *The Life of Helen Stephens*, 96.

69. The "sour grapes" line may be a slight paraphrase by Stephens's biographer. See Hanson, *The Life of Helen Stephens*, 96.

70. "Helen Stephens Is Real Girl," *Harrisburg Telegraph*, August 6, 1936.

71. John Lardner, "Good Feeling Lacking at Olympics," *The Atlanta Constitution*, August 9, 1936.

72. "Sport, Olympic Games," *Time*, August 17, 1936.

73. "Helen Stephens Is Real Girl."

74. Hanson, *The Life of Helen Stephens*, 96.

75. Canadian Press, "German Officials Ascertain True Sex of Helen Stephens," *Saskatoon Star-Phoenix*, August 6, 1936.

76. United Press, "Brundage Says Rumors About a Sex Test for Miss Stephens Untrue," *The Oshkosh (WI) Northwestern*, August 6, 1936. Brundage issued a strong denial. He said that Stephens's eligibility was the domain of the IAAF and "I, as a member of the counsel, attended all meetings and I can say flatly that the matter never even was discussed."

77. Paul Gallico, *Farewell to Sport* (New York: Alfred A. Knopf, 1938), 234.

78. Hanson, *The Life of Helen Stephens*, 96.

CHAPTER 17

1. FSFI Meeting Minutes, Technical Commission, August 6, 1936, 1. Courtesy of Musée National du Sport.

2. "Mrs. Cornell's Injury May End Career as Athlete," *Daily Herald* (London), September 28, 1934.

3. Williams, *Britain's Olympic Women*, 107.

4. Cornell said immediately after the Olympics, "Women's athletics have only been recognized by men during recent years, and it seems a pity that control should follow almost immediately upon recognition." See McKenzie Porter, "Men to Rule the Games Girls," *Daily Mirror*, August 15, 1936.

5. "Astonishing Assertion," *Belfast Telegraph*, September 21, 1934.

6. "How the Eleventh Olympiad Was Opened," *The Times of India*, August 11, 1936, paraphrases Cornell as saying, "Such a rule would be hard to enforce."

7. FSFI Meeting Minutes, Technical Commission, August 6, 1936, 1.

8. FSFI Meeting Minutes, Technical Commission, 1. Translation by Marion Renault.

9. FSFI Meeting Minutes, Technical Commission, August 6, 1936, 1.

10. Koubek, "Zdeněk Koubek: The Story of a World-Record Woman."

11. The minutes simply read, "After explanations given by Dr. Bléha, the commission decided to keep records set by Koubkova on the IAAF list." See FSFI Meeting Minutes, Technical Commission, August 6, 1936, 1. Translation by Marion Renault.

12. Meeting Minutes of the Congress of the FSFI, August 6, 1936, 1.

13. Meeting Minutes of the Congress of the FSFI, August 6, 1936, 2.

14. Meeting Minutes of the Congress of the FSFI, August 6, 1936, 3.

15. Meeting Minutes of the Congress of the FSFI, August 6, 1936, 5.

16. The FSFI discussed the next host of the Women's World Games in its meetings. Meeting Minutes of the Congress of the FSFI, August 6, 1936, 3.

17. Socolow, *Six Minutes*, 146.

18. Large, *Nazi Games*, 261.

19. "Berlin 1936 Rowing Results," Olympics.com, https://olympics.com/en /olympic-games/berlin-1936/results/rowing.

20. Large, *Nazi Games*, 265.

21. United Press, "Helene Mayer Second in Olympic Fencing," *Camden Courier-Post* (New Jersey), August 6, 1936.

22. "Former Scripps Student Second in Single Foils," *The Pomona (CA) Progress Bulletin*, August 6, 1936.

23. Large, *Nazi Games*, 266.

24. Large, *Nazi Games*, 266.

25. Minutes of the IAAF Congress, August 10–11, 1936, 1. Courtesy of Doudou Sall Gaye of the World Athletics Library, Monaco.

26. Krüger, "The Ministry of Popular Enlightenment and Propaganda and the Nazi Olympics of 1936," 36.

27. Large, *Nazi Games*, 291.

28. Minutes of the IAAF Congress, August 10–11, 1936, 2.

29. Minutes of the IAAF Congress, August 10–11, 1936, 19.

30. Minutes of the IAAF Congress, August 10–11, 1936, 21.

31. Minutes of the IAAF Congress, August 10–11, 1936, 23.

32. Alan Gould, "I.A.A.F. Approves 27 Track and Field World Records," *The Times Leader* (Wilkes-Barre, PA), August 11, 1936.

33. Associated Press, "A.A.F. Heads Pass Rule on Sex Question," *Sioux City Journal*, August 11, 1936.

34. Associated Press, "A.A.F. Heads Pass Rule on Sex Question."

35. "New York Book Indexes to Passenger Lists, 1906–1942," database with images, FamilySearch.

36. "Girl Olympic Champ Who Became Man Looks Forward to Marriage and Family," *Brooklyn Times Union*, August 25, 1936.

37. "New York Book Indexes to Passenger Lists, 1906–1942," database with images, FamilySearch.

38. United Press, "Sex Changed in Operation Because He Wants to Wed," *The Pittsburgh Press*, August 13, 1936.

39. United Press, "Woman Athlete to Become Man," *The Dayton Herald*, August 12, 1936.

40. "She Was a Girl, Now He's a Man," *The Brooklyn Daily Eagle*, August 12, 1936.

41. Advertisement for French Casino ("Tonight . . . Summer edition Folies de Femmes"), *New York Daily News*, August 15, 1936.

42. "Night Club Reviews," *Variety*, September 2, 1936, 54.

43. Harry Levin, "Girl Athlete Who Became a Man Wants to Marry and Become Father of 'Large, Healthy Family,'" Central Press, August 24, 1936; "Zdenka Koubkova la 'femme en homme' est arrivé à Paris," *Paris-soir*, November 2, 1936.

44. Levin, "Girl Athlete Who Became a Man."

45. "He Proves 'She's' a Man's Man," *Shenandoah (PA) Evening Herald*, August 15, 1936.

46. "Here's How I Used to Do It!," *The Indiana Gazette*, August 28, 1936.

47. Levin, "Girl Athlete Who Became a Man."

48. United Press, "Sex Changed in Operation."

49. Levin, "Girl Athlete Who Became a Man."

50. International News Service, "Girl Who's Now Man Wants to Wed Blonde," *Pittsburgh Sun-Telegraph*, August 12, 1936.

51. Levin, "Girl Athlete Who Became a Man."

52. "Woman Likes Being a Man," *The Decatur Daily Review*, August 16, 1936.

53. "Biggest Bargain on Broadway," advertisement, *New York Daily News*, August 31, 1936.

54. Danton Walker, "French Casino Reopens with Lively Revue," *New York Daily News*, August 27, 1936.

55. "Former 'Girl' Athlete Arrives, Now a Man," *New York Daily News*, August 13, 1936.

56. See Hy Gardner, "Night Club Newsreel," *The Brooklyn Daily Eagle*, August 28, 1936; Walker, "French Casino Reopens."

57. Levin, "Girl Athlete Who Became a Man."

58. James Aswell, "My New York," *The Evening Independent* (Massillon, OH), August 28, 1936.

59. Levin, "Girl Athlete Who Became a Man."

60. "'Woman' Athlete Who Became Man Married to 'Girl in a Million,'" *Daily Mirror*, August 11, 1936.

61. "Man, Once Woman, Weds 'Girlhood' Friend," *Daily News* (London), August 11, 1936.

62. "'Woman' Athlete Who Became Man."

63. "Mr. Mark Weston Married," *Western Morning News* (Plymouth, UK), August 12, 1936.

64. Bronner, "The Girl Who Became a Bridegroom." In the article, Weston actually says that his name was listed as "bachelor" in the marriage registry. This is probably a misstatement, since bachelors are generally unmarried men.

65. "Mr. Mark Weston Married."

66. See, for example, "Joe Williams Says: Questions of Sex Disturb Olympic Officials," *Pittsburgh Press*, August 12, 1936.

67. Associated Press, "A.A.F. Heads Pass Rule on Sex Question."

68. "Joe Williams Says."

69. "Gespräch mit Heinrich Voss," *Der Leichtathlet*, November 3, 1936. With gratitude to Berno Bahro for the copy of this article. English translation courtesy of Alexander Luckmann.

70. Brundage, "Talk for Germany Day."

71. Large, *Nazi Games*, 279.

72. Eric Dunning and Dominic Malcom, *Sport: Sport and Power Relations* (Milton Park, UK: Taylor & Francis, 2003), 150.

73. Porter, "Men to Rule the Games Girls."

74. Porter, "Men to Rule the Games Girls."

75. Hanson, *The Life of Helen Stephens*, 113.

76. Hanson, *The Life of Helen Stephens*, 119.

77. Hanson, *The Life of Helen Stephens*, 122.

78. "Off the Record," *The Brooklyn Citizen*, September 5, 1936. The date comes from Ben Schneider, "The Night Club," *Women's Wear Daily*, September 3, 1936.

79. Schneider, "The Night Club."

80. United Press, "Man-Girl Athlete Must Undergo 2D Operation Now," *The Hanford (CA) Sentinel*, October 24, 1936.

81. "Girl Who Became a Man," *Western Morning News* (Plymouth, UK), November 2, 1936.
82. "L'ex-championne Zdenka Koubkova a débarqué au Havre," *Le Journal*, November 2, 1936.
83. "Débuts au music-hall," *L'Intransigeant*, November 11, 1936.
84. Folies-Bergère advertisement, *Le Figaro*, November 8, 1936.
85. "City Limits: A Brush with Fame," *The Vancouver Sun*, April 23, 2001.
86. "Edgar Wiggins, Paris Representative, Sends Season's Greetings to Friends, Relatives and Performers," *The Chicago Defender*, January 2, 1937.
87. Quoted in Kovář, *Příběh české rekordwoman*, 207.
88. Leonard Lyons, "The Post's New Yorker," *The Washington Post*, February 5, 1937.

CHAPTER 18

1. These paragraphs about de Bruyn are sourced entirely from "A New Life: How I Changed from a Woman into a Man."
2. Robert Gawkowski, "Na tropach Smętka i Smentka (1910–1983)," *Pismo uczelni* 98 (2021), University of Warsaw, 44.
3. "Zofia Smętkówna przestała istnieć, Nowy mężczyzna rozpłakał się (Zofia Smętkówna no longer exists; a new man weeps), *Echo*, April 23, 1937. Article courtesy of Robert Gawkowski; translation by Jack J. Hutchens.
4. Gawkowski, "Na tropach Smętka," 45.
5. "Woman Who Became a Man, Former Fiancé Going Abroad to Forget," *Nottingham Evening Post*, May 1, 1937.
6. "WOMEN: About a Table Tennis, a Mermaid, and a Sex Switcher," *Newsweek*, April 24, 1937, 24.
7. "Athlete Who Changed Her Sex," *Gloucester Citizen*, April 28, 1937.
8. "Les deux ex-championnes devenues hommes vont se rencontrer sur le terrain sportif," *Paris-soir*, April 18, 1937.
9. Response to Koubek's sex marker appeal, Ministry of Public Health and Physical Education, February 12, 1937, from the fonds of the Ministerstvo veřejného zdravotnictví a tělesné výchovy (Ministry of Public Health and Physical Education), Box 892, Inventory number 3352, Národní archiv (National Archives of the Czech Republic).
10. Letter from the Ministry of Justice to the Ministry of the Interior, June 23, 1937; fonds Ministerstvo spravedlnosti (Ministry of Justice) 1918–1953, inventory number 405, signature Sb—sbírka informací, Box 1998, Národní archiv (National Archives of the Czech Republic). Translation by Barbora Bartunkova.

11. Response to Koubek appeal, May 20, 1937; Ministerstvo spravedlnosti (Ministry of Justice). Translation by Barbora Bartunkova.

12. Cornwall, "Heinrich Rutha and the Unraveling of a Homosexual Scandal," 332.

13. Cornwall, "Heinrich Rutha and the Unraveling of a Homosexual Scandal," 333.

14. Huebner, *Magnetic Woman*, 158.

15. A scan of this certificate is located in Policejní ředitelství Praha II—všeobecná spisovna (Police Headquarters Prague II—General Register) 1921–1950, Národní archiv (National Archives of the Czech Republic).

16. Kovář, *Příběh české rekordwoman*, 210.

CHAPTER 19

1. Large, *Nazi Games*, 316.

2. Large, *Nazi Games*, 319.

3. Large, *Nazi Games*, 311.

4. Large, *Nazi Games*, 313.

5. Large, *Nazi Games*, 314.

6. See generally, Hans Joachim Teichler, "Coubertin und Hitler," *Stadion* 46 (2022).

7. John Hoberman, "Toward a Theory of Olympic Internationalism," *Journal of Sport History* 22, no. 1 (Spring 1995): 26.

8. Stefan Berg, "How Dora the Man Competed in the Woman's High Jump," *Spiegel*, September 15, 2009.

9. Kluge, "Scandal About 'Dora' and the 'Bergmann Case,'" 22.

10. Kluge, "Scandal About 'Dora' and the 'Bergmann Case,'" 24.

11. Steve Jacobson, "No Place for a Jew," *Newsday*, August 21, 1994.

12. Kluge, "Scandal About 'Dora' and the 'Bergmann Case,'" 22.

13. Berg, "How Dora the Man Competed."

14. "Women's High Jump Record," *The Palestine Post* (Jerusalem), September 19, 1938.

15. Berg, "How Dora the Man Competed."

16. Kluge, "Scandal About 'Dora' and the 'Bergmann Case,'" 24.

17. "German Application to Nullify World's Record," *The Scotsman* (Edinburgh), October 1, 1938.

18. Kluge, "Scandal About 'Dora' and the 'Bergmann Case,'" 24.

19. Kluge, "Scandal About 'Dora' and the 'Bergmann Case,'" 25.

20. Berg, "How Dora the Man Competed."

21. Letter from Bo Ekelund to Avery Brundage, November 21, 1938, Series 6, Box 57, Folder 7, Avery Brundage Collection.

22. Berno Bahro, "Lilli Henoch and Martha Jacob—Two Jewish Athletes in Germany Before and After 1933," *Sport in History* 30, no. 2 (2010): 268.

23. Avery Brundage to Bo Ekelund, February 16, 1939, Series 6, Box 57, Folder 7, Avery Brundage Collection.

24. Large, *Nazi Games*, 320.

25. Guttmann, *The Games Must Go On*, 87.

26. Guttmann, *The Games Must Go On*, 94.

27. Letter from Avery Brundage to Henri de Baillet-Latour, April 23, 1940, Series 5, Box 44, Folder 11, Avery Brundage Collection.

28. Guttmann, *The Games Must Go On*, 88.

CHAPTER 20

1. Waters, "Barbara Ann Richards Designed."

2. "Sex Changes," *Pathfinder*, July 19, 1941, 3.

3. Snorton, *Black on Both Sides*, 148.

4. Snorton, *Black on Both Sides*, 158.

5. Guttmann, *The Games Must Go On*, 100.

6. Guttmann, *The Games Must Go On*, 133.

7. Large, *Nazi Games*, 40.

8. Guttmann, *The Games Must Go On*, 133.

9. Guttmann, *The Games Must Go On*, 137.

10. Guttmann, *The Games Must Go On*, 136.

11. Guttmann, *The Games Must Go On*, 137.

12. Guttmann, *The Games Must Go On*, 139.

13. Guttmann, *The Games Must Go On*, 100.

14. Heather L. Dichter, "Where Denazification and Democratization Intersect: The State Department and Foreign Office's Role in the Re-formation of the German Olympic Committee," *International Symposium for Olympic Research*, October 2006, 293–94.

15. Dichter, "Where Denazification," 298.

16. Guttmann, *The Games Must Go On*, 102.

17. Guttmann, *The Games Must Go On*, 151.

18. Chatziefstathiou and Henry, *Discourses of Olympism*, 174.

19. Chatziefstathiou and Henry, *Discourses of Olympism*, 174–75.

20. Guttmann, *The Games Must Go On*, 100.

21. John Horne and Garry Whannel, *Understanding the Olympics* (Milton Park, UK: Routledge, 2020), 182; also Dichter, "Where Denazification," endnote 3.

22. "IAAF Women's Commission Report," May 27, 1947, Series 20, Box 230, Folder 3, Avery Brundage Collection.

23. Pieper, *Sex Testing*, 31.
24. Max Dohle, *"They Say I'm Not a Girl": Case Studies of Gender Verification in Elite Sports* (Jefferson, NC: McFarland, 2020), 53.
25. Dohle, *"They Say I'm Not a Girl,"* 58.
26. "Fast Sprinting by Dutch Girl," *Daily Herald* (London), August 22, 1949.
27. Dohle, *"They Say I'm Not a Girl,"* 68.
28. Dohle, *"They Say I'm Not a Girl,"* 56.
29. Micha Peters, "The Scandalous Suspension of Foekje Dillema," *The Low Countries*, July 17, 2021, https://www.the-low-countries.com/article/foekje-dillema-and-the-biggest-scandal-in-dutch-sporting-history.
30. Dohle, *"They Say I'm Not a Girl,"* 67.
31. Pieper, *Sex Testing*, 113.
32. Pieper, *Sex Testing*, 113.
33. Guttmann, *The Games Must Go On*, 151.
34. Guttmann, *The Games Must Go On*, 109.
35. Guttmann, *The Games Must Go On*, 113.
36. Guttmann, *The Games Must Go On*, 112.
37. Guttmann, *The Games Must Go On*, 48.
38. Guttmann, *The Games Must Go On*, 114.
39. Guttmann, *The Games Must Go On*, 115.
40. "Report Concerning Women's Athletics," IAAF Congress, August 10–11, 1936, Series 20, Box 229, Folder 10, Avery Brundage Collection.
41. Carpentier, "Alice Milliat," 79.
42. "Prepaid Advertisements: Medical," *Western Morning News* (Plymouth, UK), February 24, 1937.
43. "Worried by Change of Sex," *Coventry Evening Telegraph*, July 29, 1942.
44. "New York, New York Passenger and Crew Lists, 1909, 1925–1957," database with images, FamilySearch.
45. Weston said he'd lived in that house "for the past 11 years" in "Legal Complications," *The Herald-News* (Passaic, NJ), March 3, 1967.
46. "Three Hurt in Car Crash," *The Morning Call* (Paterson, NJ), May 31, 1965.
47. "Legal Complications."
48. Clifton city directories, courtesy of Marissa Figlar at the Passaic County Historical Society.
49. Hanson, *The Life of Helen Stephens*, 140.
50. Hanson, *The Life of Helen Stephens*, 140. In an interview with Hanson, the student, Shannon Chenoweth, noted that the dean said "something to the effect of" this quote. It therefore may be a paraphrase.
51. Hanson, *The Life of Helen Stephens*, 38.

52. "Helen Gets $4500," *The Daily News and Intelligencer* (Mexico, MO), August 11, 1937.

53. Hanson, *The Life of Helen Stephens*, 237.

54. Hanson, *The Life of Helen Stephens*, 238.

55. Gawkowski, "Na tropach Smętka," 45.

56. Cited in Gawkowski, "Na tropach Smętka," 45. English translation courtesy of Jack J. Hutchens.

CHAPTER 21

1. United Press, "High Jump Mark Set by 'Woman' in '38 Was Male," *Camden (NJ) Courier-Post*, July 24, 1957.

2. "Track & Field: Preserving la Difference," *Time*, September 16, 1966.

3. See, for example, Kluge, "Scandal About 'Dora' and the 'Bergmann Case,'" 26. Kluge states that "with a probability bordering on certainty it can also be ruled out that Ratjen ever gave an interview."

4. See, for example, Rose Dosti, "A Pretty Girl . . . ," *Arizona Republic*, August 13, 1972.

5. Rose Dosti, "Olympic Roster Bulges with Beauties," *The Journal-News* (White Plains, NY), August 20, 1972.

6. Richard Sandomir, "Tamara Press, Olympian Who Faced Taunts," *The New York Times*, May 6, 2021.

7. Associated Press, "Brawn Plus Beauty," *Tampa Bay Times*, October 18, 1964.

8. Allan J. Ryan, "Sport and Health," *Meriden (CT) Record-Journal*, September 26, 1967.

9. Associated Press, "Girls Amused, Chagrined," *Asbury (NJ) Park Press*, February 3, 1968.

10. Stefan Wiederkehr, "'We Shall Never Know the Exact Number of Men Who Have Competed in the Olympics Posing as Women': Sport, Gender Verification and the Cold War," *The International Journal of the History of Sport* 26, no. 4 (2009): 556.

11. Wiederkehr, "'We Shall Never Know the Exact Number,'" 562.

12. Guttmann, *The Games Must Go On*, 158.

13. The process behind these tests is discussed in Pieper, *Sex Testing*, 51–52.

14. "Are Girl Athletes Really Girls?," *Life*, October 7, 1966, 66.

15. Mike Hughes, "Did Sex Tests Scare 'Em?," *Times Colonist* (British Columbia), August 31, 1966.

16. David Empey, "Mary Rand Built Like Real Champ," *Vancouver Sun*, February 15, 1968.

17. Alan Simpson, "I Cheated," *The People* (London), March 31, 1968.

18. Quoted in James L. Rupert, "Genitals to Genes: The History and Biology of Gender Verification in the Olympics," *Canadian Bulletin of Medical History* 28, no. 2 (Fall 2011): 346.

19. Leo Heiman, "Do Reds Beef Up Gal Athletes with Male Hormones?," *The Boston Globe*, October 14, 1966.

20. "Tamar Press," in the Central Database of Shoah Victims' Names, Yad Vashem, https://yvng.yadvashem.org/index.html.

21. Heiman, "Do Reds Beef Up Gal Athletes with Male Hormones?"

22. Guttmann, *The Games Must Go On*, 108.

23. Butterfield, "Avery Brundage," 115.

24. Guttmann, *The Games Must Go On*, 108.

25. "Competition for Women," Series 15, Box 123, Folder 1, Avery Brundage Collection. The origins of this document are slightly opaque; I'm guessing 1940s or 1950s because those were the years when the people named in it were most active in sports.

26. Mildred Schroeder, "Brundage Speaks at Safe Range," *The San Francisco Examiner*, May 11, 1960.

27. Minutes of the Meeting for the Medical Commission, July 13–14, 1968, IOC Medical Commission, reference B-ID04-MEDIC/038, Olympic Studies Centre.

28. Pieper, *Sex Testing*, 72.

29. "Polish Girl Star Flunks Sex Test," *The Berkshire Eagle* (Pittsfield, MA), September 16, 1967.

30. Alison Wrynn, "The Human Factor: Science, Medicine and the International Olympic Committee, 1900–70," *Sport in Society* 7, no. 2 (2004): 221.

31. Letter from Włodzimierz Reczek to Alexandre de Merode, October 24, 1967, correspondence folder, reference B-ID04-MEDIC/001, IOC Medical Commission files, Olympic Studies Centre.

32. Letter from Avery Brundage to Włodzimierz Reczek, November 4, 1967, correspondence folder, reference B-ID04-MEDIC/001, IOC Medical Commission files, Olympic Studies Centre.

33. Monique Berlioux, "Femininity," *IOC Newsletter*, December 1967. Accessed via LA84 Library at https://digital.la84.org/digital/collection/p17103coll1/id/28501/rec/129.

34. Circular letter from Avery Brundage, August 27, 1968, correspondence files, reference A-P05/029, IOC President Avery Brundage, Olympic Studies Centre.

35. Minutes of the Meeting for the Medical Commission, July 13–14, 1968, Olympic Studies Centre, 4.

36. "Report by Doctor Thiebault on the Grenoble Games to the International Olympic Committee Medical Committee," 1968, reference B-ID04-MEDIC/038, Olympic Studies Centre.

37. Erik Strömgren, Johannes Nielsen, Mogens Ingerslov, Gert Bruin Petersen, and A. J. Therkelsen, "A Memorandum on the Use of Sex Chromatin Investigation of Competitors in Women's Divisions of the Olympic Games," IOC Medical Commission, gender verification correspondence files, reference B-ID04-MEDIC/035, Olympic Studies Centre.

38. Letter from Avery Brundage to Alexandre de Merode, April 24, 1972, correspondence files, reference A-P05/035, IOC President Avery Brundage, Olympic Studies Centre.

39. Dosti, "A Pretty Girl . . . ," *Arizona Republic.*

40. Letter from Mary Glen-Haig to Alexandre de Merode, December 30, 1987, IOC Medical Commission, correspondence files, reference B-ID04-MEDIC/008, Olympic Studies Centre.

41. "Report by Doctor Thiebault on the Grenoble Games to the International Olympic Committee Medical Committee," 1968, reference B-ID04-MEDIC/038, Olympic Studies Centre.

42. Arne Ljungqvist, "Historical Perspective of Gender Verification," 1988, in gender verification file, reference B-ID04-MEDIC/037, IOC Medical Commission, Olympic Studies Centre.

43. Letter from Alexandre de Merode to Albert de la Chapelle, July 14, 1987, gender verification file, reference B-ID04-MEDIC/037, IOC Medical Commission, Olympic Studies Centre.

44. Letter from Hans Howald to Albert de la Chapelle, December 7, 1987, gender verification file, reference B-ID04-MEDIC/037, IOC Medical Commission, Olympic Studies Centre.

45. De la Chapelle to Howald, December 22, 1987, gender verification file, reference B-ID04-MEDIC/037, IOC Medical Commission, Olympic Studies Centre.

46. Pieper, *Sex Testing,* 62.

47. Pieper, *Sex Testing,* 83.

48. Frank Horwill, "The Evolution of the Women's 800 Metres," *Official Journal of the British Milers' Club* 3 (Spring 1999): 24.

49. Kovář, *Příběh české rekordwoman,* 211.

50. Kovář, *Příběh české rekordwoman,* 212.

51. Koubek, "Zdeněk Koubek: The Story of a World-Record Woman."

52. Kovář, *Příběh české rekordwoman,* 216.

ACKNOWLEDGMENTS

When I say I couldn't have written this book alone, I mean it. Some of my most important discoveries would not have been possible without a countless number of archivists who generously pored over finding aids, leafed through boxes, and sent over reams of PDFs in response to my out-of-the-blue emails.

An incomplete list: Doudou Sall Gaye at the World Athletics Library took my vague requests related to gender surveillance and women's sports and delivered an assortment of meeting minutes that provided the scaffolding for my sections on the IAAF; the archivists at the Olympic Studies Centre, especially Diego Girod, patiently answered my many questions and requests during my visit there; Marissa Figlar at the Passaic County Historical Society flipped through city directories to help me map out Mark Weston's time in New Jersey; Lukáš Pátý at the National Archives of the Czech Republic sent me detailed scans of all of the library's administrative files related to Koubek; the staff at the University of Illinois Urbana-Champaign Archives, especially Sammi Merritt, helped me navigate the sprawling, and often intimidating, Avery Brundage Collection; Léna Schillinger at the Musée National du Sport generously sent me a cache of documents related to the Women's World Games; and the scholar Jörg Krieger, who had spent extensive time at the World Athletics Library for his own research, shared with me a series of letters he'd uncovered from the 1920s and 1930s, one of which led me to focus on the role that Wilhelm Knoll played in the origins of sex testing. Finally, when I had yet to even start my book proposal, Kateřina Trnavská at Prague's National Museum scanned for me a copy of Koubek's essay in the *Prague Illustrated Reporter* that became the spark for all of it.

I am similarly grateful for the scholars whose writings on queer history and sports history offered a theoretical basis for much of this book. The work of Lindsay Parks Pieper, Joanna Harper, Jules Boykoff, Jules-Gill Peterson, Paisley Currah, Joanne Meyerowitz, Susan Stryker, Margot Canaday, C. Riley Snorton, and Jonathan Ned Katz were instrumental in shaping how I researched and thought about *The Other Olympians*. Scholarship is always essential, but none of us would be having this discussion in the first place if it were not for the efforts of athletes like Chris Mosier, Renée Richards, Caster Semanya, Dutee Chand, and CeCé Telfer, who have brought the discriminatory realities of sex testing into mainstream conversation, all while simply trying to play their sports.

I threw myself into this project after consulting my whip-smart agent Michael Bourret, who, after politely critiquing a string of other book ideas, told me that this was the one. The book proposal came together thanks to the generous support of the New York Public Library, especially Jason Baumann, who offered me a fellowship to excavate this story from the archives. Jackson Howard, my brilliant editor, believed in the book right away, and has been a fierce advocate for it ever since. Thanks as well to Hannah Goodwin, Brianna Fairman, Janet Renard, Vivian Kirklin, Andrea Monagle, Laura Ogar, and the rest of the team at FSG. June Park designed the wonderful cover. Suzanne Connelly, my editor at Ebury, provided thoughtful notes and guidance throughout the process. Michaela Whatnall at Dystel, Goderich & Bourret was a wonderful second set of eyes on the manuscript.

I also want to give special thanks to Meghan Forbes, whose rigorous and empathetic translation of Koubek's personal essay from the *Prague Illustrated Reporter* is the grounding for much of this book. I don't know how Meghan was able to relay so much of Koubek's personality, especially his wry sense of humor, from 1930s Czech into contemporary English, but I feel sure *The Other Olympians* would have been a lesser book without her.

My nonfiction writing journey has been a meandering one, beginning with a teen writing blog I started—too young—in eighth grade. Along the way, a number of editors took early chances on me and patiently pushed me to try once unimaginably terrifying activities, such as calling up sources on the phone. Ella Morton and Melissa Albert let me put together quirky articles when I was very young and eventually gave me the courage to write professionally; meanwhile Leah Finnegan, Zachary Crockett, and David Haglund read my cold emails and managed to see a glimmer of potential in my work. I wouldn't be a historian without my college professors April Mayes and Diana Selig, each of whom taught me to see the immense possibilities in the past—especially once you start looking outside traditional archives. I have carried their lessons with me ever since. Similarly, I don't think I'd be publishing books and articles about history without Hugh Ryan, who took my career as a historian seriously from the start and who has offered me wisdom for many years now.

I have been talking about writing a book forever, and now that it's happened, I'm kind of like, *What was I thinking?* My friends can attest to these ups and downs. Eleanor Cummins, Caroline Haskins, Melinda Fakuade, Louise Matsakis, Hannah Seo, Julia Carmel, Isabel Ling, Natasha Frost, Robbie Moscato-Goodpaster, and Hannah Popal have given me a writing community; Josephine Chiang, Erin Wiens, Eliza McCullough, Sohini Desai, Liz Stone, Tife Oluwo, Christina Djossa, Jacque Groskaufmanis, and Willie Quiroz have given me community in every other way. I remain touched to have friends like Tulika Mohan, Hannah Osland, Alex White, Shiv Pandya, Sarah Ramos, Noor Dhingra, and Amanda Mutai in my life. Camryn Garrett in particular has been there from the start, and has, now that I think about it, truly seen too much. Lastly, of course, I am grateful for my mom and dad, who raised me with such a strong sense of possibility (or maybe delusion?) that I have continued to write and pitch stories like this one even as the rejections pile up.

INDEX

A Note About the Author

Michael Waters has written for *The New Yorker*, *The Atlantic*, *The New York Times*, *Wired*, *Slate*, and *Vox*, among other publications. He was a 2021–2022 New York Public Library Martin Duberman Visiting Scholar in LGBTQ studies, and he lives in Brooklyn, New York. *The Other Olympians* is his first book.